Infographics

PRACTICAL GUIDES FOR LIBRARIANS

About the Series

This innovative series written and edited for librarians by librarians provides authoritative, practical information and guidance on a wide spectrum of library processes and operations.

Books in the series are focused, describing practical and innovative solutions to a problem facing today's librarian and delivering step-by-step guidance for planning, creating, implementing, managing, and evaluating a wide range of services and programs.

The books are aimed at beginning and intermediate librarians needing basic instruction/guidance in a specific subject and at experienced librarians who need to gain knowledge in a new area or guidance in implementing a new program/service.

About the Series Editor

The **Practical Guides for Librarians** series was conceived by and is edited by M. Sandra Wood, MLS, MBA, AHIP, FMLA, Librarian Emerita, Penn State University Libraries.

M. Sandra Wood was a librarian at the George T. Harrell Library, The Milton S. Hershey Medical Center, College of Medicine, Pennsylvania State University, Hershey, PA, for over 35 years, specializing in reference, educational, and database services. Ms. Wood worked for several years as a Development Editor for Neal-Schuman Publishers.

Ms. Wood received a MLS from Indiana University and a MBA from the University of Maryland. She is a Fellow of the Medical Library Association and served as a member of MLA's Board of Directors from 1991 to 1995. Ms. Wood is founding and current editor of *Medical Reference Services Quarterly*, now in its 35th volume. She also was founding editor of the *Journal of Consumer Health on the Internet* and the *Journal of Electronic Resources in Medical Libraries* and served as editor/co-editor of both journals through 2011.

Titles in the Series

1. *How to Teach: A Practical Guide for Librarians* by Beverley E. Crane
2. *Implementing an Inclusive Staffing Model for Today's Reference Services* by Julia K. Nims, Paula Storm, and Robert Stevens
3. *Managing Digital Audiovisual Resources: A Practical Guide for Librarians* by Matthew C. Mariner
4. *Outsourcing Technology: A Practical Guide for Librarians* by Robin Hastings
5. *Making the Library Accessible for All: A Practical Guide for Librarians* by Jane Vincent
6. *Discovering and Using Historical Geographical Resources on the Web: A Practical Guide for Librarians* by Eva H. Dodsworth and L. W. Laliberté

7. *Digitization and Digital Archiving: A Practical Guide for Librarians* by Elizabeth R. Leggett
8. *Makerspaces: A Practical Guide for Librarians* by John J. Burke
9. *Implementing Web-Scale Discovery Services: A Practical Guide for Librarians* by JoLinda Thompson
10. *Using iPhones and iPads: A Practical Guide for Librarians* by Matthew Connolly and Tony Cosgrave
11. *Usability Testing: A Practical Guide for Librarians* by Rebecca Blakiston
12. *Mobile Devices: A Practical Guide for Librarians* by Ben Rawlins
13. *Going beyond Loaning Books to Loaning Technologies: A Practical Guide for Librarians* by Janelle Sander, Lori S. Mestre, and Eric Kurt
14. *Children's Services Today: A Practical Guide for Librarians* by Jeanette Larson
15. *Genealogy: A Practical Guide for Librarians* by Katherine Pennavaria
16. *Collection Evaluation in Academic Libraries: A Practical Guide for Librarians* by Karen C. Kohn
17. *Creating Online Tutorials: A Practical Guide for Librarians* by Hannah Gascho Rempel and Maribeth Slebodnik
18. *Using Google Earth in Libraries: A Practical Guide for Librarians* by Eva Dodsworth and Andrew Nicholson
19. *Integrating the Web into Everyday Library Services: A Practical Guide for Librarians* by Elizabeth R. Leggett
20. *Infographics: A Practical Guide for Librarians* by Beverley E. Crane

Infographics

A Practical Guide for Librarians

Beverley E. Crane

PRACTICAL GUIDES FOR LIBRARIANS, NO. 20

ROWMAN & LITTLEFIELD
Lanham • Boulder • New York • London

Published by Rowman & Littlefield
A wholly owned subsidiary of The Rowman & Littlefield Publishing Group, Inc.
4501 Forbes Boulevard, Suite 200, Lanham, Maryland 20706
www.rowman.com

Unit A, Whitacre Mews, 26-34 Stannary Street, London SE11 4AB

British Library Cataloguing in Publication Information Available

Library of Congress Cataloging-in-Publication Data

Name: Crane, Beverley E., author.
Title: Infographics : a practical guide for librarians / Beverley E. Crane.
Description: Lanham : Rowman & Littlefield, [2016] | Series: Practical guides for librarians ; no. 20 | Includes bibliographical references and index.
Identifiers: LCCN 2015031113| ISBN 9781442260351 (hardcover : alk. paper) | ISBN 9781442260368 (pbk. : alk. paper) | ISBN 9781442260375 (ebook)
Subjects: LCSH: Library science—Graphic methods. | Charts, diagrams, etc.—Computer programs. | Communication in library science. | Visual communication. | Information visualization. | Presentation graphics software.
Classification: LCC Z678.93.G73 C73 2016 | DDC 020.22/2—dc23 LC record available at http://lccn.loc.gov/2015031113

∞™ The paper used in this publication meets the minimum requirements of American National Standard for Information Sciences—Permanence of Paper for Printed Library Materials, ANSI/NISO Z39.48-1992.

Printed in the United States of America

For my mother, Dee Foust, who has always supported me in all my endeavors. Her vitality at eighty-eight years of age prompts me to always look forward, continue to learn, and move in new directions—all characteristics that help me as I continue to write new books. Thanks, Mom.

Contents

List of Illustrations

Figures

Tables

Preface

Society today loves its libraries. Adults and youth also love visuals. They are constantly snapping photos, posting them on Facebook and Pinterest, tweeting messages, and texting bits of information. How can the public's interest in graphic representation, fast-paced lifestyle, and love of the library work in the library's favor? The answer is *Infographics: A Practical Guide for Librarians.*

Although the public, students, and organizations say they cannot do without their libraries, research from the Pew Research Center found that they do not know about the diverse types of services, expertise, and products offered by public, academic, special, and school libraries. The bottom line is that libraries need to do a better job telling their story. They also need to do it in a way that is interesting to a diverse audience.

A quick story emphasizes how visuals dominate today's society. I recently attended two high school graduations. Observing the students and their siblings, parents, and even grandparents, I noticed a constant use of cell phones before the ceremony to text friends and take pictures, as well as the snapping of photos when graduates entered and exited the hall. Afterward, families gathered in the convention hall where the new graduates were photographed with their families—with classmates, in family groups, and shaking hands with teachers. I can't begin to count the number of pictures that were taken in that two-hour time period. The next day, Facebook pages were full of photos telling a visual story of graduation ceremonies. This is just one illustration of how visuals are embedded in all aspects of today's society.

With increasing amounts of information, more powerful and ever-changing technology, and social media used by people of all ages—from youngsters in elementary schools to the elderly—and all types of businesses throughout the world, librarians must have a multitude of ways to transmit their stories and messages to students, clients, and patrons anytime, anywhere, and in any format. One way to capture and maintain the attention of today's audience is by using images. Infographics, which are now all the rage, present that vehicle. According to HubSpot, an inbound marketing organization, the number of searches for infographics on Google increased over 800 percent from 2010 to 2012. Because the brain actually discards much sensory information so it can store unique information presented in a novel way, well-designed infographics are an ideal venue for communicating the library's message.

The production of infographics is increasing by 1 percent every day. Companies incorporate infographics into their content marketing strategy because they bring powerful results. Web traffic to sites that publish infographics grows by an average of 12 percent more than it does for sites that do not use them. Visual content is powerful, and consumers find it more engaging than text alone because more than 50 percent of people are visual learners.

So how do you find out about and create great infographics that will captivate your audience and spread the word about your library? *Infographics: A Practical Guide for Librarians* is designed to meet that need.

Organization

Infographics can play a powerful part in any library's twenty-first-century game plan. Whether it's marketing the public library, improving students' information literacy skills in a school library, or showcasing the accomplishments of the academic library, infographics can be a vital part of the library's playbook.

Infographics: A Practical Guide for Librarians is divided into two parts containing ten chapters. Part 1: Infographics 101 comprises four chapters. Chapter 1 provides background about infographics: its history, importance in today's society, and benefits. Chapter 2 delves into the diversity of infographics, describing different types, their characteristics and uses, and the advantages and disadvantages of each. Illustrations of each type show diverse uses, and numerous examples explain how public, school, academic, and special libraries are incorporating infographics into their library plans. Chapter 3 outlines the process of creating an infographic: its components and step-by-step thought processes to creating one. Chapter 4 discusses the actual creation of an infographic. It presents resources, including design principles and elements, and identifies sample tools that will make the actual creation of your infographic easier. Throughout part 1, tips are given (e.g., how to promote the infographic). In each chapter, exercises at the end reinforce the material presented, and tables include additional resources. URLs for complete and partial infographics are given so you can go to each infographic and see it in color.

Part 2: Practical Applications encompasses chapters 5–10, containing the most common practical applications using infographics in public, school, academic, and special libraries. It describes specific ways to use infographics in libraries:

- raising funds for a public library
- teaching critical thinking and twenty-first-century skills in the school library
- illustrating why libraries matter by relaying the value of academic libraries
- describing partnerships
- improving information literacy in academic settings
- advocating for any library

Each chapter provides illustrations of the application in each type of library, along with a detailed descriptive example of the application in a particular library (e.g., school library). Numerous illustrations show portions of the infographics; links enable you to visit sites and see the complete infographic in color. Chapter 5 focuses on using infographics as teaching tools to provide insight on how infographics can facilitate one goal of a library—to educate its patrons. Chapter 6 illustrates how infographics can be used in fundraising for the library, an important task when competing for scarce resources. Chapter 7 showcases partnerships by school, public, academic, and special libraries, and the role infographics can play. Chapter 8 is designed to increase awareness of underused and new services and programs, such as database collections, makerspaces, Ask a Librarian, teen programs, and more. Chapter 9 emphasizes an all-important topic—advocating for the library by promoting its value among patrons and nonpatrons, the legislature, and business and local communities.

Chapter 10 brings it all together and provides two step-by-step demonstrations—one using Microsoft PowerPoint and the other using Piktochart. Each example guides you through the actual creation of an infographic, including both content and design. Chapters 5 through 10 also contain practical exercises that offer opportunities to create applications useful for your own library.

Some of the most popular images on the web and in media today are infographics—the colorful charts, graphs, and graphics that encapsulate data and tell a story at a glance. Today's library is not just about books. Infographics have the ability to tell your library's unique story in a concise, entertaining, visual manner. *Infographics: A Practical Guide for Librarians* provides that comprehensive guide to enable you to achieve your goal—to communicate to patrons and nonpatrons alike the value of your library by showcasing its multifaceted services, diverse spaces, equipment, events, and knowledgeable personnel.

I encourage readers to look at the infographics located at the indicated web addresses online. Viewing the whole infographic in color is much more informative than what can be represented in this book.

Acknowledgments

I undertook to write *Infographics: A Practical Guide for Librarians* as the result of my research—speaking to librarians, reading scholarly studies, and reviewing many infographics. My research struck a common chord: users love the library but they often do not know what the library offers; today's public wants information in quick, short, visual bursts. The current popularity of infographics seemed an ideal tool to help libraries meet the challenge of increasing awareness of the library's value.

A huge thanks to librarians and others who have created the wealth of infographics and given me permission to feature them throughout this book. These models can assist librarians in creating infographics for the numerous uses in their own libraries. Your examples bring infographics to life in the book.

Thanks also to Sandy Wood, the series editor, a gifted librarian, who brings the talents of a librarian—organization, dedication, and support—to her editorial role. She once again offered insightful suggestions and editorial advice to make each book I write better.

INFOGRAPHICS 101

Infographics: A Practical Guide for Librarians is divided into two sections containing ten chapters. Part 1: Infographics 101 comprises four chapters. These chapters form the knowledge base about infographics that librarians will need as they begin to use this medium in their own libraries. Chapters 1–4 emphasize important aspects about infographics, including definitions explaining what they are, reasons they are important, models to follow, principles to use in design, and tools to create infographics for the applications in part 2 that librarians will want to try.

Building a Knowledge Base

The first four chapters cover important issues to consider about infographics.

Chapter 1 provides background about infographics: its history, importance in today's society, and benefits.

Chapter 2 delves into the diversity of infographics, describing different types, their characteristics and uses, and the advantages and disadvantages of each. Illustrations of each type show diverse uses, and numerous examples explain how public, school, academic, and special libraries are incorporating infographics into their library plans.

Chapter 3 outlines the process of creating an infographic: its components and step-by-step thought processes in creating one.

Chapter 4 discusses the actual creation of an infographic. It presents resources, including design principles and elements, and identifies sample tools that will make the actual creation of your infographic easier. Understanding the design principles and following steps to create infographics will be particularly useful in chapter 10 when you create your own.

Throughout part 1, tips are given (e.g., how to promote the infographic). In each chapter, exercises at the end reinforce the material presented, and tables include additional resources. URLs for complete and partial infographics are given so you can go to each infographic and see it in its entirety and in color. It is important to review each complete infographic because they serve as models—showing unique topics, design ideas, and different ways libraries have used them.

Once you complete these four chapters, you will be ready to apply your new knowledge about infographics to applications to meet your library's needs. Common applications are discussed and illustrated in part 2.

What Are Infographics?

IN THIS CHAPTER

- ▷ Elements of today's information problem and how they affect the public
- ▷ A brief history of infographics
- ▷ Textual and visual definition of infographics
- ▷ Why infographics have become so effective in today's society

ANY DISCUSSION OF INFOGRAPHICS must begin with a bit of background on the state of information in the world today, its beginnings and how far it has come, how much information there is, and how society is dealing with it all. This is an overwhelming problem that scientists, researchers, information specialists, and the general population have been trying to cope with for generations. From businesses to the youngest schoolchild, no one seems to have the answer to managing the huge amount of information, how to distribute it, and where to get the time necessary to deal with it all.

Chapter 1 leads you through a brief discussion describing the state of the information problem. This chapter discusses information overload and elements increasing it. At the center of the discussion will be one way to handle information overload that has been receiving a great amount of publicity and has become quite popular: infographics.

The Dynamics of the Problem

The problem that needs to be addressed in today's world has several interrelated elements. One part—information overload, coined by Russian academic Alvin Toffler—is a description given to the phenomenon whereby so much information is taken in by the human brain that it becomes nearly impossible to process it. Since the phrase was first used, it has become very popular, especially in the computer age, though some say that the idea is more a time and presentation issue than an actual data issue. Besides information overload, other elements—the complicated varieties of communication, the lack of time to process it, and the presentation of information—seem to exacerbate the problem.

Information Overload

Increasing concerns about information overload have become more prevalent in today's world (Alleyne, 2011). Individuals who suffer from this dilemma may come from a variety of professions and fields, but they tend to be those most closely associated with study-intensive pursuits, or those deeply involved in communications. For example, academics or students may suffer information overload when they use too many sources too quickly while doing research. Doctors conducting research about a patient's condition or treatment options can be overwhelmed with all the materials available to them, as can an administrative assistant managing multiple schedules and channels of communication at the same time.

Communication Complexities

Increasing concerns about information overload have also become more prevalent because of the increasing complexities of the communication systems available to humans. Today's access to instant communication via e-mail, cell phones, text messaging, and instant messaging, along with thousands of academic journals on the Internet, and even more information freely distributed through blogs and amateur websites, means that information is being exchanged at rates never before experienced. Moreover, television programs and commercials train millions of brains for flashy images and scenes that quickly cut in and out so that information often becomes somewhat disjointed. Therefore, the brain must spend a longer period of time trying to connect it all together for a more cohesive picture.

Further, because anyone can distribute information on the Internet, much of it may not be original. The format may just be different. As a result, many times the reader or viewer will spend time reviewing data already received from other sources. If there are discrepancies or even small differences in the way the information is presented, this can cause confusion, leading an individual to feel more overwhelmed than ever.

Time Constraints

Despite the fact that too much information seems to be a real problem for many people, some say the real problem is time overload. In other words, the information being distributed is able to be processed, but there is simply not enough time to do it. If that is the case, the solution is not reducing the intake of information, but finding more time to process it.

Audience Habits

Another important part of the problem is the short attention span of today's audience, which seems to be getting shorter all the time. An article appearing in the *Daily Mail Online* (Smith, 2014), titled "Proof of Our Shrinking Attention Span," reports on a survey of consumer habits of two hundred British individuals. Researchers found that users switch between three favorite devices—laptops, smartphones, and tablets, and that the average person switched up to twenty-one times an hour.

Visual Processing

Additional research (Ashton, 2013) indicates that close to 50 percent of the brain is involved in visual processing. This means that the brain can process a visual by attaching meaning to it far quicker than it can attach meaning to text. Because the brain processes visuals faster than a written message, most warning signs on the road are visual. So, one way to capture and maintain the attention of today's audience is by using images (Kusinitz, 2014).

You might ask, then, why not just use pictures to get the message across? A good question; however, Mayer (2009) finds that words supported by pictures benefit learning more than pictures alone. People absorb and retain information much better when text and images are present. This principle of continuity is one reason why children's books are so effective at communicating their message—they have a clear visual element and some simple text to reinforce what is happening.

It is clear that with increasing amounts of information, more powerful and ever-changing technology and social media used by all ages—from youngsters in elementary schools to the elderly, as well as all types of organizations throughout the world—must have a multitude of ways to transmit their stories and messages to clients and patrons anytime, anywhere, and in any format.

In summary, the problem seems to be information overload along with all the elements that are a part of it. First and foremost, human beings today, at all age levels and in all walks of life, are constantly exposed to large amounts of information. Another way people are overloaded is through communication, whether they are using computers, tablets, smartphones, or other kinds of media at school, at work, or while relaxing at home. There are so many methods to transmit information that the public is bombarded with it from morning to night—perhaps in so many ways that there is not enough time to absorb it all. Enter infographics!

A Bit of History

Infographics have been around for a very long time, from early history to current times. In the early ages, cave dwellers created the first information graphics—cave paintings. Mapmaking began several millennia before writing. Icons were used to keep records of cattle and stock, and the Indians of Mesoamerica used imagery to depict the journeys of past generations. Information graphics is not a new phenomenon (Hamilton, 2014).

Examples of information graphics over time emphasize the importance of using images and text to tell stories to relate complex information in different countries and languages no matter what the subjects were. Review the history of the information graphics slideshow at http://www.slideshare.net/kehamilt/a-brief-history-of-information-graphicsinfographics. Table 1.1 presents a chronology of highlights illustrating the rise of infographics throughout history.

Table 1.1. Brief History of Infographics

DATE	DESCRIPTION
	Cavemen were the earliest infographic artists.
3000 BC	Ancient Egyptians use hieroglyphic symbols to tell stories of life, work, and religion.
500 BC	Babylonians invent the first writing system on clay tablets using images.
1510	Leonardo da Vinci blends written instruction with illustrations to create a comprehensive guide on human anatomy.
1686	Edmond Halley shows a map of prevailing winds, the first printed.
1786	William Playfair publishes the first data graphs—statistical graphs, bar charts, line graphs, circle graphs, pie charts, and histograms—that represent the economy of eighteenth-century England.
1854	During the London cholera epidemic, Dr. John Snow combines a map with data to plot cholera deaths.
1857	Florence Nightingale combines stacked bar/pie charts to illustrate the monthly number of casualties and causes of death explained during the Crimean War to help convince Queen Victoria to improve conditions in military hospitals.
1858	Visual of the complete history of humankind from Adam and Eve forward.
1869	Charles Minard charts the story of Napoleon's disaster.
1925	Otto Neurath is the forefather of pictograms of today.
1926	Fritz Kahn visualizes human metabolism as the process of industrial production.
1933	The first tube map in London shows only lines to depict public transit routes and stations.
1970–1990	Mainstream publications—*Sunday Times*, *Time*, and *USA Today*—popularize infographics.
1972	The Munich Olympics are the venue for Otl Aicher to introduce a new set of pictograms and influence modern stick figures used in public signs.
World Wars I, II	Newspapers depict war casualties and costs through images and maps.
2000–present	Web-based infographics have become more interactive, adding animation and user interaction to convey information.

Definitions of Data Visualizations and Infographics

Although infographics in different forms have been around since before written records, it has only been recently that their popularity has grown. Despite the increased use of infographics over the last several years, many people still do not know what they are, nor can they provide a definition or give a synonym for an infographic. In addition, often when defining the term, numerous words are used to express the same concept. For example, you may have heard the terms "information graphics," "infographics," and "data visualization." Are they the same, different? Do they overlap; are they interchangeable? Some of these words have a relationship that is both different and the same, so it is helpful to provide a context for the terms and how they are similar and different.

The terms "data visualization" and "infographics" are often used interchangeably. The confusion is understandable because the meanings can overlap, yet the relationships can be represented differently. Data visualizations are used to make sense of highly complex data or to change a massive data set into a more accessible form. For example, General Electric (GE) used data visualization as a way to visualize medical data to help doctors diagnose, treat, and cure patients. Figure 1.1 shows a data visualization (http://visualization.geblogs.com/visualization/curing/) that GE uses to promote its medical imaging equipment in a visual, more understandable way. The data set presents CT and MRI scans on graphs that show scanning activity (type and time of scan and location) for more than 125,000 scans worldwide during twenty-four hours. When looking at data visualizations, you'll find images ranging from dynamic interactive applications to inspirational information graphics and everything in between.

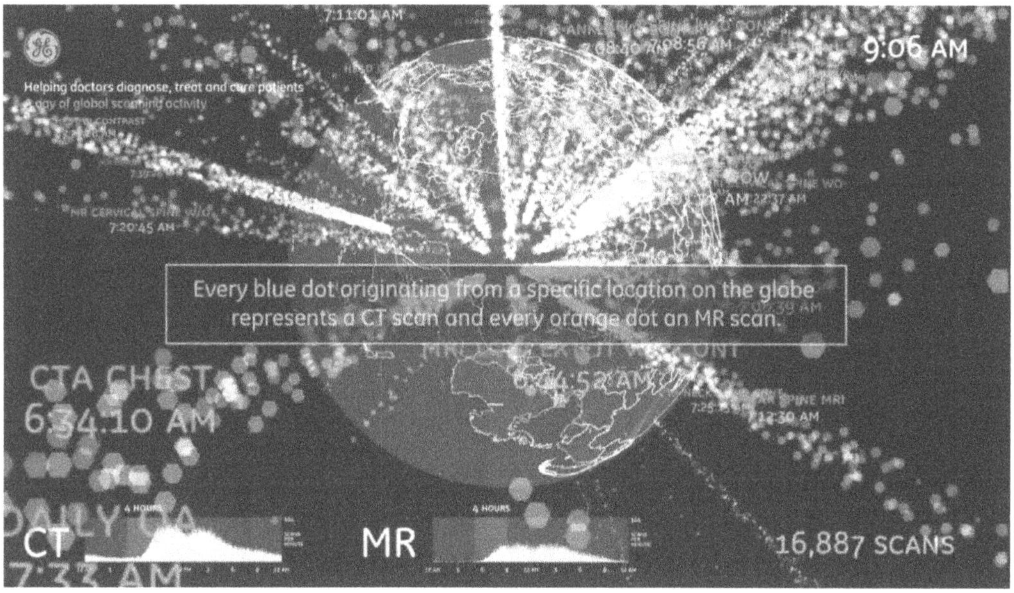

Figure 1.1. Data Visualization. By Fathom Information Design, http://fathom.info/scanning.

According to *Wikipedia* (2014), infographics are "visual representations of information, data, or knowledge intended to present complex information quickly and clearly." They use pictures, words, graphs, and other visual elements to express information. Ideally, infographics are designed so that these visual elements organize complex ideas and data into a more easily understood form in a way that enhances viewers' comprehension. Images are often an extension of the content of a written article, but infographics convey a self-contained message or principle.

An effective infographic provides information on a certain topic in a creative way and provides a conclusion. It tells a story. Thus, detailed research and editing have to be completed to convey the right message and encourage more people to share it online. Infographics now exist everywhere from journalism to technical writing, in classrooms, libraries, businesses, and government, literally anywhere information is displayed and where there is a desire to make complex information easier to understand. Compared to using only plain text, it is more interesting and permanent, similar to videos. With graphics and text combined, the information is more entertaining, and learning increases.

Since the focus of this book is infographics for libraries and librarians, definitions, illustrations, and examples are designed to meet their needs and achieve their goals.

For example, an infographic Wordle (a "word cloud") at http://www.gcls.org/about-us contains terminology for the purpose of helping libraries and librarians make their messages understandable to patrons. In this Wordle the Gloucester County Library System (GCLS) (http://www.gcls.org/about-us) emphasizes words that give the viewer the feeling of a library.

The main points of an effective infographic are summarized in the following textbox.

MAIN POINTS OF AN INFOGRAPHIC

- Provides visual presentations of information including statistics about a certain topic using graphics and text
- Uses elements of design to display content
- Is constructed in a creative way to let people easily understand the message or the story being delivered
- Conveys a self-contained message or principle with a conclusion that may be an extension of the content of a written article
- Expresses a complex message in a manner that enhances viewers' comprehension
- Is indexed by search engines on websites to gather inbound links
- Presents the right message through detailed research and editing, thus encouraging more people to share on social media, particularly Twitter and Facebook
- Helps the reader's spatial-temporal reasoning, which makes learning easier

Why Does the Brain Crave Infographics?

NeoMam Studios created a beautiful infographic reviewing brain research that illustrated why infographics are so popular. Their research (Ashton, 2013) pointed out that because the use of visualized information has increased greatly and the brain is heavily involved in visual processing, infographics—with their combination of visuals, text, color, and directed message—overcome the information overload and appeal to humans. Take a few minutes to review the entire infographic in color at http://neomam.com/interactive/13reasons/. You'll find it and the excerpt in figure 1.2 fascinating.

Tips When Creating Infographics

More and more people are creating their own infographics; however, this trend can have some bad results. Just as in a good piece of writing, an infographic should follow strict rules. No blueprint creates a step-by-step pattern you can follow to guarantee your success in writing excellent infographics, but you can avoid common, simple mistakes. Here are a few tips:

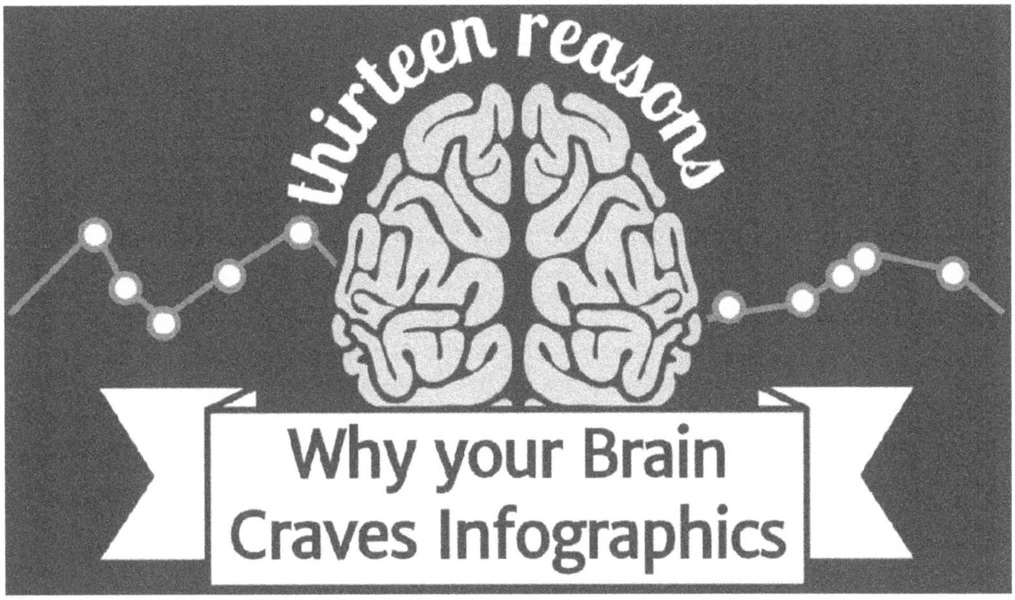

Figure 1.2. Thirteen Reasons Why Your Brain Craves Infographics. Created by NeoMam Studios and licensed under Creative Commons.

- Facts should be checked fastidiously; bias should be omitted from any statistics.
- The theme or topic should be focused and not stray from the main point of the infographic. Although there is a visual element, the focus or theme should still be central.
- Embedded links should still be central to your infographic. They should not go to unrelated sites or a link not meant to be endorsed.
- Infographics should focus on a central theme. Some have (1) too much data and try to communicate too many details all at once, or (2) they may be too long so that you keep scrolling down endlessly on an infographic that just can't seem to wrap up whatever it is trying to communicate. In either case, breaking up the data may give you more content to share and improve your infographic.
- Make sure your infographic is interesting by doing a keyword search first to see if the topic has already been done. Not all data is deserving of being immortalized in an infographic. Unfortunately, people will make an infographic for just about anything. As you research the topic for your infographic, you may find another approach that will make a more interesting infographic than your original idea.
- Your infographic will be more apt to be shared if its importance to your business or organization is recognized.

And, the most important lesson—focus on your target audience. Entertain them. Be useful. Let your passion shine through, and you'll find an excited audience as a result. Chapter 3 delves more deeply into writing infographics.

Sample Infographics

In this chapter you have reviewed some textual definitions of an infographic and identified criteria in well-written ones. Two examples illustrate different visual definitions of an infographic.

Example 1

Published by Hot Butter Studio (http://www.hotbutterstudio.com/alps/), example 1 presents a visual definition of an infographic using LEGO blocks to illustrate that a good infographic can be simple and requires very little text to convey the message. Each image depicts four elements of an infographic—data, sorting, arrangement, and visual presentation. Although the graphic is very simple, it makes the main point clearly and concisely.

Example 2

The infographic titled "What Infographics Are" (http://infographiclabs.com/?s=what+infographics+are) from Infographic Labs provides a visual, understandable, but more detailed, visual definition of an infographic. It describes each part of the infographic and how it contributes to convey the message clearly and concisely. A portion of the complete infographic is shown in figure 1.3.

To define "infographic" visually, the top of the infographic contains an image with graphics, text, and color, combined with statistics about a certain subject. As you review this image, notice the various parts contained in most infographics. In the center of figure 1.3, a short textual definition explains that an infographic contains graphics, text, and statistics about a topic. It is also creative so the audience can easily understand the story being delivered. The author uses different color arrows and text (e.g., purple, green, and orange) to indicate the color scheme. The rainbow at the top also represents the color

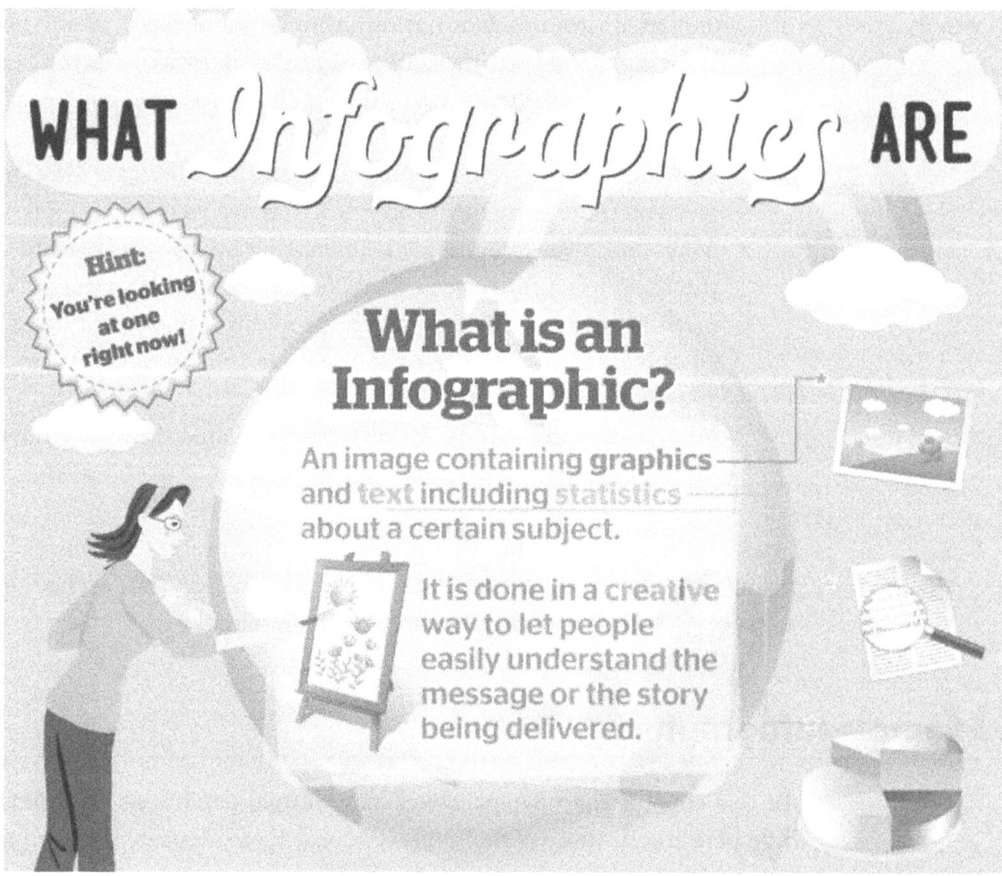

Figure 1.3. What Infographics Are. By Infographic Labs, http://infographiclabs.com/?s=what+infographics+are.

Table 1.2. Examples of Infographics

DESCRIPTION	URL
Numerous classroom infographics	http://www.pinterest.com/fibeal/infographics-in-the-classroom/
Taking notes in the twenty-first century	http://www.pinterest.com/pin/238127899022131727/
"30 Kids, One iPad? No Problem!"	http://www.pinterest.com/pin/238127899022096616/
"What Good Mathematicians Do"	http://www.pinterest.com/pin/238127899022447366/
TED talk—How to tell a great visualized story	http://www.pinterest.com/pin/238127899022448726/
"Anatomy of an Infographic: 5 Steps to Create a Powerful Visual"	http://www.pinterest.com/pin/238127899022043473/
"How to Create Infographics"	http://www.slideshare.net/library_research_service/how-to-create-infographics?related=1v

scheme. Notice the images depict the textual words—graphics, text, and statistics. So, in less than one minute you see the message, color scheme, and images explaining what an infographic is. Check out some of the links in table 1.2 to become familiar with different examples of infographics.

Importance of Infographics in Today's Society

Whether in business, nonprofits, or government, infographics have become a powerful tool for disseminating huge amounts of information to the masses. Companies large and small were some of the first to create infographics and use them to build their brands, educate their audience, and optimize their search engine ranking. Marketers present annual reports, communicate inside and outside a corporation, and create case studies through infographics. Journalists present recent trends, and bloggers highlight main points in their articles. Educators find them useful to create teaching guides for school subjects, and students prepare study materials. Whether in business, technology, education, medicine, science, marketing, and more, there is really no end to the ways infographics can be used in today's world.

Libraries—public, academic, and special libraries, such as medical—are also creating infographics to promote their messages and for many of the same reasons as other organizations. Communicating through infographics is important and of interest to staff and administrators at all levels to present information to patrons, stakeholders, and management. Senior staff and directors responsible for reporting to boards are especially encouraged to understand infographics and the power they bring to communicating their message. Librarians use infographics to market the library, raise funds, educate patrons, and more. You will learn more about uses for libraries in chapters 5–9 in part 2 of this book.

Key Points

Although infographics have become quite popular, there are still some misinterpretations about them. This chapter provides background for further discussion of infographics in chapters that follow.

- Society is overwhelmed with data. Information overload and related elements, including the complicated varieties of communication, the lack of time to explore myriad amounts of information, and the way information is presented have reinforced the popularity of infographics in today's world.
- A brief history shows infographics dating back to cavemen and continuing with contributions throughout the world from medicine, economics, warfare, and journalism to its widespread popularity today in all areas of society.
- There are misconceptions related to definitions of infographics and data visualization. Often the relationships are similar, but they may be represented differently. With the increased popularity of infographics, it is important to understand and clarify the differences.
- Creating effective infographics requires using a combination of graphics, text, and statistics to convey complex messages in a clear, concise way.
- Two examples visually define infographics and show how elements, including data, color, sorting, and arrangement are used to clearly explain the concept of an infographic.

With the groundwork laid, it will now be easier in chapter 2 to understand the types of infographics as you review them and view specific examples and when to use them.

Exercise for Chapter 1

The purpose of this exercise is to see what you learned about an infographic from this chapter.

1. In no more than two minutes each, review at least two infographics using the following URLs: https://www.customermagnetism.com/infographics/what-is-an-infographic/ and http://www.huffingtonpost.com/2012/06/26/library-infographic_n_1627784.html.
2. Write in the table at least five characteristics that are typical of two of the infographics you selected. *Note:* You don't have to be a graphic designer to identify these items!
3. You will review each component in more detail later in the book so that you can create your own infographic for your own audience for a specific purpose.

Table 1.3. Infographic Characteristics

INFOGRAPHIC A	ITEM	ITEM	ITEM
e.g., sources			
Infographic B			

Possible answers to question 2 are the following:

- A consistent color scheme
- A mix of text and graphics
- Variations in size of fonts and images
- Graphical signals to direct the eye through the infographic
- Statistics and sources to back up statements
- An embed code to spread the content
- Sources

Think about these aspects of infographics, along with your message, as you begin to work on your own infographics later in this book.

References

Alleyne, Richard. 2011. "Welcome to the Information Age—174 Newspapers a Day." *Telegraph*, February 11. http://www.telegraph.co.uk/news/science/science-news/8316534/Welcome-to-the-information-age-174-newspapers-a-day.html.

Ashton, Danny. 2013. "Thirteen Reasons Why Your Brain Craves Infographics." June 12. http://neomam.com/interactive/13reasons/.

Hamilton, K3. 2014. "A Brief History of Information Graphics/Infographics." SlideShare—Education. April 12. http://www.slideshare.net/kehamilt/a-brief-history-of-information-graphicsinfographics.

Kusinitz, Sam. 2014. "12 Reasons to Integrate Visual Content into Your Marketing Campaigns [Infographic]." *Where Marketers Go to Grow* (blog). July 18. http://blog.hubspot.com/marketing/visual-content-marketing-infographic?__hstc=28469475.3cff3ebdd35b0e511c736bfd7a1a1eca.1430826142070.1430826142070.1430826142070.1&__hssc=28469475.4.1430826142072&__hsfp=620562149.

Mayer, Richard E. 2009. *Multimedia Learning*. 2nd ed. New York: Cambridge University Press.

Smith, Jennifer. 2014. "Proof of Our Shrinking Attention Span: Average Person Switches between Devices 21 Times an Hour." *Daily Mail*, January 5. http://www.dailymail.co.uk/news/article-2534163/Proof-shrinking-attention-span-Average-person-switches-devices-21-times-HOUR.html#ixzz3Ow9Ms5xe.

Wikipedia. 2014. "Infographic." Wikipedia.org. Accessed November 19. http://en.wikipedia.org/wiki/Infographic.

Further Reading

Byrom, Matt. 2014. "The Power of Visual Communication." WYZOWL. March 3. http://blog.wyzowl.com/power-visual-communication-infographic.

Huff Post Books. 2012. "American Library Association's Library Infographic Shows Recession Budget Cuts." *Huff Post Books* (blog). June 26. http://www.huffingtonpost.com/2012/06/26/library-infographic_n_1627784.html.

Levie, W. Howard, and Richard Lentz. 1982. "Effects of Text Illustrations: A Review of Research." *Educational Technology Research and Development* 30, no. 4 (Winter): 195–232.

Mayer, Richard E. 2011. *Applying the Science of Learning*. Upper Saddle River, NJ: Pearson.

CHAPTER 2

Communicating through Infographics

IN THIS CHAPTER

- ▷ Different types of infographics and their specific characteristics
- ▷ When to use a specific type for a particular purpose and audience

CHAPTER 1 POINTED OUT the growing popularity of infographics due in large measure to information overload and the viral nature of infographics. Worldwide population in different industries, nonprofits, health care, education, and government has become more dependent upon visual representation to convey its messaging quickly and effectively. A wide range of communication devices using social media makes infographics an ideal media.

Different types of infographics are available to convey the exact message to specific audiences. Chapter 2 delves first into the elements that make up an infographic. Once you know the different parts, you can then identify various types. This chapter describes eight types of infographics, emphasizing the versatility of using them for a variety of purposes to different audiences. Examples model ways you can use infographics to meet the specific needs of your particular organization and audiences. When you are familiar enough with the types of infographics, you will be able to select those appropriate for your own purpose and audience, especially at your library.

Deconstructing the Infographic

Readers who lead busy, fast-paced lifestyles do not have a lot of time to interpret data, and so innovative ways of conveying information need to be explored. Well-designed infographics communicate key information quickly and attract the attention and maintain the focus of readers.

Information is very powerful but it can also be quite boring. Infographics can create a visual image that makes the information powerful yet understandable. However, an infographic must be designed in the right manner so that through its anatomy—its different levels and sublevels—it will not only be conceptually sound, but accurate, easily understood, and entertaining at the same time (Roy, 2009). Infographics can appear overwhelming to some because of the sheer amount of data they present, but if done right, each discrete part plays a vital role in conveying its part of the message, and they can actually be one of the most fun things you will ever create.

Anatomy of the Infographic

There are several ways to think about the structure of an infographic: levels, elements, and audience. The anatomy of an infographic has a couple of levels (e.g., one-level deep or two-level deep) depending on the complexity of the topic.

Levels

You can divide a topic into one or two levels deep both visually and textually as the topic becomes more complex.

- A one-level-deep infographic is simple, barely skimming the three core parts. It has a visual that is usually common throughout the design. It has some content to complement the visual. It imparts knowledge based on the visuals and content. The one-level design may incorporate one or two subparts from visuals and content, but the representation is very basic.
- A two-level-deep infographic is more advanced and encompasses the three core parts of the design but delves deeper by providing more details, including statistics on the topic and visuals. All data presented must be researched and backed up by established facts. Figure 2.1 shows the two levels of infographics as part of the infographic "What Infographics Are."

Elements

The core of an infographic is composed of three important parts: visual, content, and knowledge elements as shown in the infographic in figure 2.2 (http://infographiclabs.com/news/what-is-an-infographic/).

1. Visual refers to the color coding, graphics, and reference icons used in designing the infographic. Visual has the thematic-defining graphics of the design. In addition, it has reference icons to condense and compact a lot of data visually. Color coding becomes a must in this type of infographic because visually separating content via color becomes key in relaying information. *Note:* Throughout this book URLs for complete and partial infographics are given so you can go to each infographic and see it in color.
2. Content includes the statistics, time frames, and references. It not only presents factual data, but also makes references to other information and routinely relies on statistics. There may be additional pieces of data in the form of notes. With the increase in the amount of data as the design goes two levels deep, it becomes

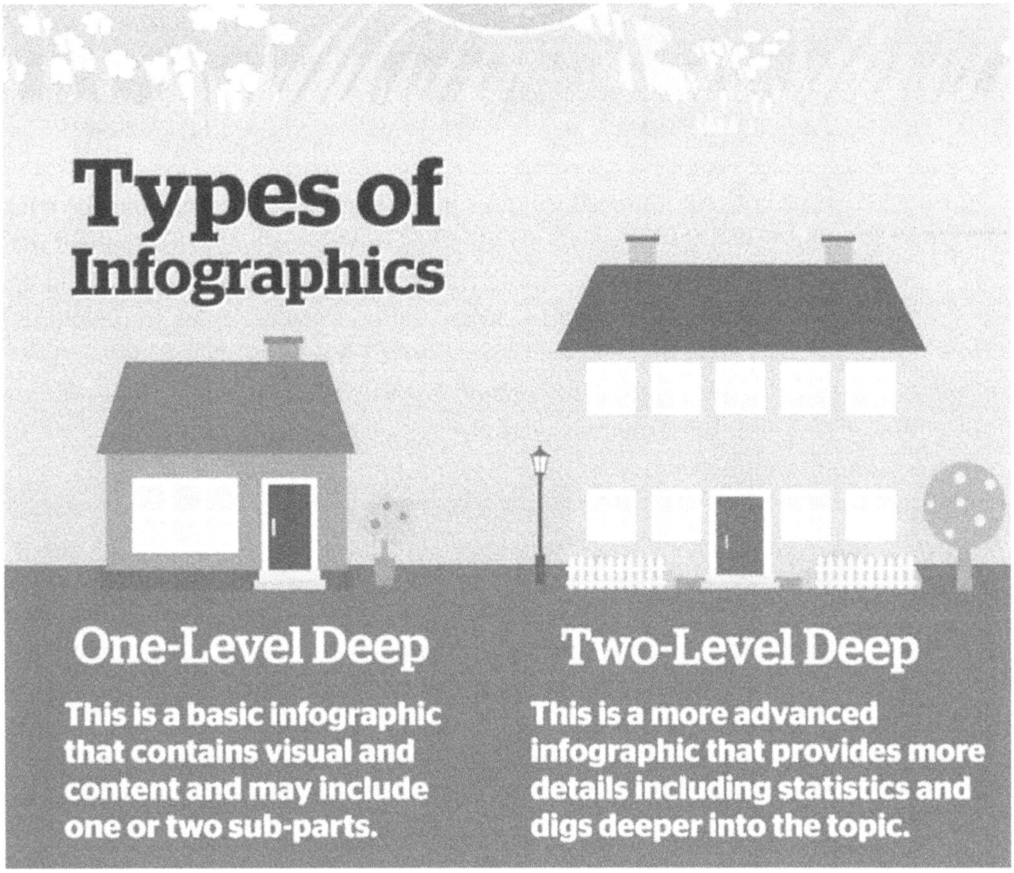

Figure 2.1. Levels of Infographics. Part of "What Infographics Are," by Infographic Labs, http://infographiclabs.com/news/what-is-an-infographic/.

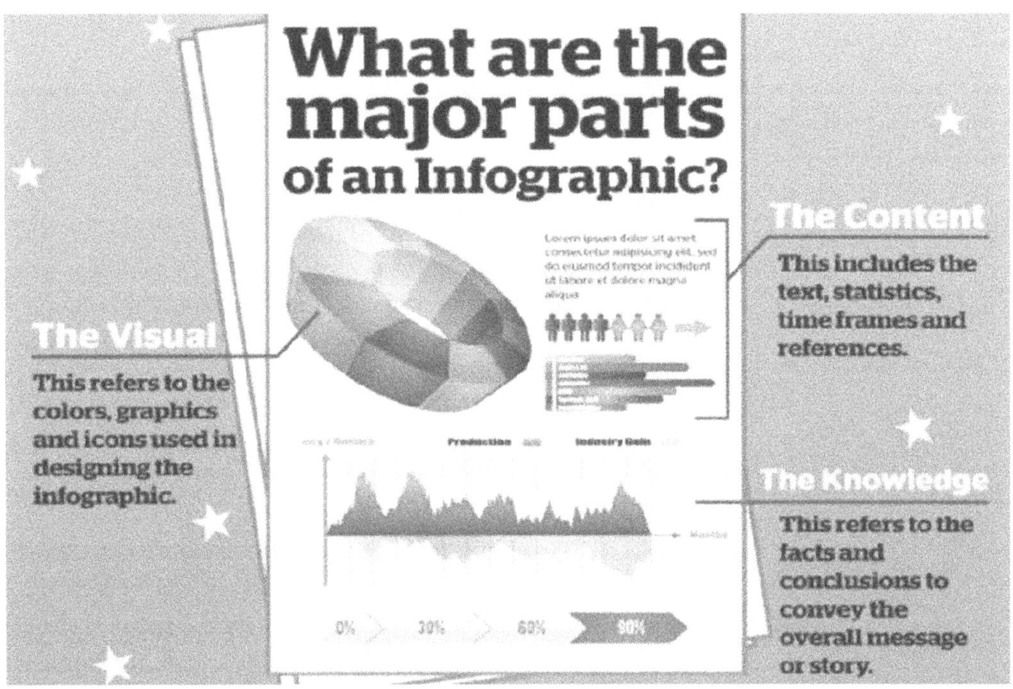

Figure 2.2. Major Parts of an Infographic. Part of "What Infographics Are," by Infographic Labs, http://infographiclabs.com/news/what-is-an-infographic/.

essential to utilize all the graphical resources available in the form of icons, images, shape groupings, color, and time frame integration. Color coding is also important to separate content.

3. Knowledge refers to the facts and conclusions to convey the overall message or story.
4. All infographics must be thoroughly researched, and the data presented must be backed up by established facts. While doing that, you will inevitably end up with piles of data. Sifting through that, you must condense and decide what information is the most relevant and how you are going to present it. The ratio of data to the graphics works best if it is 1:1, and its placement is important, too. Highlighting important content to easily generate deductions makes the knowledge that much more powerful.

Audience

Infographics can also be categorized according to how graphic information is presented to readers. The business world has gone infographic crazy, but no matter whether you are in the health care industry, work for a nonprofit or a government organization, or are the primary audience for this book—a member of the library community—you will find a need to communicate your message clearly, effectively, and concisely. Of course, if you happen to be an artist like myself, you may like reviewing infographics from a design perspective or admiring how visually appealing they are; but as a librarian, you may be wondering how useful they are for you and your library.

Just one example can show you an important advantage for your library. People love to share infographics. This can bring tons of traffic to your library website, and if you think of infographics as modern fact sheets, you can see the possibilities open up. However, there are different kinds of infographics, and the right type should match your data to your narrative to ensure that people take away your message after reading it. Therefore, the audience—the reader of the infographic—becomes extremely important in the process of creating an infographic.

Three types of infographics, as described in Adams (2011), have different characteristics and are used for different purposes:

- Static infographics present information all at once and in its entirety. These graphics have a quick and immediate impact on the reader. Examples of this kind include newspaper graphics and those in product manuals.
- Motion infographics play a major role in cinema and presentations. Information is presented sequentially and consistently. Examples of this include graphic animations and PowerPoint presentations.
- Interactive infographics engage the audience. Information is presented according to the reader's choice. For example, on the web, [readers] might select what they want to view from a complex set of instructive and simulated information.

It takes a lot more than simply writing the information to generate creative infographics. You need to offer something unique that grabs people's attention—something that is easy to understand and digest. It must also be easy to share on the web for possible viral marketing. In the end, an infographic can be as simple or as complicated as you want it to be. It is important to put yourself in the shoes of the people who are going to be viewing your infographics, and you'll design a great one!

Types of Infographics

Infographic creation is not a new phenomenon. In fact, as mentioned in chapter 1, traditional media has been using creative pictorial diagrams for years. The integration of visual information into a content-creative strategy is an optimal benefit to any organization by presenting information in a more digestible, highly entertaining way. Figure 2.3 (http://neomam.com/interactive/13reasons/) shows some of the benefits of presenting a graphic visualization:

- Color visuals are 80 percent more likely to be read.
- Sixty-seven percent of an audience is persuaded by a verbal presentation with visuals.
- People following directions with text and illustrations do 323 percent better than following directions without illustrations. People remember 80 percent of what they do, 10 percent of what they hear, and 20 percent of what they read.

In fact, publishers that use infographics grow in traffic on average 12 percent more than those that do not use infographics (Alexander, 2012).

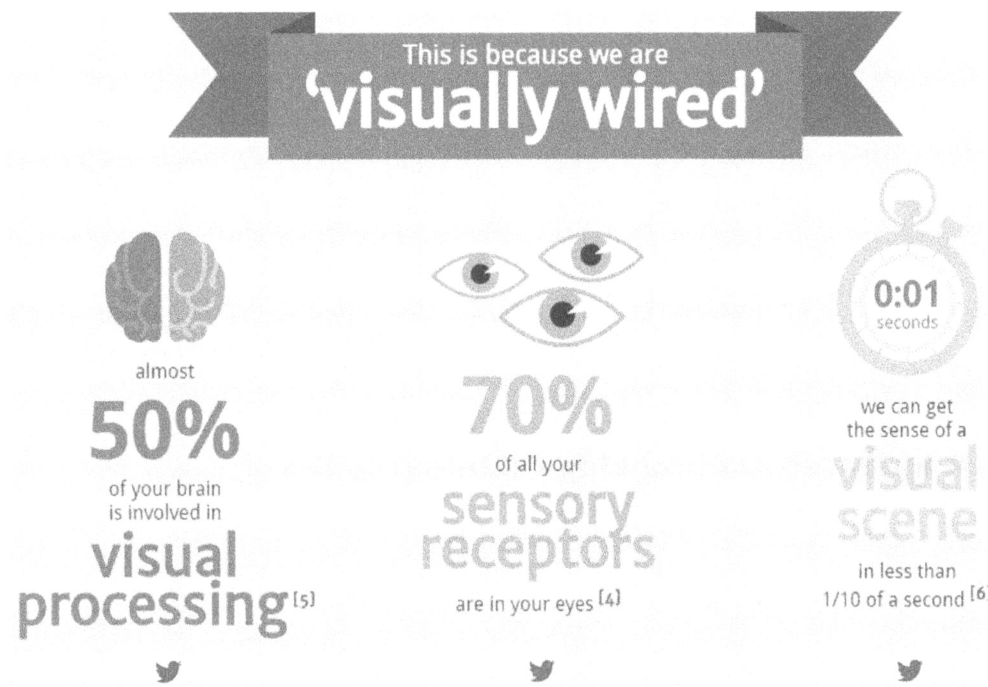

Figure 2.3. The Brain and Infographics. Part of "Thirteen Reasons Why Your Brain Craves Infographics," by NeoMam Studios and licensed under Creative Commons, http://neomam.com/interactive/13reasons/.

An infographic can be used to display information in relation to any topic. The most common types can be divided into the following eight general formats and will give you a good background to get you started. As you review the different infographics, think about the needs of your library. Which type will you use for what topic? Are there ones you might combine to convey those needs visually to your patrons? Remember, it is important to select the correct type of infographic for the topic you are working on and for the audience that will receive the message of the infographic. This means giving careful thought to the topic and audience as you choose the type of infographic. For more information about these and other types of infographics, see the URLs listed in table 2.1.

1. Statistical-Based Infographics

Certain types of infographics are targeted to people with specialized knowledge or expertise. "The secret is to choose the salient and most interesting facts within a topic in order to attract attention. Statistics are the most popular choice when creating an infographic; however, there are many variations" (Dubhaile Media, 2013).

Information graphics are visual devices intended to communicate complex information quickly and clearly. The devices include charts, diagrams, graphs, tables, maps, and lists. Among the most common devices are horizontal bar charts, vertical column charts, and round or oval pie charts, which can summarize a lot of statistical information. Diagrams can be used to explain how a system works. It may be an organizational chart that shows lines of authority or a system flowchart that shows sequential movement. Illustrated graphics use images related to the data.

The "snapshots features," up-to-the-minute news coverage of news (http://usatoday30.usatoday.com/graphics/snap/gra/gsnapshots/flash.htm) enhanced with audio and video clips used every day by *USA Today*, are good examples of this technique. Tables are common and may contain lots of numbers. Modern interactive maps and bulleted numbers are also infographics devices.

Statistical-based infographics work well with lots of content, made up of charts and numbers. Good design is needed to support data that oozes impressive numbers and is filled with data and statistics to visualize.

Applications that use infographics often present company information and industry research. Libraries use them to illustrate library demographics, collection facts, or library circulation figures. Figure 2.4 shows infographic popularity growing by the numbers using charts, color, and statistics to illustrate the increase. Note there is very little text to make the point.

2. Time-Based or Chronological Infographics

Timelines or chronologicals are a type of infographic where "visual representation of information and events" happens over time. "A timeline is the presentation of a chronological sequence of events along a drawn line that enables a viewer to understand temporal relationships quickly." Sometimes it is in the form of a "chronology that is in tabular, year-by-year paragraphs, or other form" (Ross, 2009). Presenting information on a timeline enables readers to analyze the time relationship between various stages of a process. For example, a bar chart that shows the growth in sales of a particular product over a period of time is a chronological infographic. It is made up of chronological dates that are visualized to make the graphic interesting and shareable. This type takes the user on a journey, either simple or complex, and has to be interesting or relevant enough for people to care about the trip. Some librarians might have read about one of President Roosevelt's largest initiatives to combat the Great Depression, a program called the Works Progress Administration (WPA), illustrated in the infographic timeline in figure 2.5. One of the many programs was one that constructed and repaired libraries.

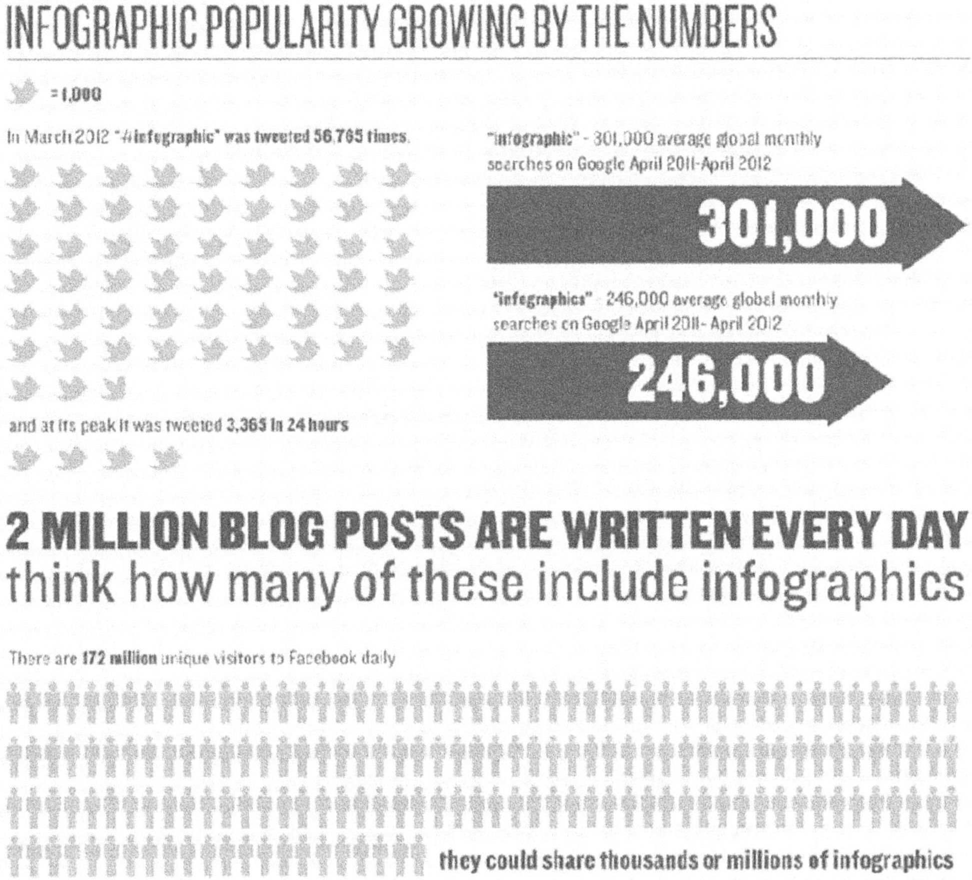

Figure 2.4. Statistical Example. From "What Is an Infographic?" by Customer Magnetism, https://www.customermagnetism.com/infographics/what-is-an-infographic/.

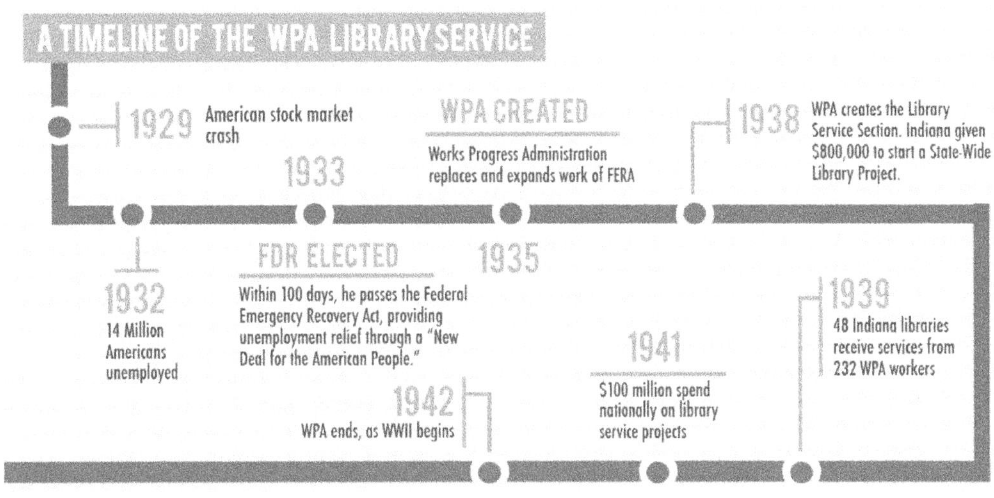

Figure 2.5. WPA Timeline. From "WPA and Libraries in Indiana," by Callie McCune, http://eduscapes.com/history/course/projects/wpa.jpg.

3. Process-Based Infographics

Process-based infographics usually can be seen in workspaces of factories or offices. You can also view them in cooking magazines that show their recipes using graphics. Often most of the food products have infographics instead of a detailed procedure on the back of their cover or box. Out of many, one important reason is to give you understanding about its uses in limited space. Using images to relate the data can produce a good example of the particular process so it's easy to understand. In libraries you may write infographics, such as how to search a database or use the online card catalog. In chapter 3 you will be going through the process of designing an infographic.

4. Location-, Directional-, or Geographic-Based Infographics

A geographic infographic is one of the most common types that you can find everywhere, from a school map to complicated astronomical graphs. City and country maps are also considered to be good examples of geography-based infographics; for example, see figure 2.6.

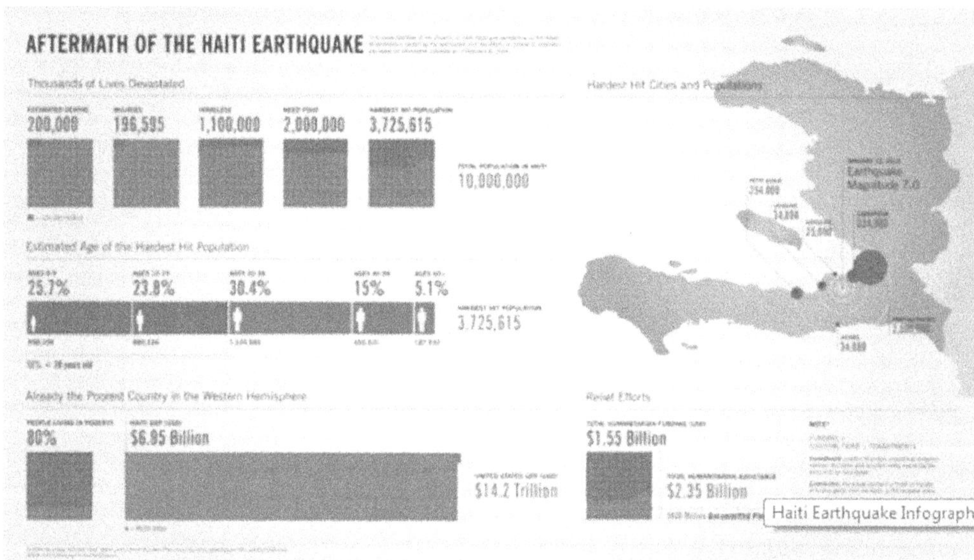

Figure 2.6. Aftermath of the Haiti Earthquake. From "Aftermath of the Haiti Earthquake, 2011," by Emily Schwartzman for a contest in *Good* magazine, http://www.emergency-response-planning.com/news/bid/46966/infographic-Aftermath-of-the-Haiti-Earthquake.

Other types of geographic infographics include symbols, icons, diagrams, graphs, tables, arrows, and bullets. You must remember that there are many types of lines (parallel, dotted, straight) used in maps to define subways, streets, highways, and railroad tracks. Traffic symbols, scale maps, and navigational aids on streets and highways are common examples. Also, many symbols and icons are used for specific landmarks like schools, churches, hospitals, banks, and so forth. Scale is the important parameter in those types as everything is marked according to particular scale or ratio.

5. Research Results Infographics

Research results infographics are ones used most often to show the results of a study or survey. Nonprofits can create an infographic based on their own internal survey of their constituents or create one jointly with other nonprofits that participated in broader research. For example, Santa Fe County (New Mexico) conducted a study with nonprofits including a local county library and an adjoining senior center to determine whether they should be part of a joint expansion project for needed county services. This project is now completed.

Upon completion of a different study in December 2011, titled "Infographics: American Public Libraries and Community Internet Access," the Bill and Melinda Gates Foundation (2012) sponsored an OCLC (Online Computer Library Center) WebJunction webinar on "Data Visualization for Advocacy," to depict the public library story of providing community Internet access and the need for increased funding to support this vital project. The research results of this study are available in the infographic in figure 2.7.

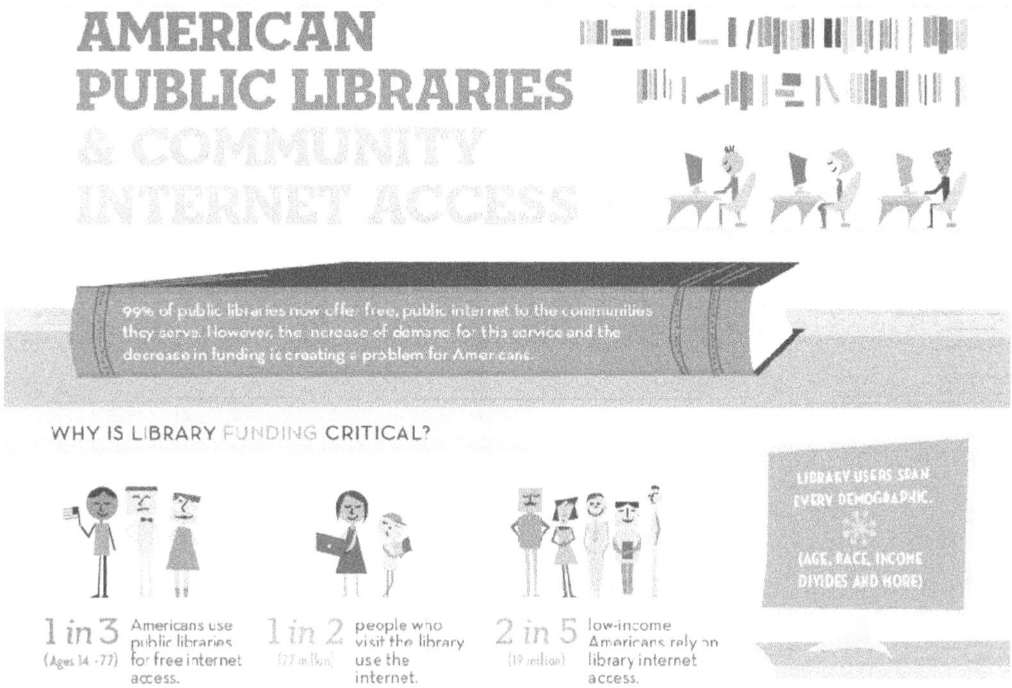

Figure 2.7. Public Libraries. From "American Public Libraries and Community Internet Access," by the Bill and Melinda Gates Foundation and licensed under Creative Commons, http://www.webjunction.org/content/dam/WebJunction/Documents/webJunction/Infographic8.5%20x%2011Color.pdf.

6. Compare and Contrast Infographics

Using compare and contrast infographics shows how something has grown or changed, for example, two or more products, ideas, philosophies, or programs as in the infographic "The Internet: A Decade Later" at http://www.bestedsites.com/the-internet-a-decade-later/. Nonprofits could showcase their history and accomplishments or their impact (how they've grown since they first started); they might compare and contrast a new way of doing something that they advocate or have adopted.

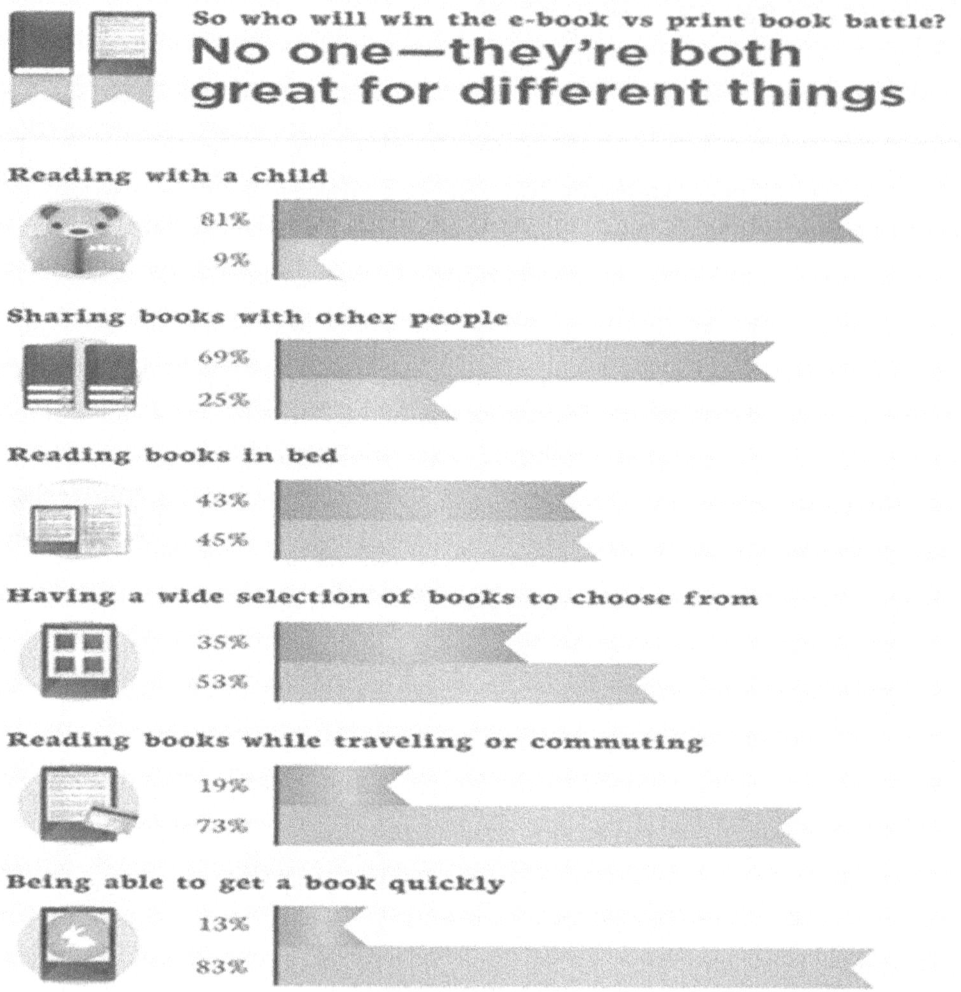

Figure 2.8. E-books vs. Print Books. From "Libraries Are Forever: E-books and Print Books Can Co-exist," by Rachel, Teaching Degree, and licensed under Creative Commons, http://dailyinfographic.com/libraries-are-forever-e-books-print-books-can-coexist-infographic.

Another compare/contrast option is to place two things in a head-to-head comparison so the differences can be visually seen. Design is important to visualize this comparison. This type works well with lots of data and has to be interesting or relevant enough for people to care about the comparison. Librarians may be interested in popularity of e-books as compared to print books, for example, which are favored and by whom (see figure 2.8).

7. Did You Know?

A type answering the question "Did you know?" would just be interested in facts without necessarily reporting on the entire results of any study—either pulling out one component of your own study or gathering data from other people's research into a unique compilation of information. Many nonprofits have fact sheets related to the people they serve or the issues they face that would make for very interesting infographics.

Using facts to support why a patron or outsider should support your library encourages an audience to visit the library either in person or online to support libraries. For example, "McGill Library and Archives Fun Facts" is a well-researched and well-

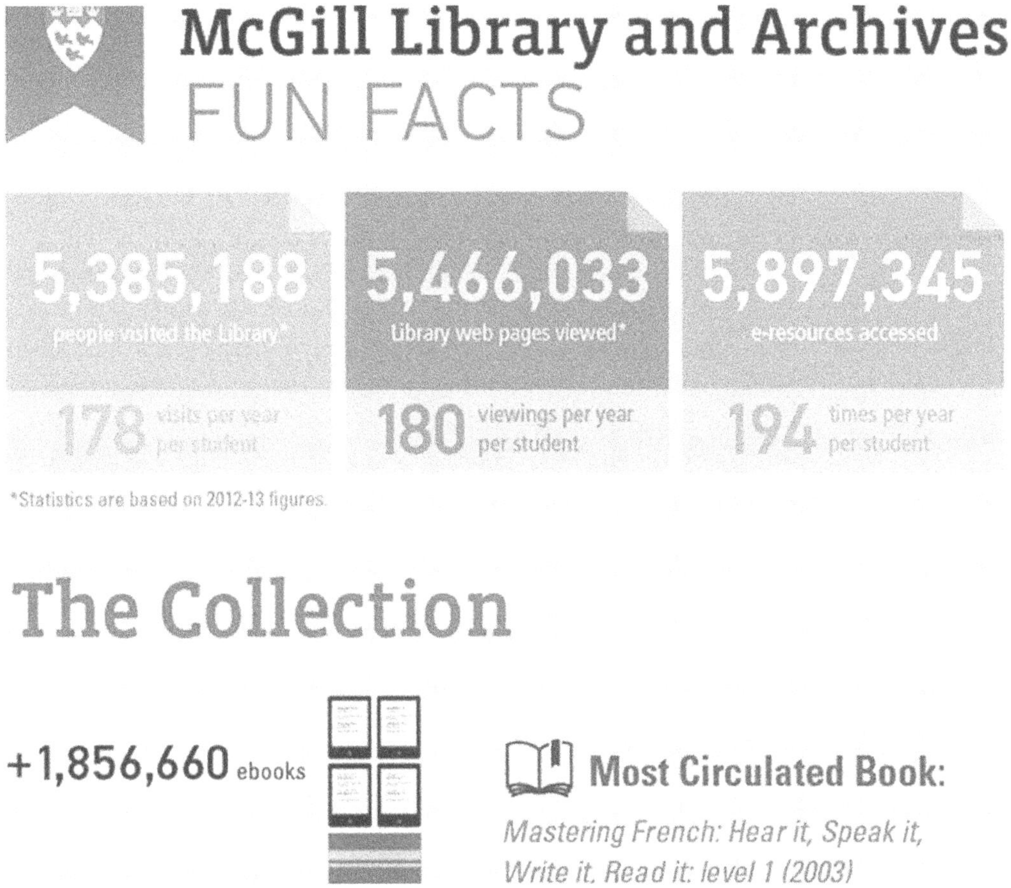

Figure 2.9. McGill Library and Archives Fun Facts. Courtesy of McGill University Advancement and McGill University Library and Archives, http://news.library.mcgill.ca/mcgill-library-and-archives-fun-facts/.

designed infographic with a complete list of facts and figures picturing the library and its importance (McGill Library, 2014). Often, there is a call to action: "Help the library in your neighborhood!" Help can take the form of obtaining a library card and regularly borrowing books in every possible form. Figure 2.9 describes important facts about the public library and its collection.

8. Demographics Infographics

Demographics is traditionally used when doing market research for a business or campaign of some kind and can be very useful information in general to put in an infographic. Nonprofits can profile their client population or the areas they serve to educate donors and constituents. In 1996 the City of San Jose, California, and San Jose State University Libraries, along with the city council and university officials, worked together to create a city-university library to service both city and university constituents. Both libraries needed more space and current space remodeling. As a result of the surveys and political meetings, the city and university came up with the idea of a joint library to service both city and university patrons. This successful joint project is a model of local government and university officials working together for a common purpose to service the tenth-largest city in California and one of the largest campuses in the California State University network. An infographic would have worked well to publicize this venture.

Other Types of Infographics

Other types of infographics have also gained traction:

Photo infographics use photos to visualize, present short pieces of content, or tell a short story. They offer a unique sign and can be helpful to visually explain something using real-life photos along with a narrative quote. Use them to answer a question, describe or explain something, or guide the reader. Design is usually simple but visually enticing.

Useful bait infographic is similar to a reference tool for information that can be used again and again, for example, explaining "how to do something." Because it is a visual reference and provides advice, people are likely to share it via social media or save it as files for use in the future. Repeated exposure for this kind of infographic almost guarantees it a long life. Infographics can not only be shared but frequently republished as well. Therefore, you can expect numerous good links to be generated for you with little effort. You can link the infographic to your home page or to your specific landing pages on your website. This would help increase website traffic and give it an SEO (search engine optimization) boost as well. Search engines would definitely note your presence on the Internet.

Advocacy infographic has as its purpose outlining an issue or problem and then inviting people to help fix it, often with a call to action. It is designed to educate and cause change, like this infographic "Stop the Texts, Stop the Wrecks" (http://www.pinterest.com/pin/278378820687125080/), a call to stop texting and driving. This call to action was picked up by several organizations such as Teen Motor Vehicle Safety, Auto Truck Group, and an insurance policy group that created their own infographics that passed on the message. Any advocacy campaign can be expressed through an infographic.

Flowchart infographics can answer specific questions by giving choices to readers so they reach the right answer for themselves. The design for flowcharts can be simple; flowcharts can be lighthearted and humorous, and they work well on social media.

Data vis (visualization) infographic is looked upon as information that is beautiful and can often be turned into something visually creative and appealing, making it seem unique and interesting. This type of infographic works with lots of data. The focus is on the design. The design can be simple but has to be effectively visualized.

Table 2.1. Types of Infographics

DESCRIPTION	URLS
Descriptions and examples of different types of infographics	http://www.instantshift.com/2009/06/07/infographic-designs-overview-examples-and-best-practices/
Statistical infographics	https://dubhailemedia.wordpress.com/2013/11/02/infographic-the-ultimate-guide-for-business/
More types of infographics	http://branded4good.com/8-types-infographics-nonprofits/
Different format timeline examples	http://bashooka.com/inspiration/stunning-timeline-designs/
Vector Open Stock template timeline	https://www.vectoropenstock.com/vectors/preview/71660/project-timeline-infographic-template http://www.freepik.com/free-vector/timeline-infographics-for-bussines-project_748613.htm
"Library of Congress by the Numbers"	https://historytech.files.wordpress.com/2012/09/loc-infographic.png

Visualized article takes on an otherwise lengthy piece of writing and makes it visual. A piece that uses a large amount of data—maybe containing statistics—may fit this model. It needs a strong title with lots of content and works well on social media.

Tips or demos infographics are great for just conveying general information or best practices about a topic directly helpful to patrons. They may start with "The Top 5"; for example, you might provide tips on the five best ways to improve a child's reading skills or tips to remember when going to a job interview.

Key Points

This chapter has demonstrated that to tell a story to meet the needs of diverse audiences, it is necessary to use different types of infographics as described. Numerous examples illustrate different styles for different purposes and diverse audiences. You will see more as you progress through this book.

- The anatomy of an infographic contains one- or two-deep levels and elements—visual, content, and knowledge.
- Infographics can be categorized according to how graphic information is presented to readers.
- There are eight different types of infographics, each with their own characteristics and specific uses.
- Other types of infographics provide more choices in addition to the more common kinds listed.
- The audience for an infographic determines in large part what type of infographic to select.
- The type of infographic should match your data and your narrative and ensure that viewers take away your message after reading it.

The popularity of infographics has spread throughout the world. Many librarians would like to tell a compelling story about their library through the medium of infographics. However, telling an effective story through infographics requires accurate data, compelling design, and visualization tools, as chapter 3 will describe.

Exercise for Chapter 2

Since you as a reader lead one of those fast-paced lives talked about in the first chapters of this book, you do not have a lot of time to interpret the data you just read. Therefore, as you read through each chapter, it is helpful to apply what you have just learned. This exercise lets you think about the concepts immediately so that you can focus on what has attracted your attention.

1. Review at least three different infographics from the sample illustrations in this chapter.
2. Divide a piece of paper in half lengthwise.
3. At the top of the left side, write the names of at least three or four types of infographics selected from the samples you reviewed. These should be ones you think

you might want to use to create your own infographic later after reading more about infographics.

4. On the right side, list three to five characteristics that stand out about each of the different types.
5. Think about a topic that would make a good infographic. Prioritize the types of infographics from high to low, one being the type you think would be best for your topic based on the characteristics you wrote down and three (or five), the least favorable type for your topic. State your reasons. Keep this information to use later in this book as you begin to compile information for infographics for your library.

References

Adams, Daniel. 2011. "What Are Infographics and Why Are They Important?" Instant Shift. March 25. http://www.instantshift.com/2011/03/25/what-are-infographics-and-why-are-they-important/.

Alexander, Anson. 2012. "Infographic Effectiveness Statistics [Infographic]." Ansonalex.com. May 21. http://ansonalex.com/infographics/infographic-effectiveness-statistics-infographic/.

Bill and Melinda Gates Foundation. 2012. "Infographics: American Public Libraries and Community Internet Access." Bill and Melinda Gates Foundation, March 12. OCLC WebJunction webinar on "Data Visualization for Advocacy." http://www.webjunction.org/documents/webjunction/Infographics_American_Public_Libraries_and_Community_Internet_Access.html.

Dubhaile Media. 2013. "Infographic: The Ultimate Guide for Business." November 2. https://dubhailemedia.wordpress.com/2013/11/02/infographic-the-ultimate-guide-for-business/.

McGill Library. "McGill Library and Archives Fun Facts." 2014. McGill University Library News. February 25. http://news.library.mcgill.ca/mcgill-library-and-archives-fun-facts/.

Ross, Anders. 2009. "InfoGraphic Designs: Overview, Examples and Best Practices." Instant Shift. June 7. http://www.instantshift.com/2009/06/07/infographic-designs-overview-examples-and-best-practices/.

Roy, Sneh. 2009. "The Anatomy of an Infographic: 5 Steps to Create a Powerful Visual." SpyreStudios. November 18. http://spyrestudios.com/the-anatomy-of-an-infographic-5-steps-to-create-a-powerful-visual/.

Further Reading

Ashton, Danny. 2015. "10 Reasons Why You Should Care about Visual Content Marketing." NeoMam Studios. February 19. http://neomam.com/blog/13reasons/.

Mortensen, Elizabeth. 2013. "Infographics: Three Formats for Communicating Information." Propoint. January 30. https://www.propointgraphics.com/blog/infographics-three-formats-for-communicating-information/.

Rocheleau, Jake. 2012. "How Do You Design Good Infographics?" SpyreStudios. June 27. http://spyrestudios.com/how-to-design-make-infographics/.

Sibley, Amanda. 2012. "19 Reasons You Should Include Visual Content in Your Marketing." *Where Marketers Go to Grow* (blog). August 6. http://blog.hubspot.com/blog/tabid/6307/bid/33423/19-Reasons-You-Should-Include-Visual-Content-in-Your-Marketing-Data.aspx.

CHAPTER 3

Creating an Infographic

IN THIS CHAPTER

- ▷ Identification and description of key components of an infographic
- ▷ Step-by-step process of creating an infographic
- ▷ Different elements of a sample infographic and how they contribute to a successful infographic

CERTAIN KEY MATERIAL IS NECESSARY in a successful infographic that gets shared and drives traffic to your website. When you create an infographic, you should consider three elements—story, design, and promotion. Each element is equally important, and none stands alone. For example, storyboarding happens as you plan the infographic and as you design it. Design takes into account the audience to whom you will be presenting your story. Each element encompasses key components that you will learn about next.

Key Components of an Infographic

Seven key components—story, style, simplicity, size, stats, sources, shareability—will assist you in creating a successful infographic (Vaughan, 2013). These components help to bring together the storyboarding, design, and promotion elements. Note that not all are required, but you should consider each one as you are working on the infographic.

1. Story

Just as with any story you write, an infographic should contain a title, a beginning, middle, and conclusion. It also needs to focus on information that is helpful to and inspires the audience you want to view the infographic.

Title. It should be short and grab attention, contain keywords, and give the reader a quick overview of what the infographic is about. The word "infographic" should be part of the title or one of the keywords.

Main idea. The main idea conveys the theme of the infographic—the information you want to share with your audience. Focus on one main idea, the central message, one that you can summarize in one or two sentences. If your infographic becomes too long or complex, segment it with visuals so that one message appears in each section as part of the total story. Because you want your infographic to be shared, the main idea should contain information that helps, inspires, and educates your audience. Visualize your information with images and text. Use graphs, maps, and data to support your content. Think about problems and challenges of addressing your target audience and how you will solve those visually with your infographic.

2. Style

The style of an infographic has several elements:

Visual appeal. Catch the eye and make the audience want to read it. The visuals should support the story and not distract from the central message.

Manageability. Provide an immediate overview of the message. If the infographic becomes too long, chunk the information into sections to delve deeper into the topic.

Hierarchy. Use headings, color, and size of text and images to showcase the important information.

3. Simplicity

Decide upon one style for your images, graphics, and photos and stick to it. Be consistent and limit fonts, restrict your color palette, and establish a flow and connection between sections with design elements or icons. Use white space to give the eyes a rest.

4. Size

Size does matter. Select an ideal horizontal width and keep the length manageable to maintain attention—longer does not mean better. If it becomes too long, consider starting a second infographic. Optimize the size for Pinterest (approximately 735 pixels wide). Compress your images for faster load time and to facilitate sharing.

5. Statistics

Use research, articles, and statistics to support your information. If using statistics, make sure they are current, factual, reliable, and on topic.

6. Sources

Incorporate reputable sources, and confirm your facts with references to your data to establish credibility for your information. Quotes from industry leaders can also support your theme.

7. Shareability

Provide readers with the tools they need to easily share your infographic. Include source information—organization name, URL, and/or logo and button to your website. Share infographics with social media—LinkedIn, Facebook, and influential bloggers in your industry. To encourage sharing, embed your infographic into a blog post to showcase it and make sure it links back to your website.

Sample Infographic Review

There are no hard-and-fast rules for creating your infographics, but it is important to consider all components as you begin. The infographic in figure 3.1 illustrates the elements just described.

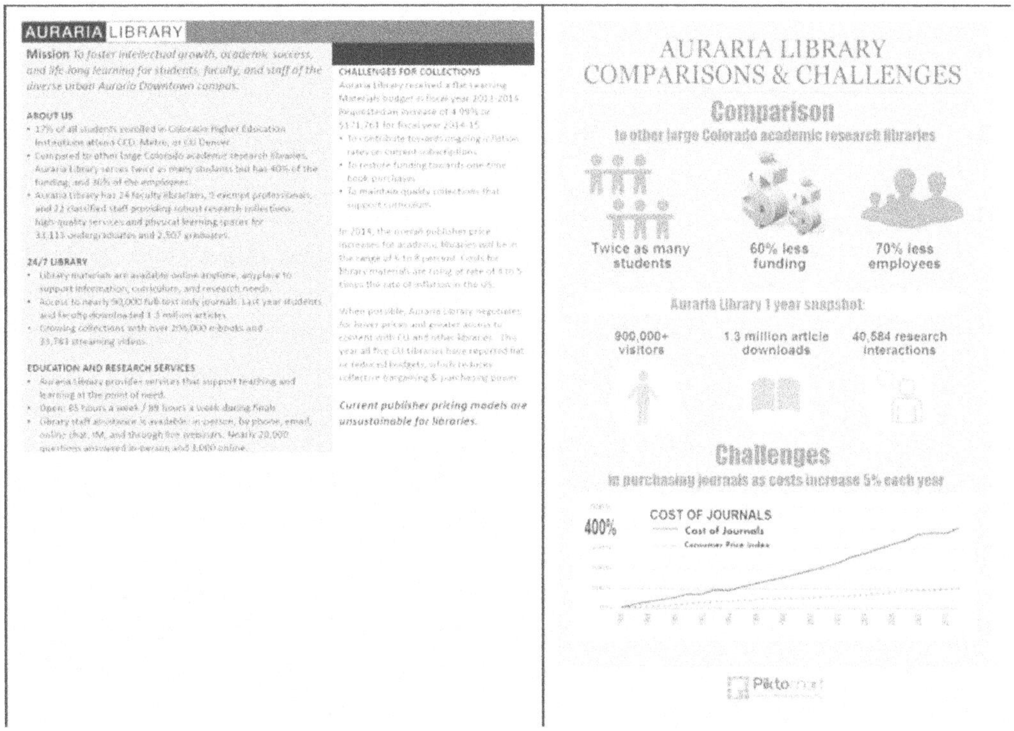

Figure 3.1. Auraria Library Infographic. By Cassi Pretlow and Jane Hood, Auraria Library, http://www.cuny.edu/libraries/conference/proceedings/Pretlow.pdf.

The most popular infographic topics are technology, business, social media, the economy, and health. Education and nonprofits have gradually joined the trend. Libraries are using infographics for a variety of purposes. The Auraria Library example (Pretlow, 2015) in figure 3.1 demonstrates how to use an infographic to communicate the value of the library and point out the challenges it faces to its users. The "before" side on the left of figure 3.1 outlines data gathered about the Auraria Library—its users, librarians, materials, and services—as well as data about Colorado libraries as a whole. It also focuses on the escalating cost of journals, the budgetary challenge facing the libraries.

The "before" column contains the collected data in text format. The author identifies a main idea or theme: to compare aspects of the Auraria Library with the other libraries in Colorado. To form the "story," she wrote down the mission, facts about the librarians, students served, the collection, and services provided by the Auraria Library. She also lists a major challenge, specifically, obtaining funding needed to pay for escalating journal costs. Statistics are included to emphasize the value and benefits of the library, as well as why funding was needed.

The infographic shown in the "after" column was based on the information gathered. It focuses on key points from the same information and data displayed in the "before" column. Once the data was simplified, two points stood out to visualize in the infographic—comparisons between Auraria Library and large Colorado academic libraries and challenges they all faced.

Divided into two sections, the infographic presents a visual representation of the information compiled about the Auraria Library. In section 1 it compares Auraria Library to other Colorado libraries in numbers served, funding, and number of employees. It also uses statistics to show the services of the Auraria Library. In section 2 a line graph illustrates the financial challenge Colorado libraries face because of rising journal costs. Each component just discussed is illustrated in the infographic:

- The title states the theme.
- The story shows the value of the library and need for funding to cover rising journal costs.
- The style includes a color palette of two colors (blue and green), a single font, a graph of journal costs, and a hierarchy of headings and size of images to visualize the information more easily. Review the infographic in color at http://cuny.edu/libraries/conference/proceedings/pretlow.pdf.
- The statistics lend authority to the information.
- Simplicity is using one font style with two sizes to show importance, a two-color palette, and simple graphics.
- Size is presenting the information concisely—not too short and not too long.
- Sources: the infographic is composed of internal data, so no sources are listed.

This example demonstrates the thinking process used to create the infographic and provides a model for libraries to follow. Table 3.1 lists more infographics to help you review how authors use different components to create infographics.

Steps to Create a Successful Infographic

As you saw in the Auraria Library infographic, a well-thought-out plan is important prior to creating an infographic. The following steps provide a guide to keep you organized as you start the process (Schrock, 2015).

Step 1

Think of an idea, a clear conceptualization of the message or story that the graphic is intended to convey; then craft an interesting story. The strength of your idea will make or break the success of your infographic. When selecting your topic, consider the following:

Table 3.1. Examples of Infographics

DESCRIPTION	URL
"E-books in America"—discusses popularity of e-books and describes characteristics of e-book readers	http://dailyinfographic.com/e-books-in-america-infographic
"A Look at Using Pinterest in Education"—covers how it's being used, tips for using it, and growth stats	http://www.teachthought.com/social-media/a-look-at-using-pinterest-in-education/
"The Book Is Not Dead"—shows that e-book/print book coexistence is more likely than conquest	http://dailyinfographic.com/the-book-is-not-dead-infographic
"Infographics & Information Literacy"—shows learning outcomes and topics presented in a library instruction session for first-year university students	http://transliteracylibrarian.com/2013/02/09/infographics-information-literacy/
"Challenged Materials in Colorado Public Libraries"	http://www.lrs.org/fast-facts-reports/challenged-materials-colorado-public-libraries-2012/
"Library Instruction: Student Success"	https://transliteracylibrarian.files.wordpress.com/2013/02/stss-follow-up-feb-2-2013.pdf
"Trends in U.S. Public Library Websites and Social Media Use"	http://www.lrs.org/data-tools/public-libraries/u-s-public-libraries-and-the-use-of-web-technologies/
Tips on improving on-page SEO	http://backlinko.com/on-page-seo?wide=1
"10 Reasons to Use Infographics in Content Marketing"	https://www.pinterest.com/pin/470907704762411675/
"Viral Sharing Tactics of an Infographic"	https://www.pinterest.com/pin/470907704763736454/ https://magic.piktochart.com/output/2209172-viral-sharing-infographics

1. Have a purpose for your infographic. Why do you want to tell the story?
    - Is it to make a complex idea understandable? Does it add value? Is it going to inform? Or, is it going to entertain? It needs to do at least one of these things, and knowing which one it is going to be can help shape the rest of the process.
    - Is the topic concise enough to be communicated in a short sentence?
    - What are the key questions or main theme on which you plan to focus?
    - Can you narrate your graphic and use illustrations to visualize the words and ideas?
2. Identify your audience. Understand the position and perspective of your potential audience to help you design the story line and later build the campaign to promote and attract that audience.
    - How will your intended audience approach the concept?
    - Will it be completely new to them?
    - Will they be skeptical and need convincing?
    - Are they experts you're trying to convince?

Step 2

Research your topic and gather data. Content is most important, and research makes the subject more meaningful.

1. Find a unique or clever angle to make the data meaningful.
    - Does the topic or concept reveal something interesting or urgent?
    - Have you showcased a trend or a truth that needs to be told and, more important, needs to be acted on?
    - Have you thoroughly researched the topic?
2. Identify statistics to provide legitimacy for your topic.
    - Are your statistics supported and verified with legitimate facts? Which facts will you share?
    - Is the data from reliable, authoritative sources? How was it collected? What are its limitations? Is it biased?
    - Have you analyzed the data? The Internet makes research easier, but you need to dig for credible data and use a variety of sources.
    - What concepts emerge from the data?
    - Is research and data suitable for creating visuals? Do you need to convert the data in any way?

Step 3

Edit the information.

- Is the topic focused on one main idea?
- Does your data support the topic's theme?
- Have you looked for more information you think will support and illuminate the topic and the infographic as a whole?

To summarize, weave together all the work you have done so far: purpose, audience, research, and unique angle. Consider where your audience is most likely positioned when they see the infographic and how you can accomplish your purpose and effect action. Every story has a beginning, a challenge, a struggle, a resolution, and hopefully, a moral. The story draws the audience in and gives them confidence, not only inspiring their own personal action, but also the need to share that discovery with others.

Step 4

Create an outline and flowchart to organize your infographic.

1. Begin with the most powerful piece of information to attract your audience.
2. Select points that will be interesting to visualize and group similar points together.
    - What form of visual will best tell the story?
    - Should the data be interactive to make it more meaningful?

3. Order the information logically and build to a clear conclusion and call for action at the end.
4. Write the connecting narrative so the data points flow together from one section to the next.
   - How will you portray your argument? Can you use a visual metaphor or analogy?
   - How will you reveal patterns or relationships? What type of infographic is most appropriate? (See chapter 2 for types.)
5. Indicate the sources of data that communicate reliability and validity of the information.

Step 5

Create a complete draft. Put all the pieces together.

1. Gather or create graphics.
   - What color palette will blend the content and graphics? Background colors and images serve as layers of messaging. Choose two or three primary colors with one for background (usually the lightest), and the other two to break up sections. Use shades of these three for variety.
   - Which visuals (e.g., icons and symbols, charts, bar graphs) will represent different sets of data? All sections should feel part of the same theme.
   - Where will you find images? Take into account copyright, and check images allowable under Creative Commons.
2. Create the layout.
   - Is all your content present within the graphic? Check for its accuracy.
   - Is it readable?
   - Can it persuasively educate the reader about the topic?
   - Can you automatically understand what the graphic is about?

Step 6

Review and refine.

1. Check and refine editorial content.
   - Is the most compelling information included?
   - Does the narrative have a beginning, middle, and conclusion?
   - Are your sources included? Are they cited? Check spelling and format.
   - Does the theme work for the topic? Are the right sections included?
   - Is there a hook, call to action, or primary takeaway?
2. Perfect the visuals.
   - Do the illustrations help you understand the topic, have no impact, or distract from really getting the information?
   - Is color used wisely?

- Do graphics and text tell the story, answer the main questions, and support the thesis?
- Is the typography appropriate to the text and graphics?
- Is all material that is not vital eliminated (e.g., redundant data, graphics that don't support the theme)?

Step 7

Share the infographic. An infographic, once created, doesn't just go viral by itself. You have to make it happen.

1. Apply sharing tools. Because infographics are appealing, the capacity for them to be shared on social networks and become viral is much higher than ordinary textual content.
   - Have you made use of social media like LinkedIn, Twitter, Facebook, Google+, and Pinterest, and included social-sharing buttons to embed on your site?
   - Do you have an embed code users can put on their own sites for further sharing?
2. Make the infographic searchable. Add the word "infographic" in your content, as a keyword, and as part of the title.
3. Roll it out on social media networks.
   - Did you submit your infographic to infographic directories?
   - Have you checked out blogs or other sites (e.g., Daily Infographic, Cool Infographics) that specialize in infographics?
4. Submit press releases to introduce your infographic.
   - Have you created social media press releases?
   - Have you submitted SEO-optimized press releases to gain publicity and drive traffic to your website? The viral nature of the infographic medium makes people link to your site, and Google will index your website higher. Review "Ten Tips for Search Engine Optimization (SEO)" below.
5. Reach out manually by checking related blogs, searching related topics, and tweeting your infographic with hashtags.
6. Share it on the right platform. Visual.ly (http://visual.ly), StumbleUpon (http://www.stumbleupon.com), and Reddit (http://www.reddit.com) are well-known platforms where you can share your infographics so that thousands of users can view them as well as vote them "up" or "down."
7. Strike a balance between a concept that is interesting and one that people will feel comfortable sharing.

Varying amounts of time are spent on each step in the process of creating your infographic. The bar graph in figure 3.2 visually illustrates the process in order of importance. Notice that the most time is spent on research for your idea and refining and perfecting the visual once you create the draft of the infographic.

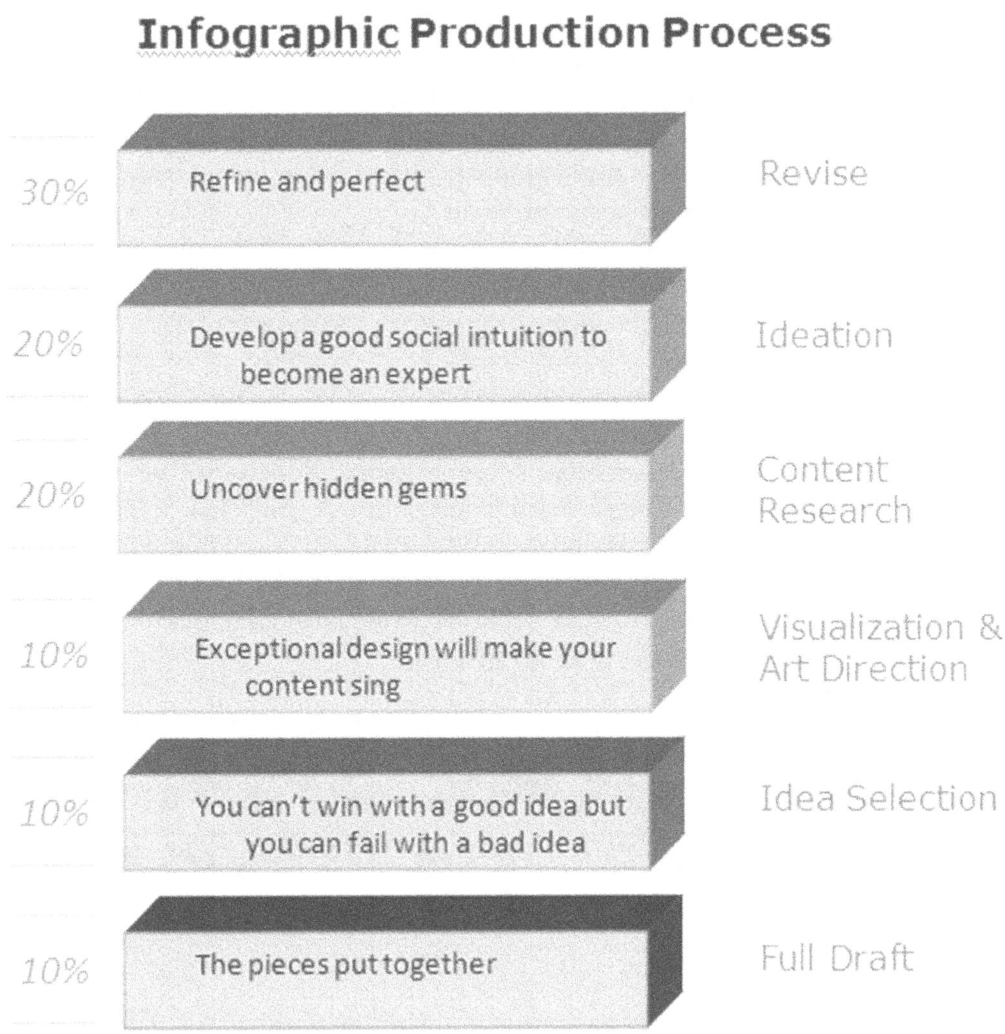

Figure 3.2. Infographic Production Process.

Ten Tips for Search Engine Optimization (SEO) for Your Infographic

To encourage more viewers to see and share your infographics, it is important for search engines to find them. Viral marketing can make that happen, but what does "go viral" mean? In simple terms, it means for content to be well received and widely shared. Viral marketing's main purpose is to circulate your message to as varied numbers of individuals as possible.

Understanding some of the components that make something viral can do a lot to make sure your content gets the attention it deserves and that you want.

Here are some tips to incorporate into the content of your infographic to increase interest and sharing through search engine optimization (SEO). Keep these in mind as you create your infographic.

1. Make the URL of the page containing your infographic short but containing keywords. Have the word "infographic" after the title. Google indicates that the first three to five words in a URL are given the most weight by search engines.

2. Start your title with a keyword, rather than have it appear in the middle or end of the title.
3. Engage your audience with images, videos, and diagrams to increase time on the page and reduce bounce rate—when a visitor quickly leaves your site.
4. Use outbound links to related pages and authorities to help the search engine home in on your topic.
5. Put the important keyword early in the content to emphasize that the content is about the keyword.
6. Add modifiers to the title, such as the year of the content and words like "review," "guide," or "infographic."
7. Compress images to boost page loading time. A page that takes too long to load is often abandoned by a potential viewer, never to return.
8. Add synonyms to your keywords. Review "Searches Related to . . ." at the bottom of Google search results or by using the Google AdWords Keyword tool.
9. Lower the bounce rate by adding internal links, writing unique copy, and creating a clean design.
10. Review figure 3.3 below to see how one author incorporated SEO tips into the content of an infographic.

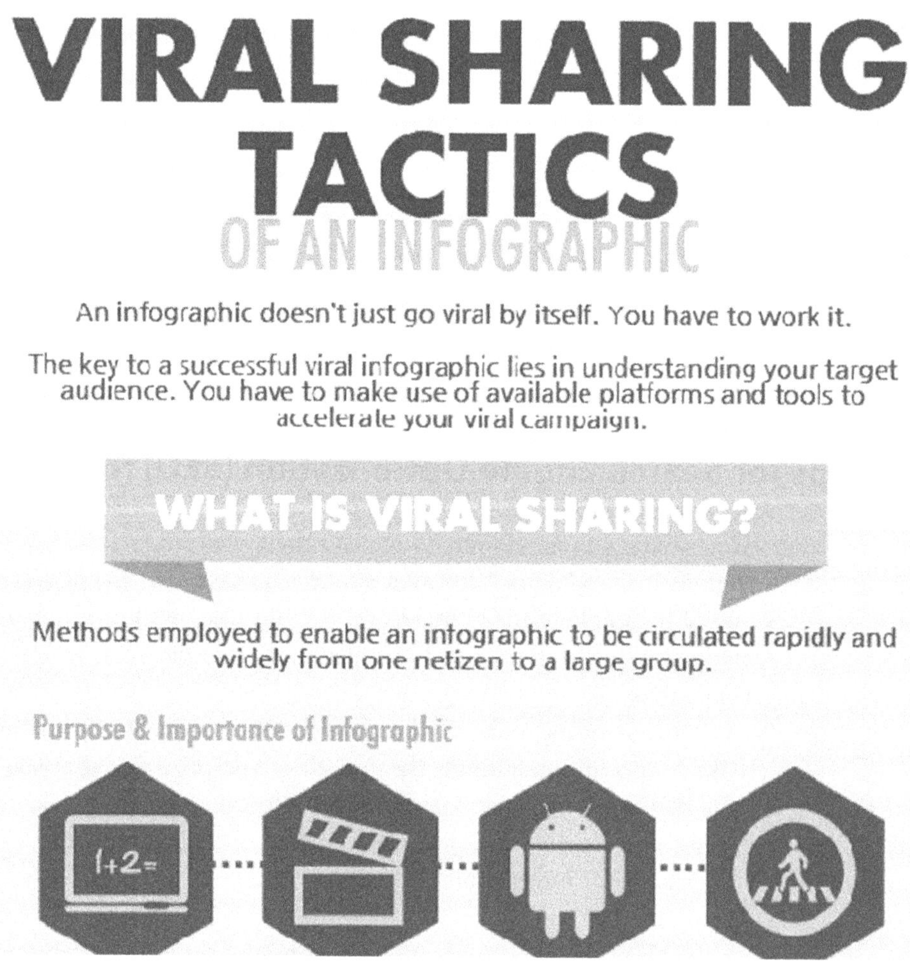

Figure 3.3. Viral Sharing Tactics of an Infographic. Created by Shuan Thing, https://magic.piktochart.com/output/2209172-viral-sharing-infographics.

Promoting the infographic is no less important than the story and design. After all, the goal of creating your infographic is to get your message out to people who will be impressed by your story and respond to your call for action.

Examples of Library Infographics

The more infographics you see, the more ideas you will have when it comes to creating your own. They enable you to see how libraries have used infographics for different purposes. They also illustrate the elements already discussed and show how the authors have weaved together text, research, and visual components, including images and color.

The seven steps just described form a framework for creating an infographic. You may follow each step depending on the purpose and audience, or you may select the steps that meet the needs of your infographic. Several examples from libraries demonstrate the results of using this step-by-step approach.

Example 1: "Capilano University Library Infographic"

The Capilano University Library conducted a survey (2013) of its users, the goal being to obtain feedback on what the library was doing well and what needed improvement. The survey resulted in valuable information that the library could use to better serve its patrons. Library staff created an overview of the results in the form of the following infographic (see figure 3.4).

The Capilano University Library decided on a topic, gathered data using a user survey, and created an outline of how they planned to present the content. They identified graphics, a color scheme, and text to represent the main ideas. Next, they created a draft to bring all the pieces together and then reviewed and revised the draft to create the final infographic. Lastly, they displayed the infographic on the university website.

As you review the infographic, you will see that the authors considered purpose, audience, images, information flow, color schemes, links, and font styles and sizes.

- The beginning of the infographic identifies the library using its logo, depicts the theme in the title "You spoke. We listened," and indicates how the information was gathered.
- The purpose and the library plans, based on what they learned from the survey, are written in the subtext under the title.
- Three sections identified with the same oval graphic and text font tell the story: who the users surveyed were, the suggestions they made, and the responses to the suggestions planned by the library.
- The color palette contains four colors: a blue background with yellow, green, and red accent colors. To see the color scheme, review the infographic at http://www.capilanou.ca/library/news/libqual-infographic/.
- Images in each section represent the different ideas: people for the users, batteries with text identifying three areas to address (people, resources, and space), and images on the batteries—people, a book, and a house—to illustrate the text.
- In section 3, light bulbs containing text outline the action items, the specific tasks to improve the library.

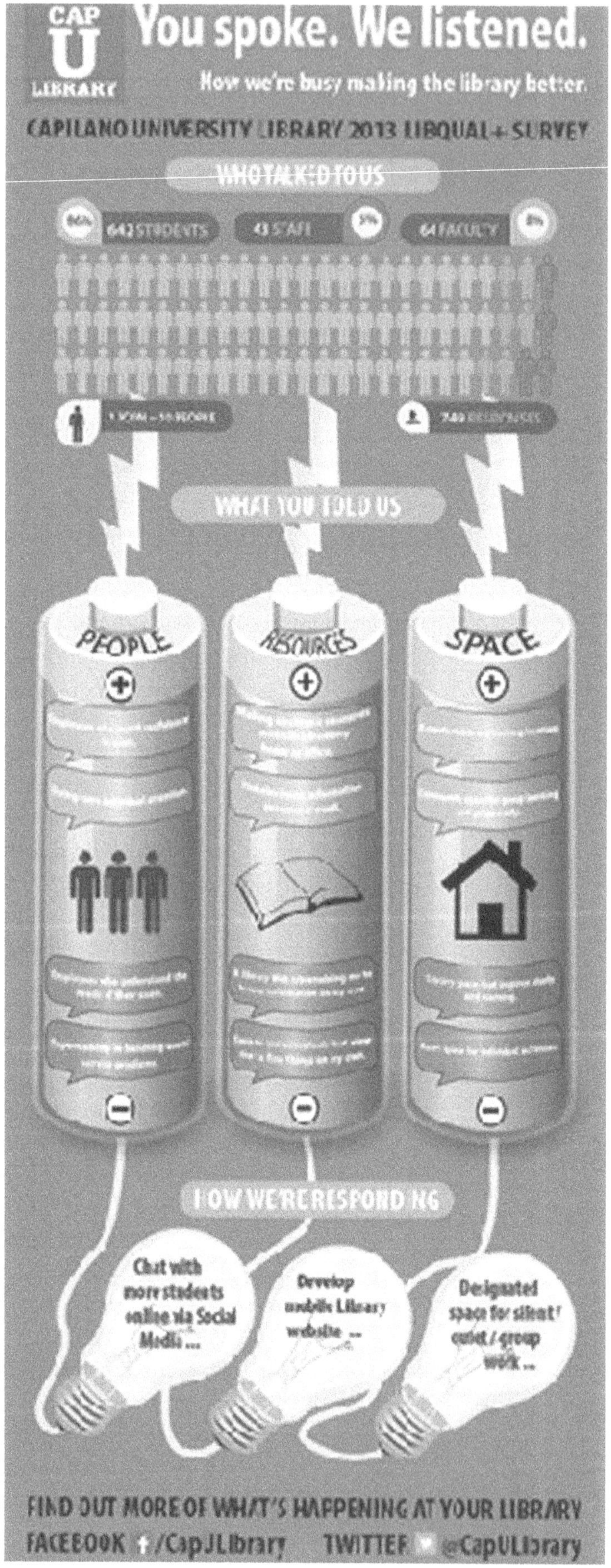

Figure 3.4. Capilano University Library Infographic. From "You Spoke, We Listened," created by the Capilano University Library, http://www.capilanou.ca/library/news/libqual-infographic/.

- Text at the end provides a call to action and allows a way for the infographic to go viral: find out more about the library using social media—Facebook and Twitter.

Once completed, the library placed the infographic on the Capilano University website. This infographic contains the components outlined for a powerful infographic and follows the steps discussed earlier. It presents the results of the survey clearly and shows its users that the library plans to focus on the suggestions made in the survey.

Example 2: "Libraries Are Forever"

The "Libraries Are Forever" infographic (TeachingDegree.org, 2012) examines the state of print books in the digital era by comparing print and e-book usage (see figure 3.5). Based on statistics about e-books and print books gathered in a study by the Pew Internet & American Life Project (Rainie and Duggan, 2012), TeachingDegree.org created the infographic "Libraries Are Forever: E-books and Print Books Can Coexist" to examine the state of print and e-books. The purpose is to show that e-books and print books can coexist. It uses statistics to highlight the differences between the two types of books.

Figure 3.5. Libraries Are Forever: E-books and Print Books Can Coexist. By TeachingDegree.org and licensed under Creative Commons, http://www.teachingdegree.org/2012/11/26/ebooks-vs-print-books/.

- The first section uses a book graphic to display the title, which also provides the theme of the infographic: libraries are forever and e-books and print books can coexist. It also identifies the color palette (complementary colors orange and aqua), and the text font that will be used in the rest of the infographic.
- Each of the four content sections, outlined in black, tells part of the story. Sections 1 and 2 provide statistics about the increase in e-readers and the reading habits of people with and without e-readers. Section 3 focuses on children's preference and reasons for using e-books and print. At the end of the third section, libraries are touted. The fourth section emphasizes the theme that no one is ready to give up print books and supports that premise with a bar graph indicating reasons for using each type of book.
- The final section states the conclusion that books, no matter what type, are here to stay. A large font emphasizes this point. See the complete infographic in color at http://dailyinfographic.com/libraries-are-forever-e-books-print-books-can-coexist-infographic.
- Visuals represent the text, for example, a teddy bear for children, an e-reader and print books with statistics, and shelves of books to depict the library.
- The ribbon image acts as a bookmark and moves the eye from one section to the next and is also carried through in the bar graph to unify the graphic.
- The template is divided within sections using double lines to indicate each sub-point and a medium-sized font.

Sources are provided to support the conclusions stated in the infographic. The organization's name—Teaching Degree—and URL make sure that once viral, the origin of the infographic is known and that it can be shared using a Creative Commons license.

As you can see, each of the sample infographics contains visual and textual components of an effective infographic. Having an outline of steps to follow helps both novice and seasoned creators of infographics organize the content and graphics for their desired purpose and specific audience.

Key Points

Following a step-by-step process will help ensure that your infographic is not only conceptually sound but accurate and easily understood. This chapter has identified components to include in infographics and a step-by-step process to follow when creating them.

- The basic elements of infographics are pretty simple: content, visuals, and the knowledge they represent.
- A theme makes it easy to identify what your graphic is about and create a story to convey a message.
- Visual elements, including colors, icons, and pictures, describe the content so you can quickly summarize data or make connections that might be difficult to perceive otherwise.
- Knowing your audience enables you to tailor your infographic to their taste to increase the chance of viral sharing among a like-minded audience.
- Planning your infographic using a step-by-step process is key to organizing your information, data, and images to convey a message.

- Incorporating search engine optimization (SEO) components into your infographics provides a better chance for them to go viral.
- A well-planned and well-designed infographic can be shared across social media platforms and can go viral on relevant websites.

Infographics are popular because they simplify concepts that would otherwise be difficult to understand or are simply overwhelming to consider. While the attention spans of Internet page visitors are diminishing, expectations for quick and compelling content are increasing. Users not only want to be able to parse information quickly, they demand an enjoyable experience doing so.

Knowing the different parts that comprise an infographic and having a plan to follow to create one enables you to transform tedious data into graphic-rich content, designed specifically to be easier to digest, more engaging, and highly shareable. The graphic visual representations of information and data make content more fun to understand because they present complex information quickly and clearly. Chapter 4 identifies tools that will make the actual creation of your infographic easier.

Exercises for Chapter 3

By completing the following tasks, you will practice what you have just learned about creating an infographic. To begin, select an infographic from those listed in table 3.1, and analyze it to identify components used and the steps you think were followed. Then complete the following tasks and answer the questions.

1. List the components. What important elements, if any, are not included and why do you think they were omitted?
2. State the purpose and audience. What parts of the infographic emphasize the purpose and give you a clue about the audience?
3. Provide an outline. What are the main and supporting points that create the story?
4. List support for the main and supporting ideas to make them believable. How does the support add authority to the topic? If statistics are used, what makes them credible?
5. Check the research. What type of research supports the ideas (e.g., statistics, surveys, organization data)? Are sources listed? What types of sources are included (e.g., varied, authoritative, Internet only)?
6. Review the visuals. What is the color palette? How do font type and size help to organize the infographic? How does the creator move your eye from beginning to end? How do the images help convey the points of the story (the message)?
7. Identify how to share the infographic. Who is the creator? Where can the infographic be shared?
8. Based on your answers to the questions, what is your overall opinion of the infographic related to purpose for a specific audience, combination of text and graphics to tell the story, research/support to lend authority to the topic, and use of visuals?
9. What are the strong points of the infographic and what suggestions would you give the creator to make it better?

Reviewing infographics of others will help you as you start putting together your own story, content, and design.

References

Capilano University Library. 2013. "Library Survey Results." October 24. http://www.capilanou.ca/library/news/libqual-infographic/.

Pretlow, Cassi. 2015. "From Data Snore, to Data Score: Communicating Library Assessment Data Visually through Infographics." Auraria Library, Denver. Accessed January 30. http://cuny.edu/libraries/conference/proceedings/Pretlow.pdf.

Rainie, Lee, and Maeve Duggan. 2012. "E-book Reading Jumps; Print Book Reading Declines." Pew Internet & American Life Project. December 28. http://libraries.pewinternet.org/2012/12/27/e-book-reading-jumps-print-book-reading-declines/.

Schrock, Kathy. 2015. "Infographics as a Creative Assessment." Accessed May 15. http://www.schrockguide.net/infographics-as-an-assessment.html.

TeachingDegree.org. 2012. "Libraries Are Forever: E-books and Print Books Can Coexist." *TeachingDegree.org* (blog). http://www.teachingdegree.org/2012/11/26/ebooks-vs-print-books/.

Vaughan, Pamela. 2013. "The 7 Key Components of a Knockout Infographic." *Where Marketers Go to Grow* (blog). November 11. http://blog.hubspot.com/marketing/knockout-infographic-components.

Further Reading

Haughney, Christine. 2012. "Young People Frequent Libraries, Study Finds." *New York Times*, October 22. http://mediadecoder.blogs.nytimes.com/2012/10/22/young-people-frequent-libraries-study-finds/?ref=technology&_r=0.

"Infographics & Information Literacy." 2013. Transliteracy Librarian. February 2. http://transliteracylibrarian.com/2013/02/09/infographics-information-literacy/.

Qualey, Ellen. 2014. "What Can Infographics Do for You? Using Infographics to Advocate for and Market Your Library." *AALL Spectrum*. February. http://www.aallnet.org/mm/Publications/spectrum/Archives/Vol-18/No-4/pr.pdf.

Rainie, Lee, Kathryn Zickuhr, Kristen Purcell, Mary Madden, and Joanna Brenner. 2012. "The Rise of E-reading." Pew Internet & American Life Project. April 4. http://libraries.pewinternet.org/2012/04/04/the-rise-of-e-reading/.

Roy, Sneh. 2015. "Anatomy of an Infographic: 5 Steps to Create a Powerful Visual." SpyreStudios. Accessed January 28. http://spyrestudios.com/the-anatomy-of-an-infographic-5-steps-to-create-a-powerful-visual/.

CHAPTER 4

Resources to Create Infographics

IN THIS CHAPTER

- ▷ Graphic design principles
- ▷ Visual design elements
- ▷ The importance of design principles when creating an infographic
- ▷ Graphic design tools used to create infographics
- ▷ Design principles and elements in infographic examples

AS DISCUSSED IN CHAPTER 1, visual communication has great impact on an audience. Communicating visually is the most effective means to get your message perfectly conveyed. And in doing this, infographics play a crucial role in this digital world.

There's no doubt that infographics are a great means to attract readers to your content information. If you ask a reader to pick between a lengthy one-thousand-word article and an infographic with pictures that requires a few scrolls, the reader will most likely go for the infographic. Reasons include: the way the human eye sees and reads content, diminishing attention spans, growing information overload, an infographic's unique ability to tell a visual story, and the enormous viral sharing potential allowed by the medium. An infographic at http://visual.ly/6-reasons-visualize-your-data illustrates reasons infographics have become so popular.

Visual Design Principles and Elements

Visual literacy is increasingly becoming an important skill for lifelong learning. Today's students will be expected to be visually literate as they enter the workforce. Visual literacy is highly dependent upon information literacy, and visual literacy activities provide librarians with the opportunity to teach both visual and information literacy skills. Add digital tools into the mix, and you'll also be developing digital literacy skills.

A definition by Association of College and Research Libraries (ACRL) (2011) explains visual literacy and its importance:

> Visual literacy is a set of abilities that enables an individual to effectively find, interpret, evaluate, use, and create images and visual media. Visual literacy skills equip learners to understand and analyze contextual, cultural, ethical, aesthetic, intellectual, and technical components involved in the production and use of visual materials. A visually literate individual is both a critical consumer of visual media and a competent contributor to a body of shared knowledge and culture.

On the *Designer Librarian* blog, Amanda Hovious (2013) writes about infographics as the "intersection between information literacy and visual literacy." Creating an infographic requires a high level of information literacy to find, understand, and evaluate data and a high level of visual literacy to display that data clearly.

Proven design principles and elements will give you ideas to consider whether you are creating the infographic yourself or need to provide ideas to a graphic designer who is doing it for you.

- Principles of design are the artistic guidelines to organize or arrange the structural elements of design. Ten principles of effective design are common: alignment, balance, contrast, emphasis, hierarchy, proportion and scale, proximity, repetition/pattern, rhythm/movement, and unity.
- Elements of design are the components or parts that can be isolated and defined in any visual design. They structure the infographic. Basic elements of design are common throughout the field of designing: color and value, dominance/size, line, shape, space, texture, and typography and fonts.

Since this book is not a design manual, a few tips should get you started. The URLs in table 4.1 at the end of this section on design provide additional resources if you want to delve more deeply into the area of design.

You can express your thoughts and intentions for your infographic with the elements of design and do it effectively by incorporating the design principles. Consider the following principles. Then select the elements you think will achieve your purpose and have the desired effect on your audience.

Principles of Design

Design principles are guidelines to follow. Principles tell us how you should organize design elements on the page to convey your message. You don't have to follow any one principle, but before going against one, you should understand why it exists as a principle and what not adhering to it communicates.

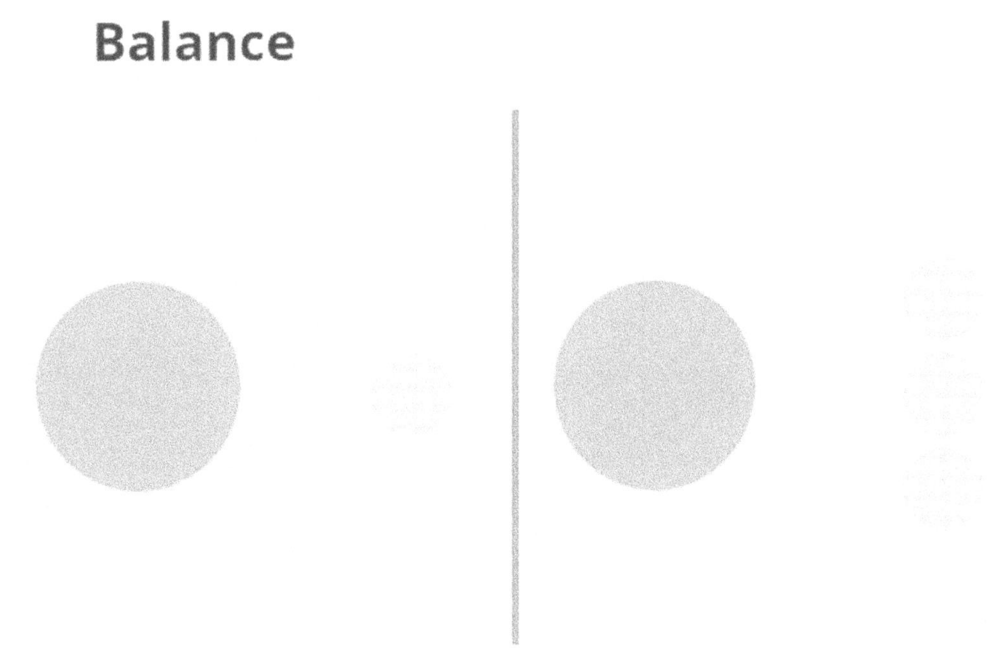

Figure 4.1. Example of Balance Principle. From "The Five Principles of Design and What They Can Do for You," by Sean Kirkpatrick, 2014, for the Canva Design School blog, https://designschool.canva.com/blog/five-principles-design-can/.

Alignment. Create start and endpoints on a page. Avoid using more than one alignment and stay away from having the information (e.g., text, images) centered on the page.

Balance. Position elements so they appear unified on the page and do not compete with each other. The design should have equal weight on both sides (see figure 4.1).

Contrast. Use contrast to help organize and create interest on a page, as well as emphasize or highlight key elements in your design. Create contrast using large and small type, old or new fonts, thick or thin lines, warm or cool colors, and vertical or horizontal lines. Vary the size of the shapes according to importance. As you design your page, also consider using blank space, asymmetrical design, or large and small text, some very bold or minimal. These elements will also create visual interest. Use a color wheel (see figure 4.2) to select visually pleasing color combinations such as complementary colors.

Emphasis. Stress one element over another in your design so it stands out to grab the attention of your audience. You can do this by using the size, color, or placement of the object to increase the focus on a certain part of the infographic. Make your text bolder or an image larger, or use a color brighter than your background.

Hierarchy. Use a visual hierarchy to help the reader pick out the most important information. It controls how the human eye perceives the order of the information on the page.

Proportion and scale. Recognize that you are communicating different messages by placing elements in and out of proportion, and make appropriate decisions based on what you want to communicate. Proportion helps create unity in a design. Elements out of proportion evoke emotion and call attention to themselves. If done on purpose, out-of-proportion elements can exaggerate the message of an element.

Play with the scale and size of your objects, shapes, type fonts, and other elements to add interest and emphasis. Scale lets you show contrast between different elements as well as similarity in groups of elements. Make sure that both text and image get a fair

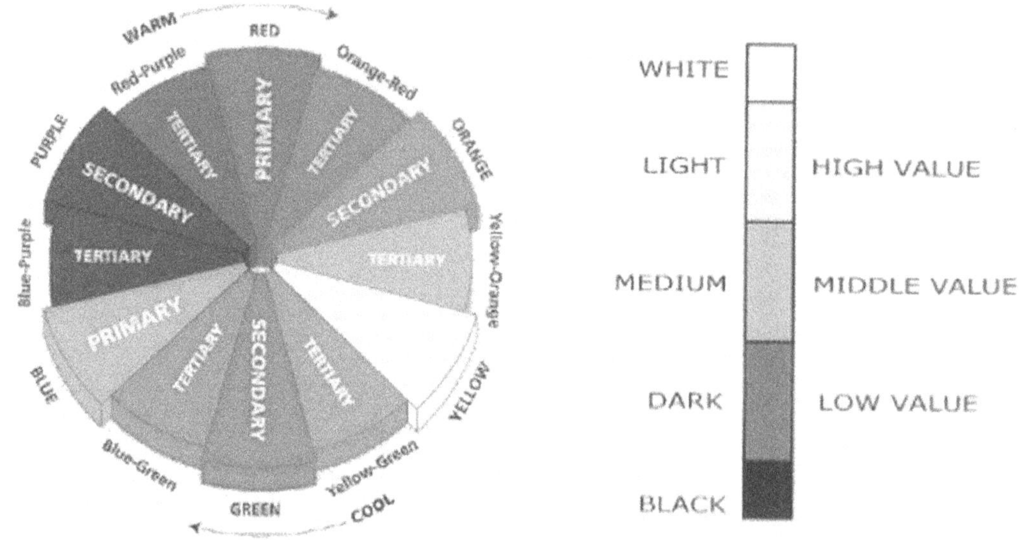

Color Wheel *Value Scale*

Figure 4.2. Color Wheel. From "Elements and Principles of Design," slide 18, by Pooja Jindal, ADMEC Multimedia Institute, http://www.slideshare.net/admecinstitute/principles-of-design-30520900?related=6.

share of the page. Put the image as the first thing you see so it is sure to catch your eye and attract you first.

Proximity. Group related elements together into closer proximity to automatically organize your infographic. Allow space to identify various parts of your design. Proximity determines the placement of elements together and apart from one another. It also makes the text more readable. Avoid too many separate elements on a page and leaving equal amounts of white space between elements.

Repetition or pattern. Unify and strengthen the infographic and create visual interest. Repetition communicates that certain elements are at a particular level in the hierarchy. Use bullets; a bold font; and color, line, and format design elements to create repetition (see figure 4.3).

Rhythm and movement. Repeat one or more elements of design to create a feeling of movement. To encourage the eye to move sequentially from one point to the next, try using a curved line that moves through your text from image to image. To keep rhythm exciting and active, variety is necessary.

Unity. Arrange elements so that all parts of the design form a coherent whole. Designs must be in harmony so that all sections seem as one complete unit.

Elements of Design

Design elements are the items you actually use in a design. You create elements or objects, and you place them on the page according to a set of design principles. An infographic of elements of design is available on slide 1 at http://www.slideshare.net/mohi_t/elements-of-design-14334177?related=1.

Become familiar with the following design elements so that you can use appropriate ones to communicate your message to a specific audience when you are designing your infographic:

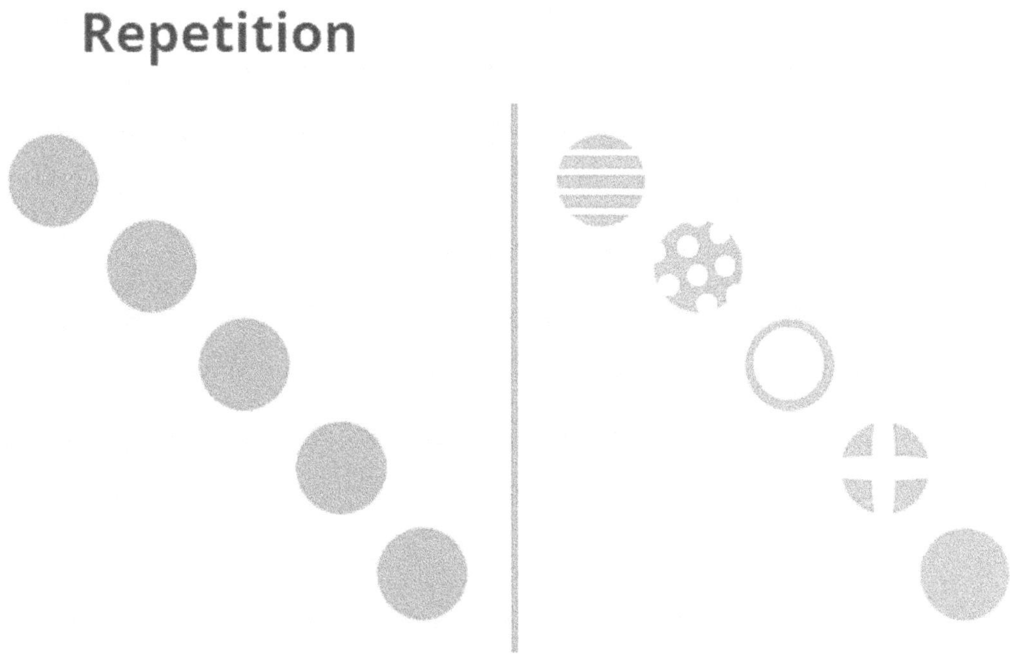

Figure 4.3. Example of Repetition Principle. From "The Five Principles of Design and What They Can Do for You," by Sean Kirkpatrick, 2014, for the Canva Design School blog, https://designschool.canva.com/blog/five-principles-design-can/.

Color and value. Transmit mood and emotion with color. Color contributes to unity, emphasizes important elements, and leads the eye through your infographic. For example, use warm colors (e.g., red, yellow, and orange) to make the viewer feel happy and optimistic or angry and irritated. For feelings of peace and tranquility, try cool colors (e.g., blue, green). Value is the lightness and darkness of color and can be used for emphasis.

If something is well designed but has poor color choices, it will not be successful because of the way the brain works. Knowing a bit about color theory, the field of study that examines how colors affect sensory experience, will help you select colors that are appropriate to use together and ones that fit the purpose and audience of your infographic. Review the color wheel in figure 4.2, a tool that organizes color, and try different color combinations. Even if you don't know much about color theory, links in table 4.1 at the end of this section on design list sites that offer free resources to pick colors that work well together.

Dominance/size. Make elements more noticeable by changing the size of images and text. The dominant element should be the largest and the first one on the page (e.g., title that states the purpose). Use size to create a focal point or starting point in your design and create a visual hierarchy.

Line. Draw your viewer's eye into an image, define space, emphasize, and create texture with line. Line can also tell the viewer how to feel—for example, curved lines for a soothing mood, vertical lines for power, and diagonal, converging lines for depth.

Shape. Try different types of shapes: geometric, free form, or abstract. Use them to add or sustain interest, organize or separate elements, and direct the eye through a design. For example, choose a geometric shape to suggest order and formality, and a free-form shape (e.g., a curvy or irregular object) to draw attention to important page elements. Limit the number and size of shapes where possible for clarity in conveying your message.

Space. Use space to both separate and connect elements to show relationships. White space does three things: creates groupings of elements, provides emphasis and hierarchy, and improves legibility (Bradley, 2010). It gives a place for the eye to rest in order to absorb the message you're trying to communicate. Less space makes sense. More densely packed information allows readers to compare the data more quickly. You'll want enough space so each bit of information can be clearly seen and understood, but not so much that it makes it hard to compare and contrast them.

Texture. Add texture to provide visual richness, to make a page appear to have more depth, and to make the colors blend more smoothly. Texture can also create drama or visual interest. Use texture to create a focal point, provide contrast, and help visually balance your design.

Typography and fonts. Help your viewer scan the text by electing a good typeface to make your message more effective (LibGuide Penn Libraries, 2015). A few tips to keep in mind:

- Mixing fonts can add visual interest, but less is best. Start with just two, and try not to use more than three. Use a different typeface for headers and body text to make important words stand out.
- The most important quality of your typeface is that it must be readable.
- Don't take spacing for granted; experiment with different distances between letters to change the effect of your text.
- Indenting, line spacing, and placement can provide cues during the reading.

As you look at different resources on design, you may see elements listed differently. The important thing is to think of the overall elements of design as a way to edit down the visual pieces of your existing infographic in order to organize and make them more cohesive.

The example in figure 4.4 (https://commons.wikimedia.org/wiki/File:Cambria_fontsample.svg) shows variations in the design element typography from font, color, and size of text to types and examples of typography. Altering these elements may cause your infographic to appeal to a different audience or change the purpose.

Knowing these elements and principles won't make you the next Monet or Picasso; they should, however, make it easier to think about designing your infographic. Table 4.1, mentioned earlier, contains resources (e.g., free fonts, color palettes, how-to tutorials) and ideas to help you in your design efforts. Follow these tips to make sure your design is solid and your information stacks up to scrutiny. Remember the importance of visuals and the beneficial effects they will have on your audience to achieve the purpose for which you've created your infographic.

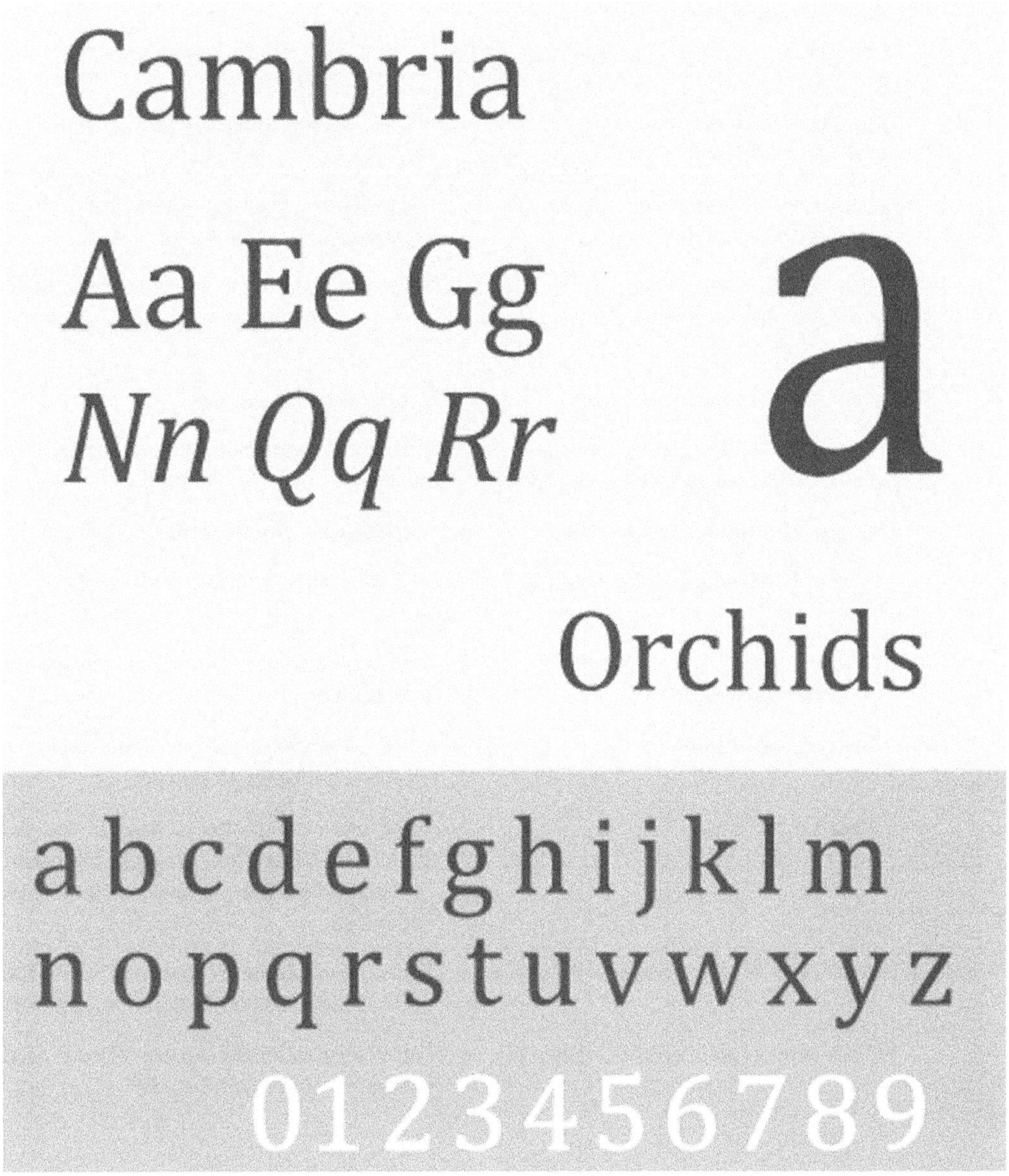

Figure 4.4. Design Element Typography. A sample of the public-domain typeface Cambria. Created by Hans Hoogglans / Wikimedia Commons, https://commons.wikimedia.org/wiki/File:Cambria_fontsample.svg.

Table 4.1. Design Resources

DESCRIPTION	URL
Instruction video of infographics design from Penn Libraries	https://www.youtube.com/watch?v=hE0SyO1pzMo
Infographic outline of file formats, color models, and other design jargon	http://www.crafted.co.uk/latest/blog/infographic-a-guide-to-graphic-design-jargon
"How to Do a Visual Analysis (A Five-Step Process)"—from the Visual Communication Guy	http://thevisualcommunicationguy.com/2015/01/12/how-to-do-a-visual-analysis-a-five-step-process/
Color palettes to use in designs	http://design-seeds.com/
"Design for Non-Designers"—design elements and advice for choosing them	http://www.jasonshen.com/2013/design-for-non-designers/
"Design 101: Design Elements, Part 1"	http://acrl.ala.org/techconnect/?p=1067
"Design 101: Design Elements, Part 2: Typography"	http://acrl.ala.org/techconnect/?p=1251
"Graphic Design Tips to Make Your Infographic Stand Out"	http://spyrestudios.com/graphic-design-tips-infographics/
"Principles of Design"	https://www.getty.edu/education/teachers/building_lessons/principles_design.pdf
"Basic Color Theory"	http://www.colormatters.com/color-and-design/basic-color-theory?utm_source=CMblog&utm_medium=link&utm_campaign=10-basic-elements-of-design
How to use design principles with Canva	https://www.youtube.com/watch?v=5tomNzVd_18&list=PLNaEwbQaxEWC-ijlGhCpJlyJoAiS3GX2B&index=4
"The Elements and Principles of Design"	http://www.slideshare.net/admecinstitute/principles-of-design-30520900?related=6

Tools to Create Infographics

Different types of tools are available to help designers and nondesigners create infographics. The following tools have become quite popular, especially among those who are novices at creating infographics. A snapshot of each tool lists its particular strong points and design features.

Microsoft PowerPoint (http://www.powerpoint.com)

PowerPoint is a tool with which most users who are planning to create an infographic will be most familiar. It's a good choice for beginners because most users know the basics of the program already. It includes some basic shapes and quite a bit of clip art. You'll probably want to edit most of your images in another program and then import them to Power-

Point. HubSpot provides ten free PowerPoint templates to get you started. An excellent tutorial created by HubSpot at http://blog.hubspot.com/blog/tabid/6307/bid/34223/5-infographics-to-teach-you-how-to-easily-create-infographics-in-powerpoint-templates.aspx will help you as you begin to create your infographic in PowerPoint (see figure 4.5).

PowerPoint Features

- Easy-to-make charts from Excel data
- Editable shapes and clip art
- More customizable than web-based tools
- Cannot embed videos
- Easily accessible to students and educators
- Save in PNG format

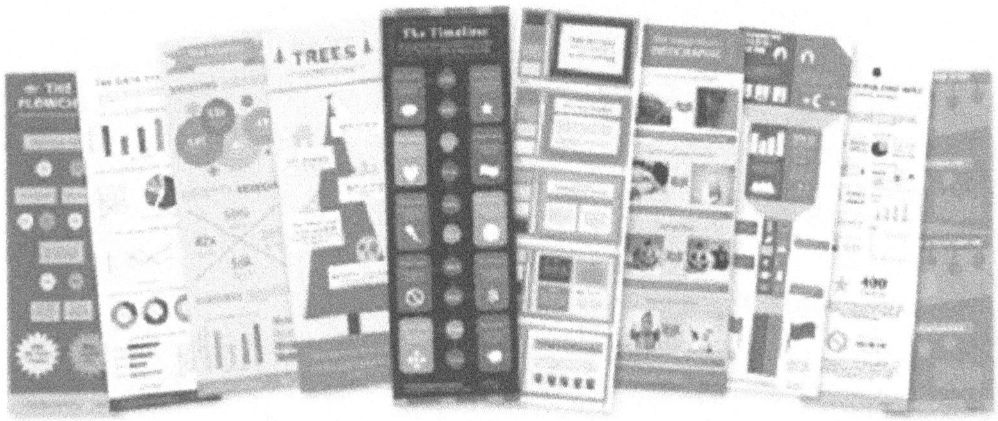

Figure 4.5. PowerPoint Example. From HubSpot, Inc. (templates at http://hubs.ly/y0VLjn0).

Canva (http://www.canva.com)

Canva lets you easily create infographics, slides, flyers, and photo collages using a drag-and-drop process. It contains templates, pictures, clip art, textboxes, icons, and more. You can upload your own images. The completed infographic can be downloaded as PDF and PNG files. Figure 4.6 shows a variety of free icons available in Canva.

Free Version Canva Features

- Templates and large library of clip art and photographs or start with blank page
- Easy-to-use drag-and-drop background and images
- Easy photo editing
- Collaboration with anyone anywhere to share and edit designs
- Own images uploadable to use in graphics
- Completed projects downloadable as PDF and PNG files or linkable to online graphic

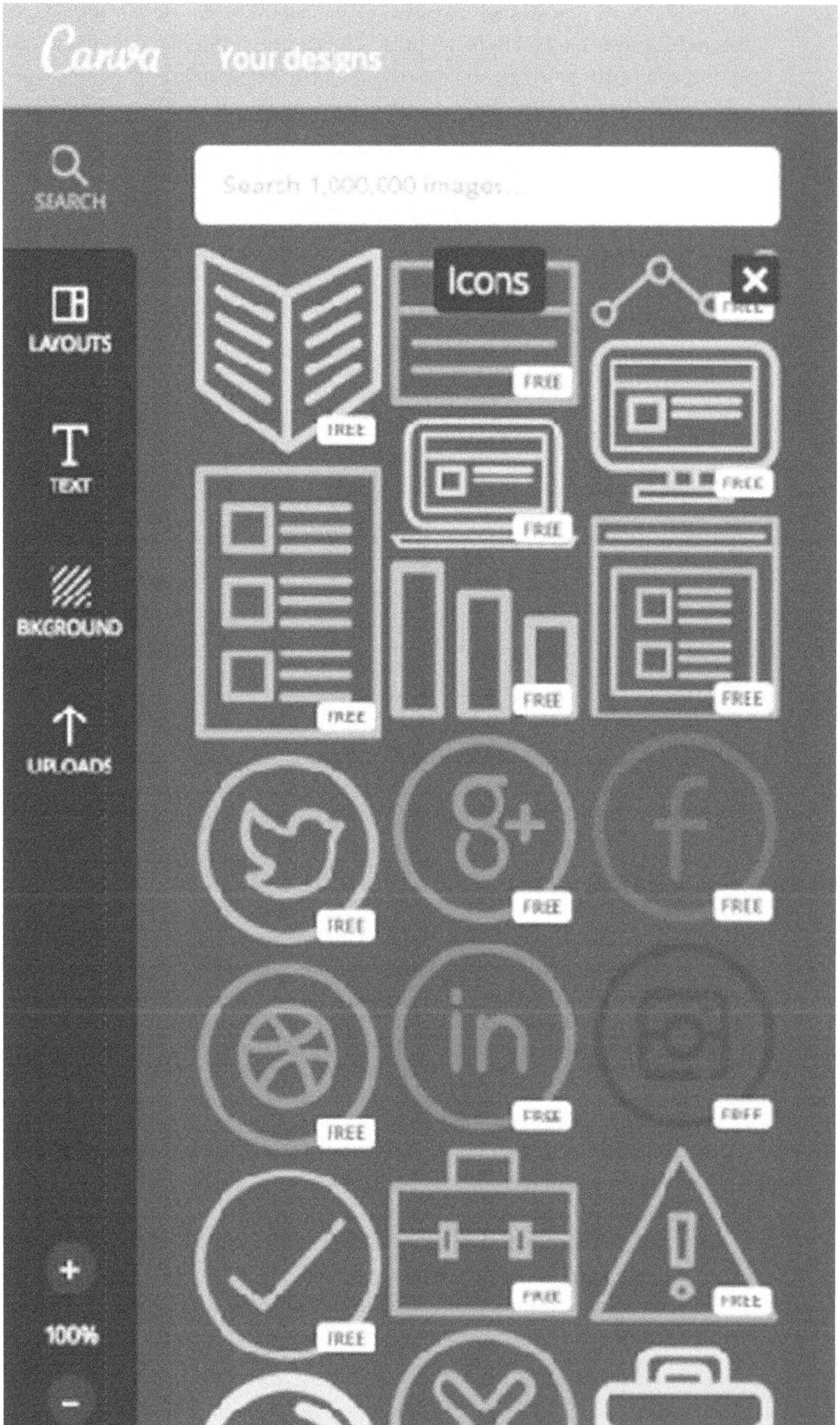

Figure 4.6. Canva Example. From Canva, https://www.canva.com/features/free-icons/.

Piktochart (http://picktochart.com)

Piktochart is a web-based tool. You can make infographics by dragging and dropping. Six themes are available for free; however, the professional version of Piktochart offers more themes with more customization options. A watermark will appear on the infographic in the free version. Infographics can be saved as PNG or JPG formats. PDF format is available in the pro version as well and can be exported to SlideShare and Evernote.

Free Version Piktochart Features

- Free fully customizable themes with templates, icons, and graphics
- Easy-to-use point-and-click editor
- Extensive image library or an option to upload your own files
- Downloadable templates or videos and photos to embed in a website
- Branded with watermark on infographic
- Online or print in high-resolution publishing
- Tutorial resources

By following three steps—insert an element, find it on the menu, and drag and drop it on the canvas, you can create professional-looking infographics, reports, and marketing materials. The Piktochart website provides numerous resources to help you get started, including video tutorials and how-to basics. Articles on different aspects like the canvas, graphics, charts, formats, edit tools, and common issues that might arise will also help you in the creation process. Figure 4.7 showcases different examples using Piktochart to create an infographic. This infographic also has a presentation mode such as for use at a conference.

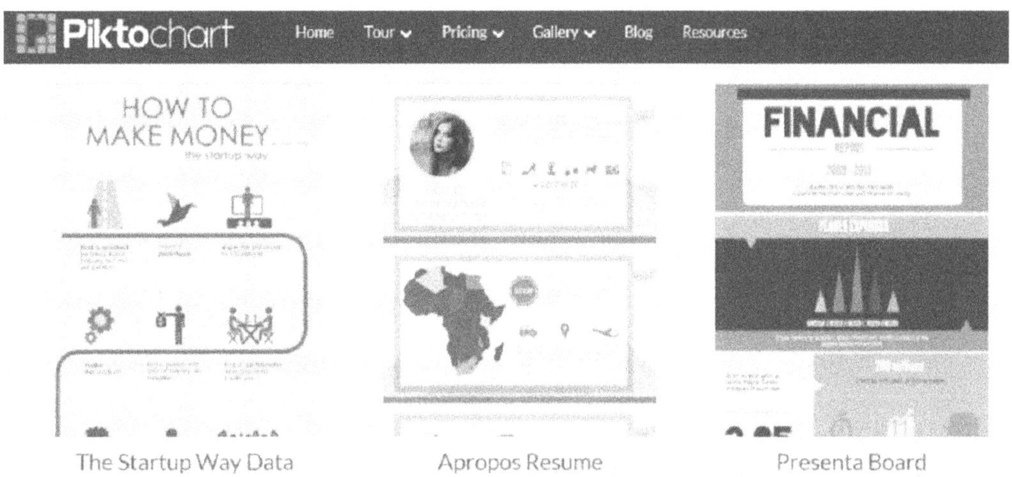

Figure 4.7. Piktochart Example. Created by Piktochart, http://piktochart.com/.

Infogr.am (https://infogr.am/)

Infogr.am, an easy-to-use, web-based tool, allows you to create simple and meaningful infographics. Users do not need to download or install any software. You can directly make infographics utilizing real data. There are lots of options available about charts, including map charts, scatter charts, bubble charts, radial bar charts, and much more.

Another benefit is that you can easily embed infographics and charts in any web page, but you cannot download your creations onto your computer. At this time it is not mobile friendly.

Free Infogr.am Features

- Interactive visualizations
- Small selection of infographic templates
- Connect live data sources from XLS, XLSX, CSV files to infographics, charts, and visualizations
- Many chart and graph types (e.g., bar, line, map) integrated from Excel
- No image library; must upload own image assets
- Easy data editing
- Downloadable as PNG version
- Online publishing

The mission of Infogr.am.org, the creator of Infogr.am, is to increase global data literacy, so it offers outreach activities, including workshops, webinars, and other resources and events. Figure 4.8 provides an example of visual trends created with Infogr.am. Review instructions for creating infographics with Infogr.am at https://about.infogr.am/5-tips-for-good-infographic-design/.

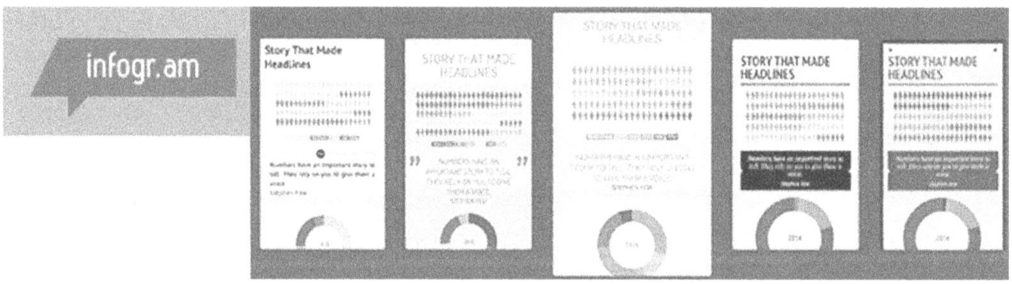

Figure 4.8. Infogr.am Example: Story That Made Headlines Template. Created by Infogr.am, http://www.infogr.am.com.

Easel.ly (http://www.easel.ly)

Easel.ly is a theme-based web app for creating infographics and data visualizations. A web-based tool, Easel.ly has a user-friendly interface and offers a number of themes. Using this website, you can easily create and process flows, maps, pictographs for storytelling, and much more. Easel.ly provides many objects and icons in order to create intuitive and informative infographics such as the one in figure 4.9 that depicts an infographic resume.

Free Easel.ly Features

- Easy to drag-and-drop design elements
- Basic templates available or upload your own background image and start from scratch

- Small library of design assets and themes
- Commended by the American Association of School Librarians (AASL) for being user friendly, intuitive, and simple enough for a sixth grader to use
- Easy to edit, change, and customize objects on the canvas
- Downloadable in low- and high-quality JPEG and PDF formats
- Three ways to share content: Shareable Link, Embed Code, and Group Share with anyone in your group
- How-to section for beginners not available
- Infographic not savable while working on it
- Often used to create visual resumes

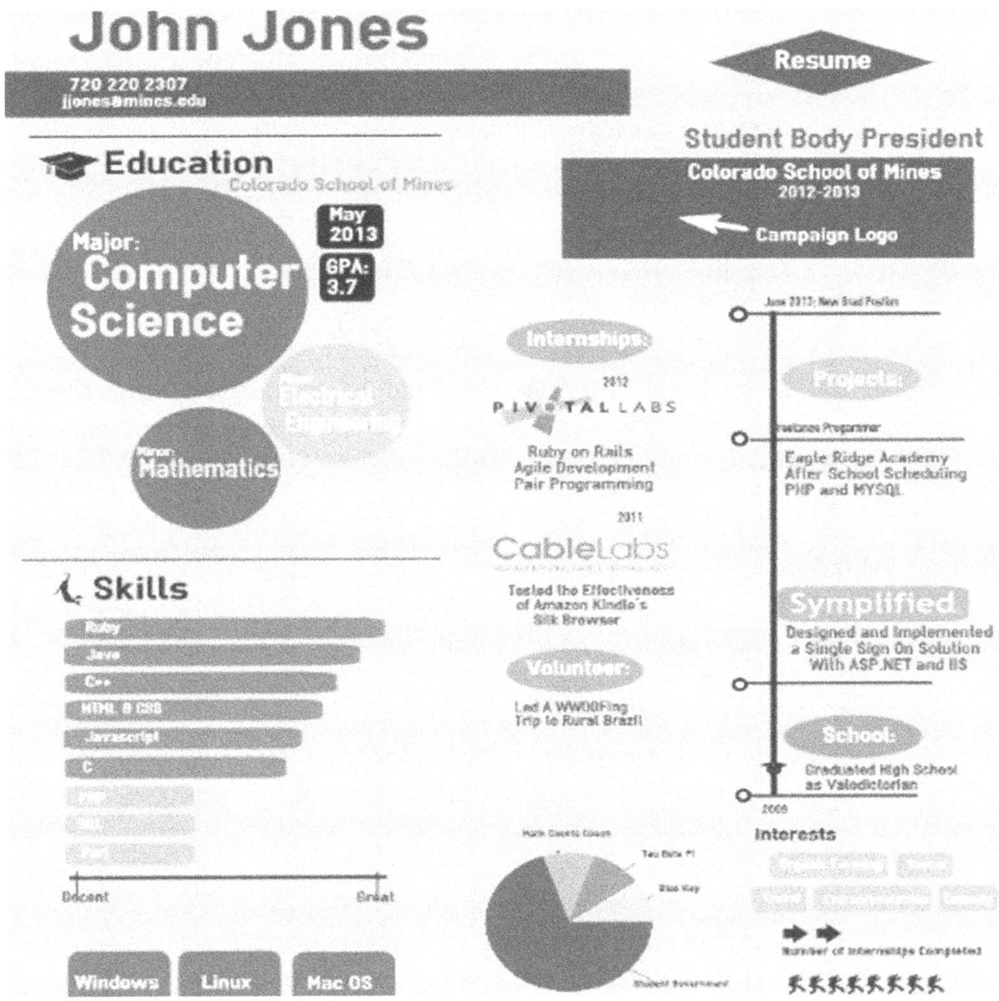

Figure 4.9. Visual Resume Created with Easel.ly. Created by author using Easel.ly, http://www.easel.ly/.

Other tools for creating infographics are listed in table 4.2, "More Tools for Creating Infographics." If you are familiar with graphic programs such as Microsoft Publisher, Adobe Photoshop, InDesign, or Illustrator, you can also use them to create your infographic. Note that tools may change so it is important to check them out as you decide which one you want to use.

Table 4.2. More Tools for Creating Infographics

DESCRIPTION	URL
Creately: makes interactive diagrams and charts using various templates.	http://creately.com
Many Eyes: offers ready-made visualizations that can be filled in with data.	http://www-958.ibm.com/software/data/cognos/manyeyes/
Wordle: generates word clouds from provided texts.	http://www.wordle.net
Stat Planet: creates visualizations to share with other users. Embeddable in browsers.	http://www.statsilk.com/software/statplanet
Glogster: used mostly by educators for teaching in the classroom. A good tool for K–12 librarians.	http://edu.glogster.com/
Vengage: contains a free version with limited themes and templates, charts, and icons and number of infographics you can make. Branded with Vengage on infographics.	http://vengage.com
Visual.ly: offers templates to create infographics and share on social media. Also easy to create Venn diagrams.	http://visual.ly

Table 4.3 contains reusable templates and design elements to use in your infographics. You can download predesigned clip art and illustrations and copy and paste them into your own infographics. How-to videos will help you get started with the infographic tools.

Key Points

This chapter has focused on principles and elements of design that will help you create your own infographics.

- Ten principles of effective design are common: alignment, balance, contrast, emphasis, hierarchy, proportion and scale, proximity, repetition/pattern, rhythm and movement, and unity should be reviewed when creating infographics.
- Basic elements of design, including color and value, dominance/size, line, shape, space, texture, and typography and fonts, enable you to structure the infographic.
- Infographic programs, such as Piktochart, Easel.ly, Infogr.am, PowerPoint, Canva, and more help you to easily create infographics.
- Compare the features of infographics programs in order to select the appropriate one to create your infographic.
- Analyzing design principles and elements in different infographics will serve as models as you prepare the design for your own infographic.

Table 4.3. Resources for Creating Infographics

DESCRIPTION	URL
Gallery of infographic samples	https://www.pinterest.com/rtkrum/cool-infographics-gallery/
Resources about infographics for teaching and learning	http://larryferlazzo.edublogs.org/2010/01/04/the-best-sources-for-interactive-infographics/
A collection of "best lists" on infographics	http://larryferlazzo.edublogs.org/2011/04/09/a-collection-of-the-best-lists-on-infographics/
Wylio contains pictures for use under Creative Commons licenses	https://www.wylio.com/
How to create an infographic using Canva	https://www.youtube.com/watch?v=nShmwzh879g; https://www.youtube.com/watch?v=kyROcitFW0w
Sixty free customizable templates from HubSpot to use when creating PowerPoint infographics	http://offers.hubspot.com/templates-shareable-graphics-social-media?&__hssc=20629287.1.1422412845038&__hstc=20629287.0532610bf0cb30254ac3061a8d3528bf.1417562913295.1422328118099.1422412845038.7&hsCtaTracking=86a964ca-2f72-4bdc-ac8f-5bb9016293ba%7C8a40680e-50a1-44b7-9200-21f7c2437fb5
"How to Make Infographics with PowerPoint"	http://www.free-power-point-templates.com/articles/how-to-make-infographics-for-powerpoint/
Free PowerPoint templates for different purposes	http://slidemodel.com/templates/tag/infographics/ http://www.free-power-point-templates.com/
Animated infographic with infographic icons	http://www.free-power-point-templates.com/articles/animated-infographics-template-for-powerpoint/
Six reasons to visualize your data	http://blog.hubspot.com/blog/tabid/6307/bid/32255/Why-Marketers-Should-Invest-in-Visual-Content-Creation.aspx/

Exercises for Chapter 4

To reinforce what you learned in chapter 4, complete the following exercises:

1. Use the starter challenges in Canva (https://www.canva.com/about/?create) to become accustomed to using the tool.
    a. Add a background to a page and change the color.
    b. Search for your favorite image and drag the image into a frame and resize it. For example, use food images.
    c. Choose a layout and upload one of your own photos.
    d. Put a title on your canvas; change the color and size of the text.

2. Watch the videos at the following URLs and try the tasks yourself as the designer shows you how.

    a. https://www.youtube.com/watch?v=YLEBRT2InhQ&list=PLNaEwbQaxEWC-ijIGhCpJIyJoAiS3GX2B&index=5—use contrast
    b. https://www.youtube.com/watch?v=yROyYPOeI9E&list=PLNaEwbQaxEWC-ijIGhCpJIyJoAiS3GX2B&index=10—create an image for Pinterest
    c. https://www.youtube.com/watch?v=89NksAINg2Q&index=16&list=PLNaEwbQaxEWC-ijIGhCpJIyJoAiS3GX2B—use icons in your design
    d. https://www.youtube.com/watch?v=RhZZ20nhXDc&index=17&list=PLNaEwbQaxEWC-ijIGhCpJIyJoAiS3GX2B—create your branding

3. Go to the website for each infographic tool listed in table 4.2, "More Tools for Creating Infographics." Review the features, pricing, and examples to see which one you think you might want to use. Write down reasons why one appeals to you more than the others.

References

ACRL (Association of College and Research Libraries). 2011. "ACRL Visual Literacy Competency Standards for Higher Education." http://www.ala.org/acrl/standards/visualliteracy.

Bradley, Steven. 2010. "How to Use Space in Design." Vanseo Design. June 21. http://vanseodesign.com/web-design/design-space/.

Hovious, Amanda. 2013. "Infographics: The Intersection between Information Literacy and Visual Literacy." *Designer Librarian* (blog). April 7. https://designerlibrarian.wordpress.com/2013/04/07/infographics-the-intersection between-information-literacy-and-visual-literacy/.

LibGuide Penn Libraries. 2015. "Graphic Design Resources." Accessed January 30. http://guides.library.upenn.edu/content.php?pid=477001&sid=3906822.

Further Reading

Curkovic, Frank. 2010. "Understanding Graphic Design Slideshare." February 17. http://www.slideshare.net/elemICT/understanding-graphic-design.

Lupton, Ellen, and Jennifer Cole Phillips. 2008. *Graphic Design: The New Basics*. New York: Princeton Architectural Press.

Williams, Robin. 2014. *The Non-Designer's Design Book*. 4th ed. San Francisco: Peachpit.

PRACTICAL APPLICATIONS

Infographics play a powerful role in any library's game plan. Whether it's marketing the public library, readying students in a school library to be information literate, or showcasing the academic library's databases, infographics can be a vital part of any library's playbook.

Part 2 describes five ways infographics can achieve and promote a library's mission. Each chapter identifies one specific use and provides examples to illustrate those uses in school, academic, public, and special libraries. While each application is obviously from one library of a specific type (for example, a public library), the points made are relevant and adaptable by almost any library regardless of type.

List of Applications

As you read each application, pay particular attention to how each infographic handles content and design principles and elements. The following applications are covered in chapters 5 through 9 and will provide you with ideas and ways you can adapt infographics for use in your own library.

Chapter 5. Educate the public/users/students (e.g., job and technology training, free services).

Chapter 6. Fund the library (e.g., importance of libraries, why to support libraries).

Chapter 7. Showcase partnerships in academic libraries (e.g., teachers/faculty, embedded librarians, flipped classrooms), special, and public libraries (e.g., university-city).

Chapter 8. Increase awareness of new and underutilized services (e.g., database collection, teen program, makerspaces).

Chapter 9. Advocate for the library (e.g., communicate value, usage statistics).

Chapter 10. "Bringing It All Together: Creating Your Own Infographic" provides two demonstrations, one in PowerPoint and the other using Piktochart, to show you step by step how to use these programs to create your own infographics.

Examples of Infographics

The following examples describe portions of a sample infographic, illustrating different types used to convey library messages and other nonlibrary topics. You have read about these types in chapter 2. The analysis of each one gives you points to consider as you begin viewing the model infographics for specific purposes designed for library audiences in chapters 5–9 and the demonstrations of how to create infographics in chapter 10.

Example 1: Flowchart

The infographic in figure P2.1, created by NeoMam Studios, forms a flowchart using a question/answer format. Based on answers to questions you ask yourself as you follow the flowchart design, you reach decision points that identify different types of infographics (see figure P2.2).

Part 2 of the flowchart infographic illustrates each type of infographic in short text with an example. Review chapter 2 for more information on these and other infographic types. URLs under each image enable you to go to the site and see the entire example infographic in color. This infographic can be helpful as you decide on the topic of your infographic, the design principles you will follow, and the elements you will use in your design.

Example 2: Visualized Article

An example of a decision point in the flowchart is the "Visualised Article" (http://visual.ly/what-gumball-3000-infographic) in figure P2.3 (part 2 of the flowchart) and is ideal for an annual report or a long article. This type needs a catchy title to generate interest in the topic and a large amount of content that is rather unique so someone will want to read it. Unique content is appealing to share and has the potential to go viral on social media. In this case, the black-and-red color scheme is also vibrant to catch the reader's eye.

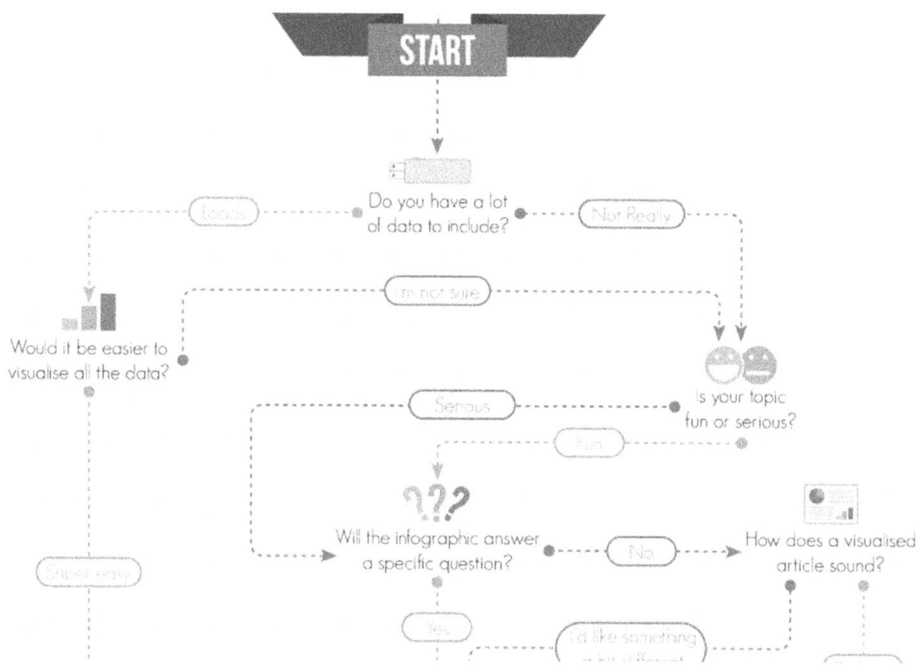

Figure P2.1. Header for Flowchart Infographic. Created by NeoMam Studios, http://neomam.com/infographics/which-infographic-is-right-for-you.

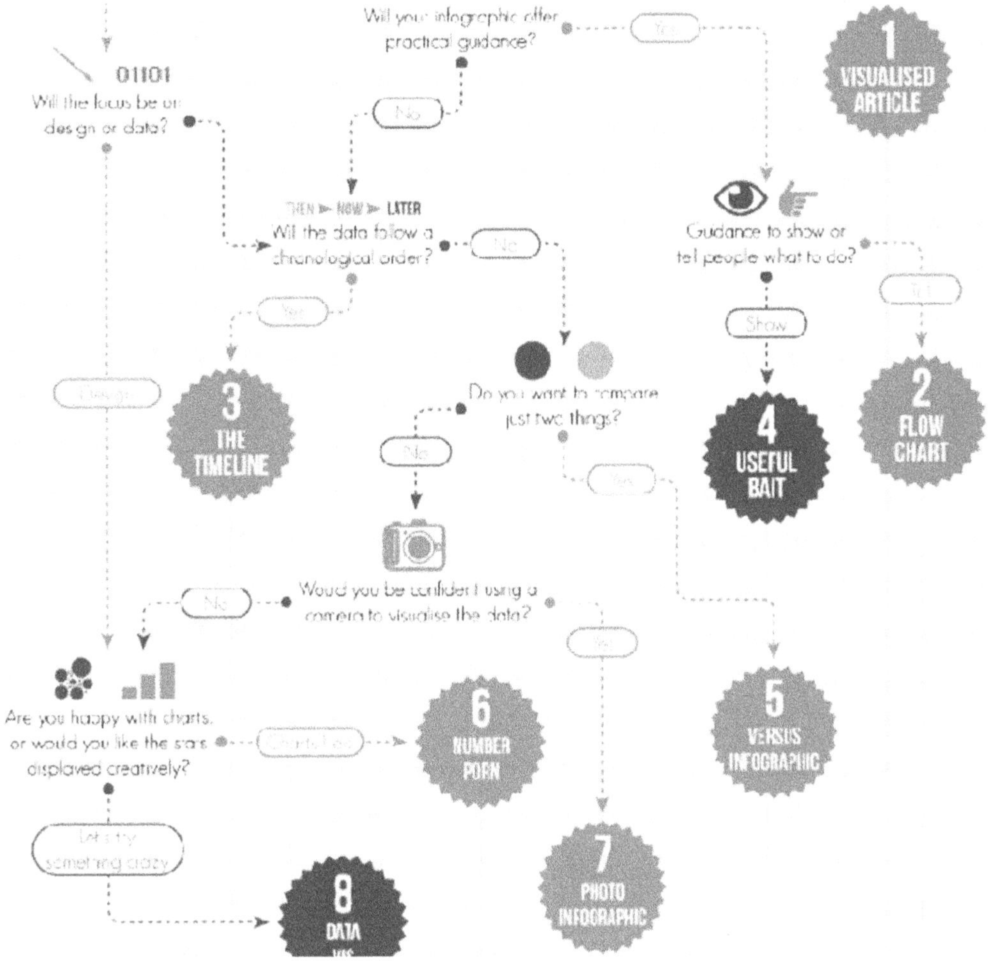

Figure P2.2. Decision Points for Flowchart Infographic. Created by NeoMam Studios, http://neomam.com/infographics/which-infographic-is-right-for-you.

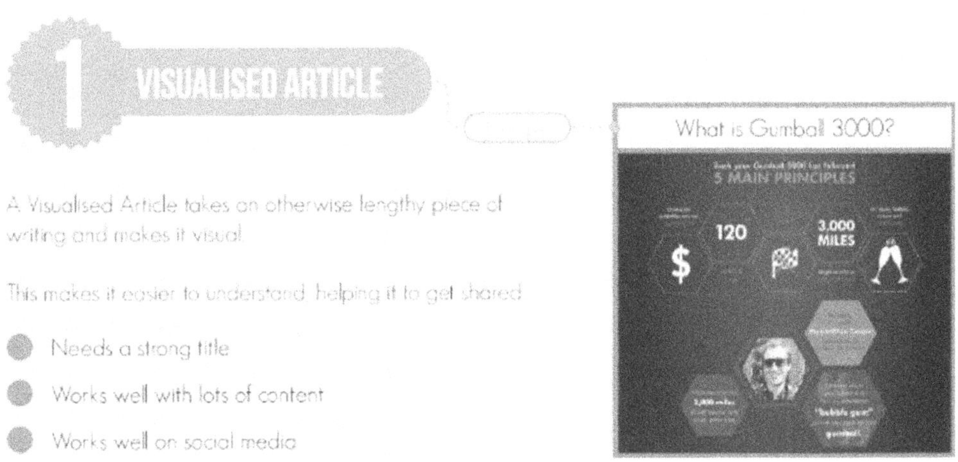

Figure P2.3. Visualised Article. Designed by NeoMam Studios, http://neomam.com/infographics/staticImages/which-infographic-is-right-for-you.jpg.

Example 3: The Timeline

The timeline, decision point 3 in the flowchart, takes the reader on a journey and can be useful to visually explain historical events over time, paths taken by travelers, individual development, and more. Again, interest and relevance are important components of a timeline infographic so the reader cares about the journey (see figure P2.4).

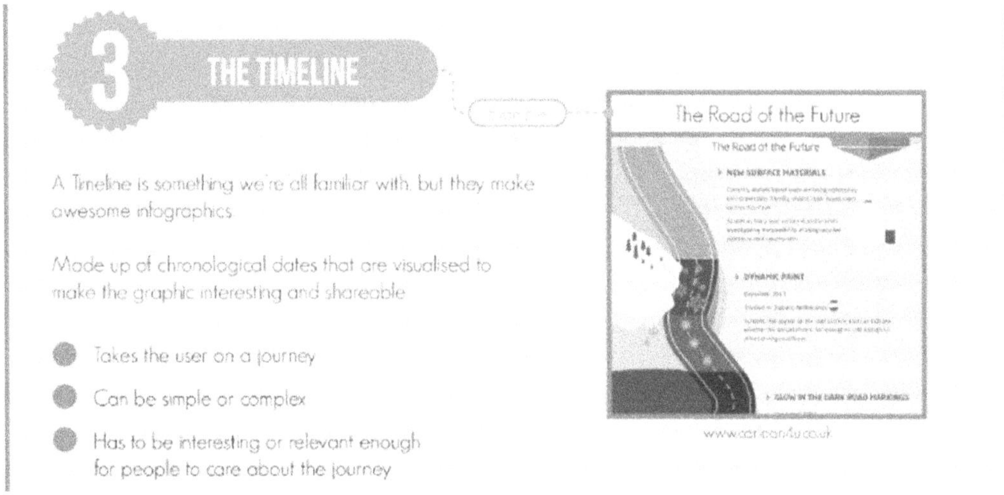

Figure P2.4. The Timeline. Designed by NeoMam Studios, http://neomam.com/infographics/staticImages/which-infographic-is-right-for-you.jpg.

Example 4: Useful Bait

Figure P2.5, "Useful Bait," explains visually how to do something; in this case, the infographic is a kitchen guide for cooks in the United Kingdom who need help converting numbers to the metric system. With its simplistic, one-page design, the infographic can also be hung on the refrigerator for easy viewing. The important aspect of this type is clarity. Readers want a clear explanation of the process, and they want to be able to reference the instructions as they proceed. A complex or overwhelming design can get in the way of understanding the message.

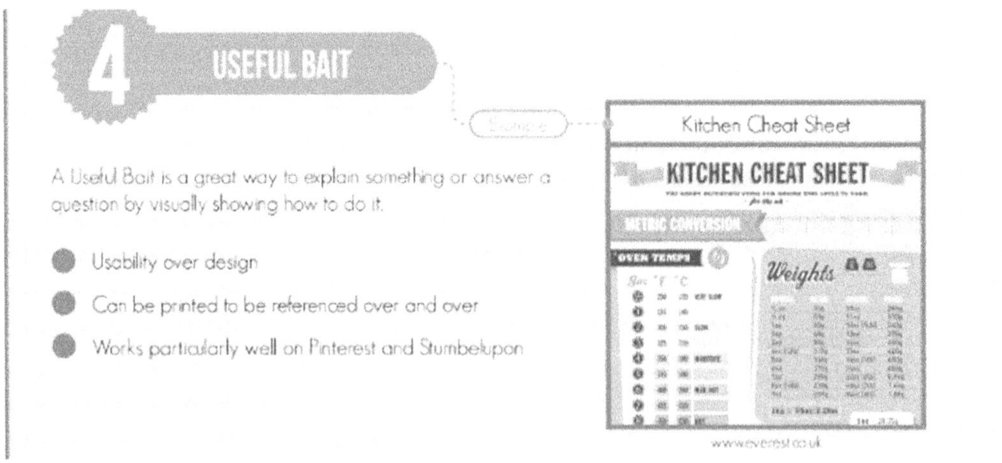

Figure P2.5. Useful Bait. Designed by NeoMam Studios, http://neomam.com/infographics/staticImages/which-infographic-is-right-for-you.jpg.

Example 5: "What Makes a Good Infographic?"

The infographic in figure P2.6 represents a different type. It uses a Venn diagram to tie together relationships among four points. There is minimal text to identify each factor. Overlapping sections of the diagram indicate the problems with an infographic that does not contain each piece.

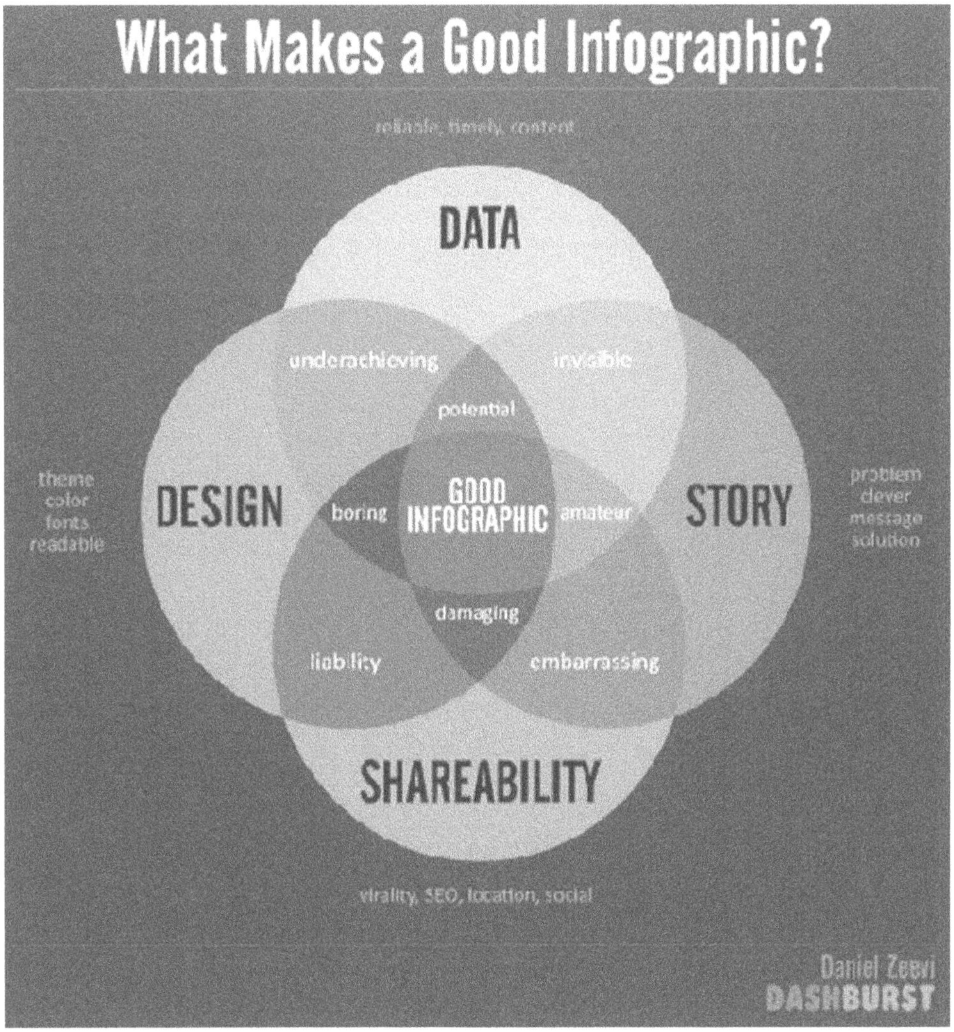

Figure P2.6. What Makes a Good Infographic? Designed by Daniel Zeevi, Dashburst, Licensed under Creative Commons, https://www.flickr.com/photos/dashburst/8448339735/.

Notice also in chapters 5–9 that infographics are designed for web or mobile device viewing, so you will see many that are very long. They may not be easy to print, but viewers can scroll down online to take in the entire infographic. Consider content and design points as you review the following models. In most examples in this book, you will see a portion of a longer infographic. Review the URL for each infographic so you can see the infographic in its entirety and in color, an important component of an infographic's message. Finally, keep in mind as you review the next chapters that infographics often have visual themes that help convey the message. Consider what theme you might use to convey your visual data successfully. Also remember that you want to make sure the visual display is as high quality as the data. If the data isn't readable because of the colors or images used, then it has no value. This is another reason why simple is good.

CHAPTER 5

Teaching with Infographics

IN THIS CHAPTER

- ▷ Models of infographics that show libraries using infographics to present data
- ▷ Librarians and teachers partnering in a learning project to teach students
- ▷ A K–12 project step by step that enables students to view and create infographics

A LIBRARY CAN USE INFOGRAPHICS in many ways: to promote partnerships with teachers, to educate students, to publicize the library and its collection, and to train teachers and students on technology, to name a few. Sometimes a school librarian can achieve more than one purpose with an infographic. One of a librarian's goals is to work together with classroom teachers, often to help them with research on a student project, instill information literacy principles, offer support on technology, and ultimately help prepare students for a life after high school.

The purpose of this chapter is to provide insight on how infographics can facilitate one goal of a library—to educate its patrons. Educating library users is a part of any library's mission. For example, in partnership with classroom instructors, school and academic librarians might be teaching students how to conduct research for a class project or providing one-on-one tutoring to find appropriate sources. Public librarians might offer a class showing patrons how to search the Internet or familiarize them with job or health resources. Special librarians may conduct a small-group training session on using PubMed or other authoritative databases to complete their research. All libraries create learning aids such as LibGuides, videos, and more.

This chapter describes samples of infographics whose purpose is to educate. It reviews a project created by a K–12 classroom teacher and shows how a partnership between a teacher and school librarian can enhance project-based instruction by providing students working on a unit in science with tools to research, write, learn about science, and present information with self-created infographics. This detailed step-by-step process can serve as a model to help you create infographics to teach your own students. Note that this application can also be used as a model for librarians teaching students at any level who are researching a topic whether in a school, academic, special, or public library.

Model Infographics

Educators use infographics because they're popular and quick to read. The combination of text and graphics also helps many readers remember the information more easily because they are designed to make complex materials easier to understand. It is important for students to be able to read and interpret visual representations of information. Not only do charts, graphs, and maps show up on standardized tests of all kinds, but whiteboard technology has made the graphic depiction of information that much more useful and ubiquitous in classrooms. Research on Bloom's Taxonomy (Wilson, 2013) and the brain (Smickilas, 2012) supports the use of infographics.

Prior to creating an infographic, it is always important to review some samples to acquire ideas and gain an understanding of how other educators are using this medium.

Example 1: School Library

In this first example, the "Big 6 Research Process" was created using Glogster EDU to illustrate the research process. Glogster is an online website where users can build posters and other designs for different purposes (see figure 5.1). It provides a simple format for educators to have students begin the process of creating multimedia presentations, designed for a specific purpose and audience. Templates make it easy to incorporate text, images, video, graphics, and voice into a "glog" (graphic blog). Elements in the glog can also be interactive so that you can click images to link to further information. Glogster offers a preliminary step before creating more complex infographics.

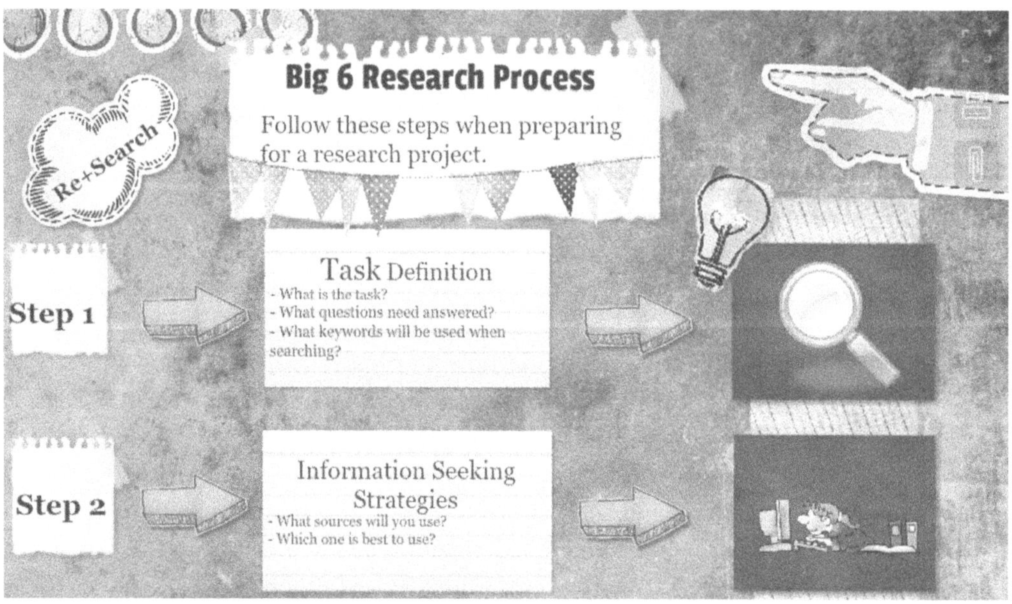

Figure 5.1. Big 6 Research Process. Created by Barb Kim, 2007–2015, Glogster a.s. All Rights Reserved, http://lesd27.edu.glogster.com/big-6-research-process/.

Example 2: Academic Library

Dr. Tim Chartier (2014), a professor of mathematics at Davidson College in Davidson, North Carolina, decided to have his undergraduate students learn to tell stories with data through creating infographics. Learning to graph data is an important tool for the modern mathematical student. As a means to this end, students in Chartier's math classroom developed infographics. The classes ranged from a general education class to a higher-level one. This project could as easily have been done with high school students using data from across the curriculum.

First, he wanted to raise students' awareness of an infographics' role in modern communication. From magazine ads to news stories, data is often displayed and tells an important part of the story. Next, the professor showed two graphics: one, a simple graphic he had created on degrees of connection among Oscar contenders (http://www.huffingtonpost.com/tim-chartier/eccentric-oscar-predictions_b_2720301.html), and two, an interactive infographic on the same topic with similar data created by the *New York Times*. When students were asked which one they preferred, they overwhelmingly selected the *Times* infographic (http://www.nytimes.com/interactive/2013/02/20/movies/among-the-oscar-contenders-a-host-of-connections.html).

He then had his students review examples from the *New York Times* (http://www.nytimes.com/newsgraphics/2013/12/30/year-in-interactive-storytelling/) and other sources, including multimedia stories, data visualizations, explanatory graphics, and breaking news. These samples enabled students to see the kinds of topics that would make good infographics and how varied they could be. Articles provided background on the subjects, and visuals and interactive features exemplified some of the data.

Next, in groups, students were asked to create their own data visualizations. The data used was from campus groups and local nonprofit organizations. The idea here was for students to learn to do something that would benefit their community prior to graduation. Figure 5.2 shows one student's infographic created for the local Habitat for Humanity office.

Example 3: Public Library

Public libraries have a wide range of uses for infographics that they promote daily through social media. They range from information literacy teaching tools such as an infographic on Boolean commands to teaching about social media in "The History and Power of Hashtags in Social Media Marketing" to digital devices and technology such as helping patrons with stress with their smartphones and with digital citizenship.

Interesting examples of uses come from the West Melbourne Public Library in Florida. The library has Pinterest boards for the library (https://www.pinterest.com/westmelbourne/) on which they post helpful information for their patrons. One board, titled "Pins for Parents and Homeschoolers," contains useful infographics to help parents understand their children's reading needs—"Why Reading at a Young Age Matters," "Inside the Brain of a Struggling Reader," and "Ways to Encourage Children for Reading." Another infographic, "Your Newborn Survival Kit," illustrates the information a new mother needs to know about her newborn. The board "Book Lists for Children" contains infographics on books that librarians can show to children and teens to guide them toward good books to read—fiction and nonfiction, sports, folktales, storybooks, and more. These visual lists can be used to motivate young people to read, especially when schools close for the summer. A board, titled "Research & Online Study Tips," shown in figure 5.3, offers tips on study habits, the SAT versus ACT tests, brainstorming techniques, and how to get college grants. All of these infographics are useful and help teach adult patrons and students at all levels who visit the public library.

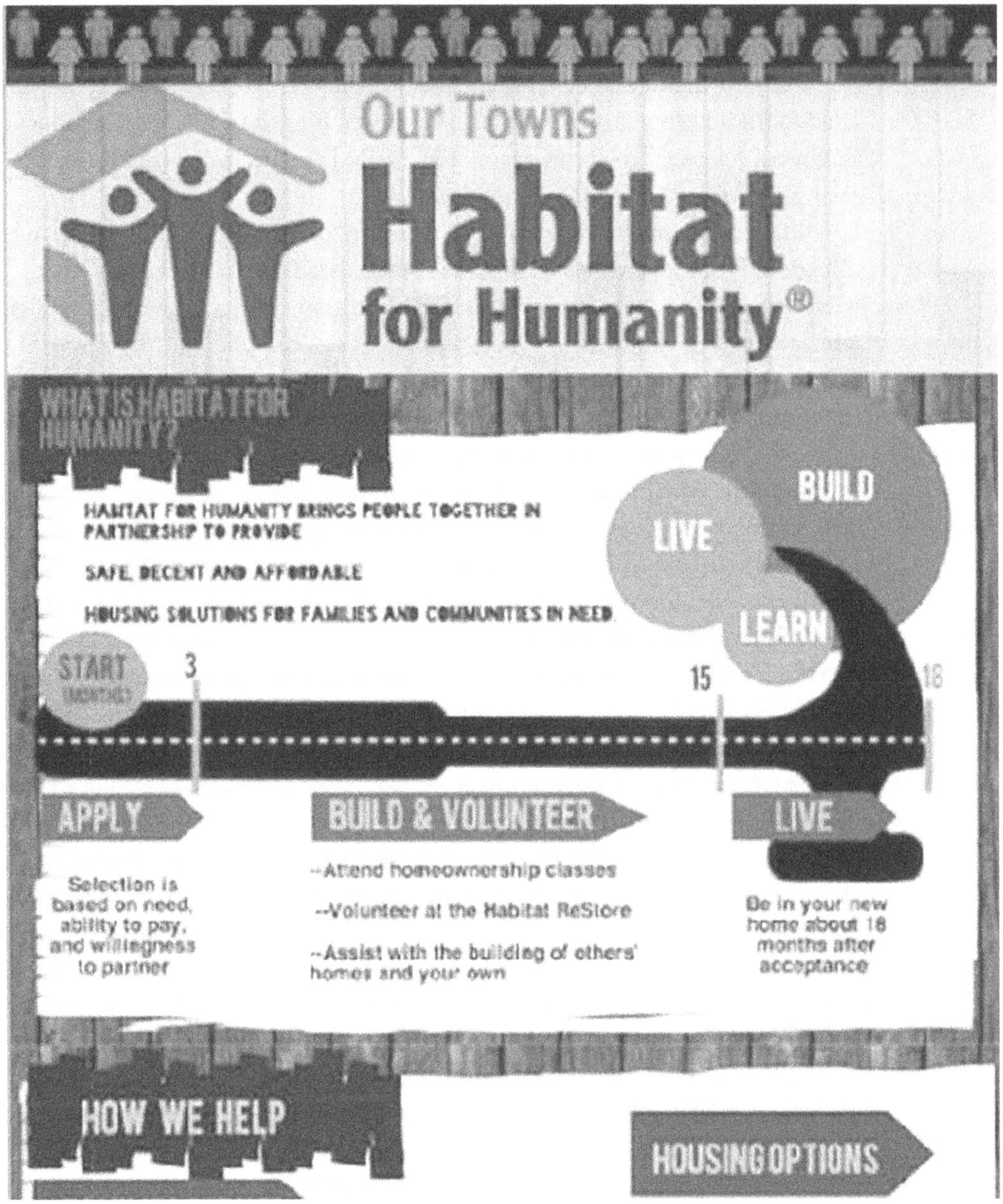

Figure 5.2. Habitat for Humanity Infographic. Credit: Designed by a student at Davidson College under the guidance of Professor Tim Chartier, http://graphics8.nytimes.com/images/blogs/learning/pdf/2014/DavidsonStudentExamples.pdf.

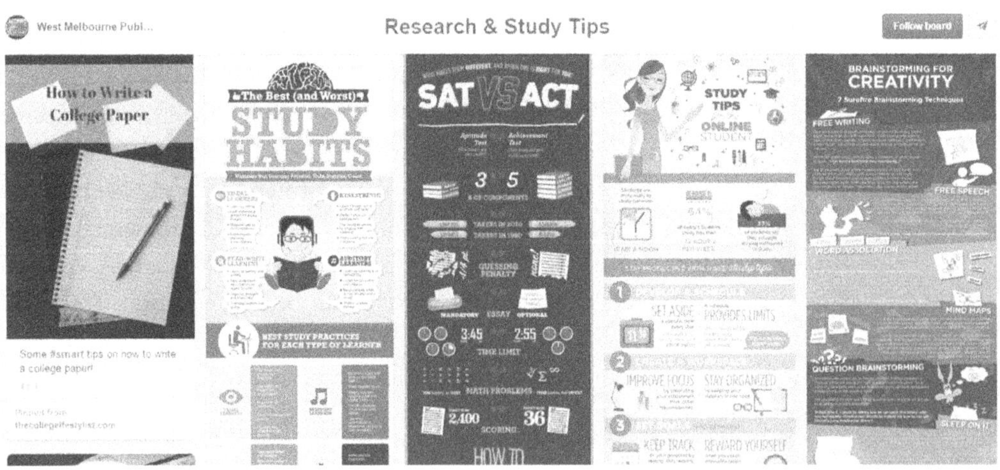

Figure 5.3. Research & Online Study Tips. Board created by West Melbourne Public Library, https://www.pinterest.com/westmelbourne/research-study-tips/.

Table 5.1. Infographics to Help Library Patrons

DESCRIPTION	URL
"Boolean Commands"	https://www.pinterest.com/pin/366621225892028870/
"Digital Citizenship"	https://www.pinterest.com/pin/396598310909515677/
"Is Your Smartphone Stressing You Out?"	https://www.pinterest.com/pin/396598310909586032/
"The History and Power of Hashtags in Social Media Marketing"	https://www.pinterest.com/pin/396598310909525250/
"Why Reading at a Young Age Matters"	https://www.pinterest.com/pin/396598310912551353/
"Inside the Brain of a Struggling Reader"	https://www.pinterest.com/pin/396598310909691223/
"Your Newborn Survival Kit"	https://www.pinterest.com/pin/396598310909230905/
"SAT vs. ACT"	https://www.pinterest.com/pin/396598310911554008/
"Study Tips for the Online Student"	https://www.pinterest.com/pin/396598310911085305/
"Brainstorming for Creativity"	https://www.pinterest.com/pin/396598310910164324/
"How to Get Free Money for College"	https://www.pinterest.com/pin/396598310909515697/
"Which Books Should You Read This Summer?"	https://www.pinterest.com/pin/396598310908042495/
"Research & Study Tips" (board)	https://www.pinterest.com/westmelbourne/research-study-tips/

Because of the viral nature of infographics, not only are they useful to West Melbourne Library patrons, but they can also be accessed online through Pinterest by other librarians, patrons, and students around the world. Review the URLs of the infographics mentioned on the Pinterest boards in table 5.1.

How Viewing and Creating Infographics Educate Users

Whether you are a school, special, or academic librarian, or a librarian in a public library, you may be called upon to teach your patrons. Your responsibility may be to provide information literacy instruction, teach students how to use databases, offer small-group technology training, or give one-on-one help to patrons who need to find health- or job-related information. Infographics can be useful to achieve any of these goals.

Using infographics can help librarians communicate and connect better with their audiences, enabling them to demonstrate their true depth of understanding. A multiple-choice test, for example, shows only that they recognize the right answer rather than that they understand why it's correct. An infographic is a good example of how combining information and graphics conveys more meaning than words alone in a list or paragraph. It's also quite important for students to understand aspects of design. A good design and layout of information enhances understanding; a bad presentation can confuse meaning. The National Science Foundation thinks so, too, by funding a $1.3 million grant to the University of Colorado at Boulder to improve STEM (science, technology, engineering, and math) literacy education with infographics. Part of the grant will be a class in infographic design to high school students (Bolkan, 2015). Part of an infographic from

"Why Support Your Local Library" is an excellent visual depiction of the importance of local libraries and why you should support them. One section emphasizes the library's value in educating children by providing statistics about library educational programs for children and the increase in number of library resources children are using. Check out the entire infographic at http://www.swissarmylibrarian.net/2012/08/22/why-support-your-local-library-infographic/. This same infographic will also give you ideas for other uses outlined in later chapters.

A Step-by-Step K–12 Project That Incorporates Infographics

Librarians and teachers at all levels are now using infographics to teach their students and patrons. Some use them as examples, illustrating how graphics and text make complex information easier to understand by communicating a story with a specific purpose to a particular audience. Others have started with examples and carried the project one step further to have their students create their own infographics. Either case enables the librarian and teacher to improve students' critical thinking, research skills, and information and visual literacies.

The framework that follows offers a plan you can adapt to bring this type of instruction into your library or classroom. In this section, you will review a step-by-step example incorporating infographics created by Diane Laufenberg, an eleventh-grade history teacher. Whether a school librarian was actually involved in this project or not, the project lends itself to a partnership between the librarian and the teacher or aspects that might be the total responsibility of the librarian. Added notes where the role of the librarian would make a difference are also provided. As the project unfolds, you will see that infographics may be useful for viewing, or you may want your students to create them. Note that academic or public librarians could adapt this structure for their own content, purpose, and audience. See examples of other projects using infographics in table 5.2.

The process is divided into steps just as you would if you were writing a research paper as shown in the infographic "Steps in the Research Process" (https://www.pinterest.com/pin/204984220514146260/). Presenting information, data, or content in appealing and innovative formats offers librarians opportunities to present instruction and resources that will engage students. Each step is listed with an example from the K–12 project that shows using infographics as models for instruction and creating infographics as part of the project. This research project incorporating infographics offers a multitude of suggestions on how teachers working with K–12, academic, or public librarians could use infographics to promote higher-level thinking while teaching about the research process, information literacy, current issues, and more.

Planning and Creating the Unit Project

The topic under investigation was designed to focus on a global environmental issue and one that would have national impact. K–12 history teacher Diane Laufenberg (2010) initiated this project following the huge oil spill in the Gulf of Mexico in 2010. She used the oil spill as a starting point for a unit to incorporate infographics to tell stories of the top ten worst man-made environmental disasters in American history. She included both consuming infographics and creating them as part of the investigation.

Table 5.2. Examples of Infographics That Educate

DESCRIPTION	URL
"Turning a Classroom Research Project into an Infographic"	http://www.edudemic.com/educational-infographics/
"A Planning Cycle for Integrating Technology into Literacy Instruction." Made with Glogster EDU	http://cailinjane.edu.glogster.com/3-2-1-framework/?=glogpedia-source
"What Is the Role of the Librarian in the Delivery of Evidence-Based Information?"	https://magic.piktochart.com/output/717224-create-your-own#
"Creating a Book Trailer Using Piktochart"	http://www.pinterest.com/pin/205828645445660060/
Infographics by librarians for library purposes	http://librariandesignshare.org/category/infographics/
Infographic stations activity	http://www.techchef4u.com/ipad/integrating-infographics-into-the-iclassroom/
"How Real Kids Create Real Infographics"	https://www.edsurge.com/n/2014-04-27-how-real-kids-create-real-infographics
Student example of infographic on the Civil War	http://gabriellexrdg1112.edublogs.org/2014/03/09/analyzing-the-civil-war/
North vs. South student example created with Piktochart	https://magic.piktochart.com/output/1453527-create-your-own
Model infographics students can look at before creating their own	http://www.somethingsosam.com/
"Data Visualized: More on Teaching with Infographics"	http://learning.blogs.nytimes.com/2011/04/08/data-visualized-more-on-teaching-with-infographics/?_r=0

Part 1: Consume Infographics to Provide Background

Following a process helps to ensure creation of a successful infographic that has a good chance of being shared. Tasks in each step are discussed (Elliott, 2014), followed by a description of the K–12 project, and notes on the role a librarian could play as a partner.

Step 1: Pick a Topic

Selecting a topic provides the theme and determines the type of infographic to create. The topic must adhere to the curriculum or academic course content. Essential questions can form the basis for the story line, the data gathered, and the infographic design. Choose a subject where there's a lot of information or a hypothesis to explore, such as in science. When deciding on a subject, the librarian and teacher can partner to help formulate the project topic. Searching the Internet and finding other sources in databases and the library that show different points of view on a subject are the forte of the librarian and will help the teacher promote information literacy in students.

The purpose of the project, created by Diane Laufenberg, was to design infographics that explained a global issue. The resulting infographics were to present a thesis supported by clear, carefully researched evidence presented graphically. In 2010 the Gulf oil spill dominated the news, so plenty of information was available. As Diane contemplated what problem her students would investigate, she first conducted a large amount of research on the Internet and searched authoritative databases in the school library. She also looked at numerous infographics on environmental problems. She set the goal to create infographics to tell stories of the top ten worst man-made environmental disasters in American history, but to use study of the Gulf spill as a framework for comparison.

In addition, she knew her students would need background on infographics. Diane surveyed infographics that told a story—both good and bad—to serve as models for her students. She also looked at tips for designing infographics because creating them was to be part of the project. Once she felt confident in her own knowledge of content and infographics, she identified the broad topic of man-made disasters. Next, she gathered resources and planned activities around a set of "essential" questions (Gallagher, 2014):

- What is the balance between the interests of the individual and the interests of business with regard to the environment?
- What role should the government play in regulating that balance?
- How do the country's past actions inform its current policies related to environmental issues?

Involving the librarian. At the project planning stage while designing the project, librarians can contribute specific feedback on the project plan. For example, do the essential questions sound engaging based on what they know about students' interests? Do they have alternatives or modifications to suggest? Are there literature connections or digital media resources the teacher might not have considered?

If librarians know about an upcoming project, they can help to create curiosity even before the project begins. Library book, picture, and artifact displays or book clubs can help whet students' appetites for upcoming projects.

Step 2: Gather Data

Use data from your own research, open data on the web, or review library resources. Be thorough—not having all the data means you don't have the full story. Having authoritative data to support the topic and its main points is critical to an infographic's success and whether it will go viral or not.

Find stories—trends, unusual angles to a topic, or counterintuitive results (i.e., data illustrating something different from what you would expect). Also read source articles to find out whether the multimedia you are viewing is from authoritative sources. Collect information, reference materials, infographics, and links. Create an interactive bibliography to review the best sources. If infographics are to be part of the project, view some about research to come up with ideas for your project.

Project example. In Diane's project on oil spills, she had students focus first on the Gulf oil spill as a whole class investigation. This activity required them to conduct research. Students read articles from the *New York Times* that included a variety of media—interactive oil spill information, slideshows investigating the cause and oil spill remedies, live videos of the spill, photos showing where oil made landfall, a time-lapse map of the oil spreading, photos from the explosion, an interactive map showing effects on marine life, a history of major oil spills, and video depicting threats to wetlands' ecosystem and local residents' livelihood. Much of this information was found in the Gulf of Mexico oil spill multimedia collection at http://www.nytimes.com/interactive/us/spill_index

.html?ref=us&ref=us. These articles provided different viewpoints as background on the subject. They also contained statistics that could then be culled to use in the infographics they would create. To keep up with the news as it happened, students also regularly read and discussed information from an interactive infographic at http://www.nytimes.com/interactive/2010/05/01/us/20100501-oil-spill-tracker.htm that tracked oil concentration by date. Review an interactive visualization of the oil spill's effects on wildlife at http://www.nytimes.com/interactive/2010/04/28/us/20100428-spill-map.html. To learn more about infographics, the teacher had her students look at samples of both effective and less effective infographics on the spill. Students were also to review examples from Randy Krum's "10 Tips for Designing Infographics" at https://digitalnewsgathering.wordpress.com/2010/04/24/10-tips-for-designing-infographics/.

As class activities she asked journal questions—for example, "Based on the *Times* infographic, describe the potential impact on the wildlife living in the Gulf." Students would then read or view other videos on a segment of the subject.

Next, Diane randomly assigned one of the ten disasters to collaborative groups of three to investigate. Students had time in class and the library to do outside research and resolve collaborative challenges: what information to select, how to use infographics effectively to tell the story, what design elements to use to represent the information graphically, and what tasks each would perform to create the infographic to bring to the whole class discussion.

During this part of the project, students researched the topic and collaborated on the assignment. They had to

- develop understandings about the essential questions and do further inquiries;
- evaluate what parts of their disaster was most important to tell and how best to represent each piece of information both visually and with text;
- present the work of the collaborative groups to the whole class;
- make predictions for connections to other events, present or future, based on trends and patterns observed in their investigations; and
- reflect individually, in groups, and as a class on successes and challenges.

Throughout the process, students had to call upon skills in design, research, presentation, collaboration, and inquiry.

Students also needed guidance on infographics. Tutorials and videos identified what an infographic is and what makes a good one. To help them with the design of their own infographics, students also reviewed examples for format, organization, design elements, and how data was incorporated into them. *Note:* Many useful resources on infographics are listed in chapter 4.

Involving the librarian. Librarians can help guide the research process both in finding and analyzing information. They can help by identifying library resources, including specialized databases and primary sources on the topic. They can also provide minilessons on smarter searching, such as having students pick out keywords from their questions to locate sources and go beyond Google searches.

In addition, librarians may facilitate connections with classes or experts on the topic in other parts of the United States or the world. Using Skype or Google Hangout, they can help arrange video conferences in the library with experts students want to consult. Table 5.3 provides a list of resources for this sample unit.

Table 5.3. Resources for the Unit

DESCRIPTION	URL
National Archives Library Information Center with journals, periodical literature, and teacher resources	http://www.archives.gov/research/alic/
"Infographics Webinar" video	https://www.youtube.com/watch?v=OzYAFaHu2Ys&feature=youtu.be
Diane's lesson plan on oil spills	http://learning.blogs.nytimes.com/2010/08/27/teaching-with-infographics-a-student-project-model/?_php=true&_type=blogs&pagemode=print&_r=0
Oil spill article with interactive map	http://www.nytimes.com/interactive/2010/05/27/us/20100527-oil-landfall.html
An infographic about critical thinking using research and Bloom's Taxonomy levels—good for elementary level	https://www.pinterest.com/pin/AfGQBbp8g-G_qMKrRbuPQYQN-CbQgrAIPKuMrcY5rBW7hLSHOQYzjrE/
Sample infographic to practice analyzing. Contains numerous sources to find information	https://www.pinterest.com/pin/27725353927813137/
Graphics on oil spills	http://www.nytimes.com/interactive/2010/12/26/us/20101226-deepwater-horizon-rig-video-diagram.html
NY Times infographic examples for social studies, history, civics, and economics	http://learning.blogs.nytimes.com/2010/08/23/teaching-with-infographics-places-to-start/
"America's 10 Worst Man-Made Environmental Disasters"	http://www.mnn.com/earth-matters/wilderness-resources/photos/americas-10-worst-man-made-environmental-disasters/the
"Environmental Historians Respond to Gulf Oil Spill"	http://aseh.net/teaching-research/environmental-historians-respond-to-the-gulf-oil-spill/copy_of_ehresponsetoGulfOilSpill.pdf
"10 Tips for Designing Infographics"	http://digitalnewsgathering.wordpress.com/2010/04/24/10-tips-for-designing-infographics/

Step 3: Analyze Data

If the data set is too large, more analysis may be necessary to distill it down to the essential parts. This will help in determining what type of chart or graph, if any, to use in the infographic.

Project example. In Diane's project, students turned to the *New York Times* to find examples of infographics that displayed data in a compelling way. They analyzed infographics to explain in detail what points in the graphic were effective to let readers quickly understand the data. They had to interact with the essential questions to develop understandings, make further inquiries, and meet challenges, including:

- Decide what they wanted to say, what point to make
- Determine who their audience is (level of writing and viewing format such as mobile or computer)

- Examine their disasters and the Gulf disaster to discover trends that were common to both

The goal was to create an infographic that told the story of their disaster, the public and governmental response directly after the incident, and the actions of the government and public over time.

Involving the librarian. Librarians play a key role in helping students build and apply information literacy skills. Students need to know how to ask good questions and also how to research effectively. Critical thinking prompts help them consider the accuracy and reliability of sources. Workshops about fair use and copyright explain how to cite sources properly.

Part 2: Create Infographics

You have planned your infographic considering your purpose and audience and researched your project. With your knowledge of infographics, you are now ready to organize and lay out the content you've gathered.

Step 4: Create the Infographic

Make a wireframe, a mock-up of the entire infographic including content and design. Select the content and statistics that tell the story. Decide on the type of graphic and the design elements—color, font, charts/graphics—discussed in chapter 4—that are most appropriate for your audience and purpose. Make sure to include your sources. Once you create the wireframe, it might be worthwhile to review other infographics to see how yours compares.

Project example. Upon completing their research and determining the design, students wrote the infographic. They had to decide what they wanted to say, what points to make, and who their audience was (i.e., what level of writing and viewing format such as mobile or computer). They examined each disaster to discover trends that were common to both so that the infographic told the story of their disaster, the public and governmental response directly after the incident, and the actions of the government and public over time. Each group member was assigned a task to complete. They also had to work out collaborative challenges. Then each group presented the completed infographic to the class for review.

Involving the librarian. Project-based learning puts students in situations where they work in teams. With practice, students get better at working with peers and also managing their own learning. School libraries offer environments for teams to work semiautonomously on projects. Some libraries provide access to technology such as 3D printers and recording equipment.

Step 5: Review, Revise, Reflect

At this stage the creator must review the draft infographic to make sure it is readable, interesting, eye catching, informative, and well substantiated. Having others critique it and offer suggestions will also help in the revision process. Once the final infographic is ready for publication, it is important to reflect on the process and ask questions, including what was successful and what the creator would do differently.

Project example. Diane's class hung their creations on the wall and viewed them as if they were in an art gallery. They discussed which infographic was "best" based only on their feelings, not on project requirements. The favorite was one on the *Exxon Valdez* oil spill based on layout and visual appeal. Next, students read the content of each infographic. In the second class discussion, they realized that the most visually appealing one did not have the best information. Finally, they reflected individually, within their groups, and as a class on learning successes and outcomes to determine difficulties related to working together and creating the infographic.

They also discussed similarities and differences between their disaster and the Gulf disaster. Next, they projected forward to predict future behaviors of the American public, the government, and business interests based on lessons learned from the past. Students revisited the essential questions and responded in writing, followed by a class discussion of insights gained. They then were asked to make predictions for other events based on the trends and patterns they had observed in their investigations.

Involving the librarian. Libraries offer a public place to display and curate the work that results from high-quality project-based learning. Often schools hold project culminating events in the school library, inviting parents and other classes to provide feedback on what students have accomplished.

Building an infographic is a project that lends itself to teamwork because the modular design allows members to divide the work along logical lines. The teamwork exists not only between students but between the teacher and librarian. The tasks in this project provided students with an opportunity to evaluate specific presentations of data, discuss the aspects that are effective or misleading, revise the graphics as they go, and work in a collaborative way to create knowledge and understanding. With a teacher-librarian partnership, you can build on this experience to develop an infographic assignment tailor made for your curriculum to educate students in the classroom and the library. By analyzing content in this manner and engaging in such critical thinking, students develop higher-order thinking skills—a goal of twenty-first-century learning. And, it produces a win-win situation for both the teacher and librarian (see figure 5.4).

Key Points

This chapter presented examples and a step-by-step process of using infographics for educational purposes.

- A primary goal of school, academic, public, and special libraries is to educate patrons. Based on characteristics of students and other library users today, infographics can be a powerful teaching tool.
- Using effective and not-so-effective infographics as models builds awareness of structure, purpose, audience, design, and authoritative content needed to create a successful infographic.
- A project that incorporates infographics mirrors tasks students will perform in life. It requires selecting a subject that appeals to a specific audience, conducting research from sources, telling a story supported with data, condensing information into an effective design that includes graphics and text, and making decisions with others to create a successful infographic.

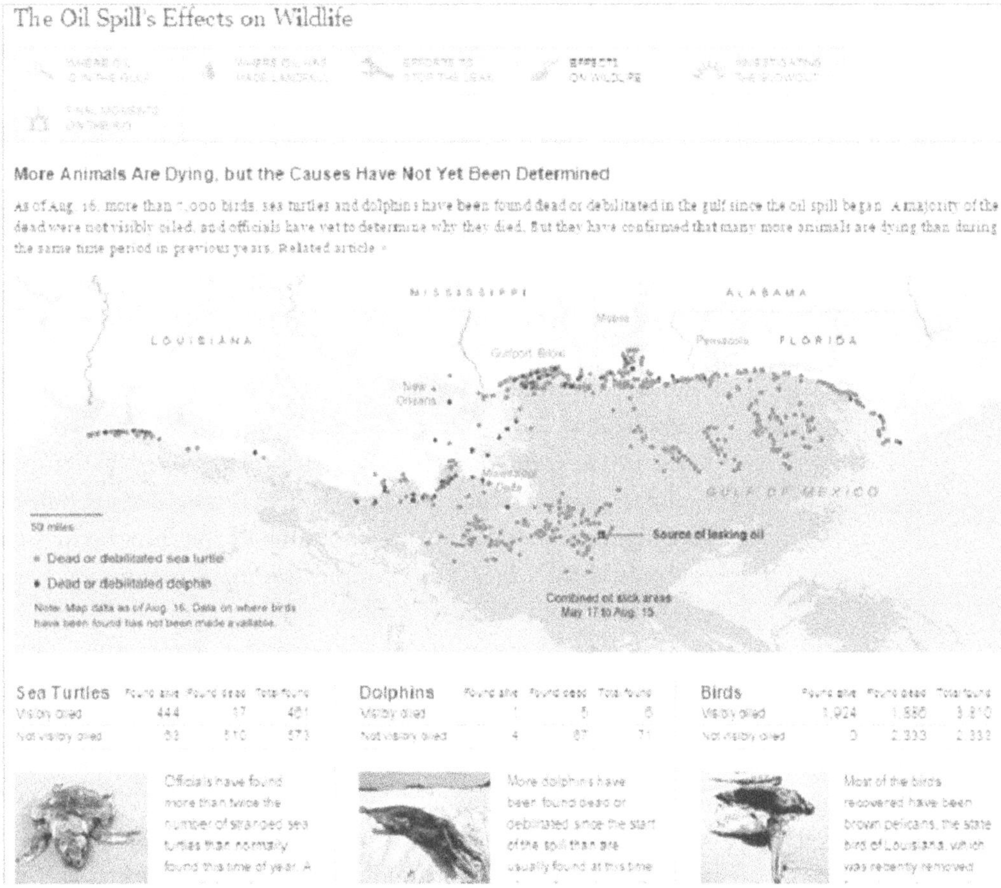

Figure 5.4. Librarians Are Ready. Created by Jennifer LaGarde, http://www.slideshare.net/jlagarde/librarians-are-ready.

- Educators have found that creating infographics can enhance a learning project, making it more interesting to students and building critical thinking skills at the same time. It also encourages collaboration, a twenty-first-century skill.

The theme of this application encompasses just one role of today's librarians—to educate their users. It also points out advantages of a teacher-librarian partnership. You will learn more about library partnerships in chapter 7. Librarians working together with teachers in classrooms or librarians teaching in the library can adapt a project similar to the example outlined in this chapter to fit their audience and purpose. Using infographics can enhance this educational process.

Exercises for Chapter 5

Review content from this chapter by completing the following tasks:

1. Using Google, search for a topic you might use with students and add the word "infographic" to your keywords. For example, search for "tornado infographic." For best results, search Images. In your journal, make a list of sites (e.g., name, description, URL) on the topic(s) you select. Over time continue this process. You will have resources you can return to when you need to decide on a project.

2. Do a search on the word "infographic." Choose different images to review a variety of infographics. Analyze several based on qualities of a successful infographic discussed in this chapter.
3. Create a student project. Have students look through sites like Flowing Data (http://flowingdata.com) and Information Is Beautiful (http://www.informationisbeautiful.net) to find a few examples of data visualizations that give them "moments of insight" to make them want to learn more. Have them collect examples to display and discuss. What did the infographics make them understand that perhaps a written version of the same data likely wouldn't?
4. Find two or more data visualizations that present data about the same groups—for example, the interactive map (http://www.nytimes.com/interactive/2011/03/06/weekinreview/20110306-happiness.html?_r=1&) that shows well-being in the United States, and Mapping America (http://projects.nytimes.com/census/2010/explorer?ref=us), which presents United States census data from 2005 to 2009. Investigate how the information in one of the infographics confirms, explains, or contradicts the other. For example, the maps mentioned here might lend themselves to a study of how income and education level may affect job satisfaction or health problems in an area. Taking it a step further, create an infographic to illustrate your conclusions.
5. Find an article that could benefit from the addition of a graph to illustrate statistical data found in the article. Draw a line or bar graph or pie chart that illustrates the data from the article. Include information that readers would need to read and interpret your graphic.
6. Practice using visual examples by creating your family tree at http://www.nytimes.com/interactive/us/family-trees.html. For models, look at the trees for Michelle Obama (http://www.nytimes.com/interactive/2009/10/08/us/politics/20091008-obama-family-tree.html) and the Kennedys (http://www.nytimes.com/interactive/2009/08/26/us/kennedy-family-tree.html).

References

Bolkan, Joshua. 2015. "U Colorado Boulder to Tackle STEM ED with Infographics." *Campus Technology*. June 23. http://thejournal.com/articles/2015/06/23/u-colorado-boulder-wins-1.3-million-to-improve-stem-ed-with-infographics.aspx.

Chartier, Timothy. 2014. "Telling Stories with Data: Davidson College." *New York Times*, August 26. http://learning.blogs.nytimes.com/2014/08/26/reader-idea-telling-stories-with-data/.

Elliott, Ann. 2014. "How to Turn a Classroom Research Project into an Infographic." *Edudemic* (blog). November 20. http://www.edudemic.com/how-classroom-project-infographic/.

Gallagher, Kerry. 2014. "How Real Kids Create Real Infographics." edSurge. April 27. https://www.edsurge.com/n/2014-04-27-how-real-kids-create-real-infographics.

Laufenberg, Diane. 2010. "Teaching with Infographics—A Student Project." *New York Times*, August 27. http://learning.blogs.nytimes.com/2010/08/27/teaching-with-infographics-a-student-project-model/.

Smickilas, Mark. 2012. "Infographics and the Science of Visual Communication." Social Media Explorer. July 3. http://www.socialmediaexplorer.com/digital-marketing/infographics-and-the-science-of-visual-communication/.

Wilson, Leslie O. 2013. "The Second Principle." http://thesecondprinciple.com/teaching-essentials/beyond-bloom-cognitive-taxonomy-revised/.

Further Reading

Anderson, L. W., and D. R. Krathwohl, eds. 2001. *A Taxonomy for Learning, Teaching, and Assessing: A Revision of Bloom's Taxonomy of Educational Objectives*. Boston: Allyn & Bacon.

Clark, Donald. 2010. "Bloom's Taxonomy of Learning Domains: The Three Types of Learning." *Big Dog & Little Dog's Performance Juxtaposition.* http://www.nwlink.com/~donclark/hrd/bloom.html.

CHAPTER 6

Fundraising

An Essential Goal of Any Library

IN THIS CHAPTER

- ▷ The importance of using infographics in fundraising
- ▷ The value of the library for the purpose of fundraising
- ▷ Successful examples of infographics for fundraising used by other libraries
- ▷ Points to incorporate in infographics to raise funds
- ▷ Steps in the process to create an infographic useful for fundraising
- ▷ An example of an infographic for the purpose of fundraising

DO YOU CHOKE UP at the thought of asking someone for money? Even though you get this queasy feeling when it's time to ask, you know it's something you've got to do if your cause is going to get the money it needs to deliver its work. Library fundraising is critical, and it demands increased professional and skillful efforts to meet the increasing needs of library users in a time of increased competition for public and private resources.

This chapter addresses the need for fundraising and how infographics can be an important tool in the librarian's toolkit. A number of libraries are already using infographics in their fundraising efforts to describe different roles the library serves in local, academic, and school communities. This chapter discusses the importance of promoting library services and resources to emphasize the value it brings to its patrons. Funding the library adequately can depend on this promotional effort.

The Need to Communicate Value

In Pew Internet studies (Zickuhr et al., 2013), one aspect mentioned quite often, both in focus groups and in qualitative work from previous research, is that people wish they were more aware of the full range of services offered by their libraries. One focus group member (Zickuhr, Purcell, and Rainie, 2014), loved her local library and rated it highly in all areas—except communication: "There's so much good stuff going on but no one tells anybody." Another said, "They do so many fabulous things, but they have horrible marketing." Focus group members emphasized that having resources and events listed on their library's website wasn't enough—as several participants pointed out, they probably weren't going to go to the website to look for events. Many of the librarians in the in-person focus groups agreed that it was difficult to reach patrons and tell them about all the services the library offered. Several said that almost daily, they would be speaking with a patron who had come in for a specific service and would mention other services or resources and hear the patron reply, "I didn't know that was available" (Zickuhr, Rainie, and Purcell, 2013).

Staff members who participated in the online panel commented that they felt patrons were not always aware of the research assistance librarians can offer. They also indicated that patrons didn't know about the research resources offered by the library other than books: "Most students have no idea what a database is and, therefore, get their information from Google, while the tremendous resources available online from our library go unknown and unused."

These responses from the research indicate that libraries must spend more time and effort communicating about their services and activities to patrons to emphasize their value. This promotion must be a vital part of library fundraising efforts.

As discussed in earlier chapters, telling the library's story is something that an infographic can do well. In addition, infographics can now be designed interactively, in video format, animated, and created to ensure mobile compatibility. Infographics can entice an audience better than some of the past attempts to point out the library's value. For example, survey results may be cumbersome in a lengthy text format, but represented visually they become eye catching, while tables of statistical data can lose the fleeting interest of a reader. Moreover, comparison research will have a more dramatic effect with visuals. And, when targeting a multilingual audience, visuals are more easily understood.

Infographics cut straight to the point, simplify complex information, and can capture the reader in an instant. As with any piece of content, an infographic must be relevant, interesting, and meaningful; it should not rely solely on eye-catching artwork, nor should the content be overwhelming. An effective infographic elicits an instant reaction and entices people to want to learn more—most useful when asking for a donation. Through graphics and text, the infographic in figure 6.1 illustrates the crisis faced by the public library and demonstrates with statistics why funding is so vital to continuing services of interest to patrons (ALA, 2012).

The examples that follow introduce infographics and model how public, academic, school, and special libraries are using them in their fundraising efforts.

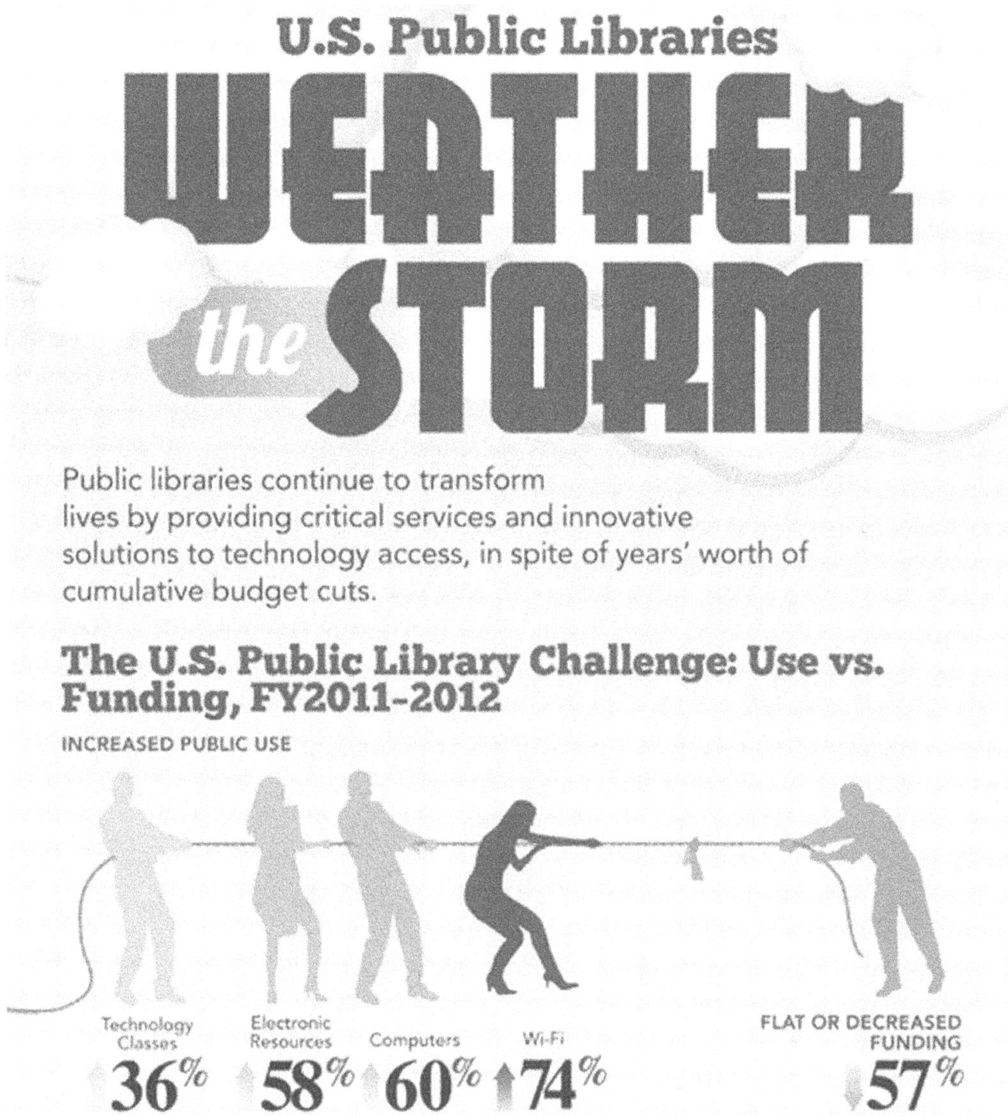

Figure 6.1. U.S. Public Libraries Weather the Storm. Used with permission from the American Library Association. "Weathering the Storm Infographic, a Supplement to Libraries Connect Communities: Public Library Funding & Technology Access Study 2011–2012," http://www.ala.org/research/plftas/2011_2012/weatheringthestorm.

Models of Infographics for Fundraising Efforts

From print fundraising appeals to digital annual reports to compelling storytelling through tweets and status updates, online behavior confirms again and again that messages are most effectively communicated through images. Infographics express complex issues in a compelling way. They can also demonstrate the role of the library—its services, products, and expertise. Moreover, they tend to be shared widely via digital media. In the article "Can Infographics Improve Fundraising?" at http://www.advice-for-good.com/blog/tag/infographic/, several sample infographics used by nonprofits show their power.

The next examples provide models where libraries used infographics to enhance their fundraising efforts. Go to the URL of each example to see the infographics in color, often a vital part of an infographic's message.

Example 1: Fundraising in Public Libraries

Today's public libraries are vital community technology hubs that millions of Americans rely on for their first and often only choice for Internet access. Despite increased demand for library computers, however, libraries typically have not seen a corresponding increase in budgets, and many are challenged to provide enough computers or fast enough connection speeds to meet demand.

The example "NYPL by the Numbers" (http://www.richertschnorr.com/new-york-public-library-annual-report), an infographic created by the New York Public Library, illustrates a section of its *FY12 Annual Report*. Using statistics, the infographic describes usage of the main library and its branches, including library visits, classes at the library, circulation figures, technology use, and reference inquiries. It also describes the user community, including social networking use and library membership.

The annual report is an important fundraising tool for a library, and the New York Public Library expanded its reach by adapting the infographic into print and online versions to communicate a core message encompassing breadth and depth of the library's services.

Example 2: "Why Support Your Local Library?"

The infographic "Why Support Your Local Library?" is an excellent example that illustrates the vital role the public library plays in the local community. It also clearly states why libraries should be supported in today's economic climate.

The infographic begins by stating the problem: budget cuts are affecting the local library and asks why you should care. This statement makes viewers want to continue reading to see how this problem might affect them. Each of the next three sections focuses on a specific problem that can affect users—unemployment, need for government services (e.g., health information), and help to educate students. Subpoints illustrate ways the library provides assistance for each problem. Using more statistics and comparisons, the infographic goes on to show that the library is becoming more popular with an increasing user base. This emphasizes that the subject of the infographic affects a wide-ranging population. At the end, the infographic issues a call to action by restating the initial problem and providing specific ways patrons can help the library and the advantages of doing so.

The design uses statistics, graphics, color, and text hierarchy to move the viewer's eye from one point to another. This infographic is quite long. To get all the details and view the different design elements, review it at https://pinterest.com/pin/254875660132510559/.

Example 3: Making the Case for School Librarians

School libraries have been experiencing budget cuts that have resulted in the elimination of certified librarians and even the closing of school libraries in many school districts. Library Research Service (LRS, 2013), based on numerous national and Colorado-based research studies, created an infographic demonstrating the positive effects of school librarians on student achievement.

In figure 6.2, this two-color infographic states its purpose concisely using a combination of statistics from the research studies and graphics to deliver the message that students in schools with endorsed librarians score better on standardized achievement tests in reading. A bold font and larger images are used at the beginning in a simple math equation (1 + 1 = 2) to focus attention on the main point: School + Librarian = Improved Reading Scores. It also outlines other school library characteristics associated with improved test scores. With the support of authoritative statistics, this simple and clearly stated message promotes the advantages of having a school library staffed by an endorsed librarian.

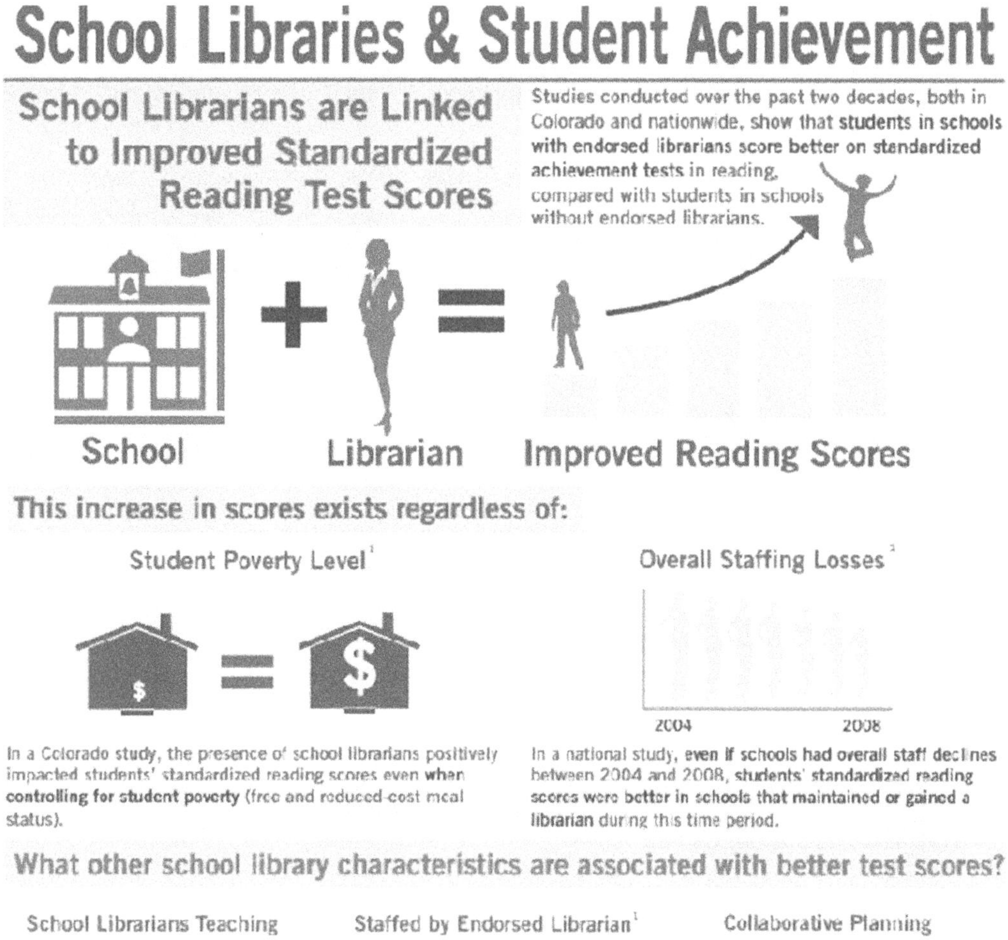

Figure 6.2. School Libraries & Student Achievement. Created by Library Research Service (LRS) staff at the Colorado State Library, https://creatingthefuture2020.files.wordpress.com/2013/03/school_library_impact.jpg.

Example 4: Funding Academic Libraries

The financial climate in today's academic library is challenging. The library's annual budget alone can no longer support the high cost of electronic information and new technologies, as well as the annual cost increases for library materials and programming. Therefore, fundraising efforts must be developed to augment the library's funding.

In "Library Science 101" (http://librarysciencedegree.usc.edu/resources/infographics/library-science-101-ig/) the University of Southern California (USC) has created an infographic outlining the advantages of a library science degree. It explains what library science is, what librarians do, and why their services are important. University libraries can use infographics as a means to solicit students, and as in this case, highlight special collections and services like Ask a Librarian. Promoting the library can be helpful in increased funding from the university, as well as donor contributions from alumni, faculty, and staff.

Table 6.1 contains additional models of fundraising infographics, as well as infographics that illustrate fundraising techniques.

Table 6.1. More Model Fundraising Infographics

DESCRIPTION	URL
An annual report in infographics for Newton Smith High School	http://newtonsouthptso.org/2013/06/check-out-the-librarys-annual-report-infographic/
Annual report using infographics of a public library in Arlington, MA	https://www.google.com/search?tbm=isch&tbs=rimg%3ACY4-20bBMfJUIjjb2iTG2IL5k3zEZFyLAgZc7YDGwheFSdGaejlMewJzMPNfflITjFpeDL3mX6Tj-BqD208nMfQmxioSCdvaJMbYgvmTEU6grdhvxsgQKhIJfMRkXIsCBlwRHjQVHwHxcRgqEgntgMbCF4VJ0REVi14Za9TJaCoSCZp6Mgx7AnMwEcmgvPY6K4vxKhIJ819-WVOMWI4RHKy_10BYOvvgqEgkMveZfpOP4GhGdsl0aWQbYxSoSCYPbTycx9CbGES_193Pj2T330&q=fund%20raising%20in%20public%20library
"How to Write an Annual Fundraising Appeal Letter"	http://bloomerang.co/blog/infographic-how-to-write-an-annual-fundraising-appeal-letter/
"Strong School Libraries Build Strong Students," created by AASL	http://www.ala.org/aasl/sites/ala.org.aasl/files/content/aaslissues/advocacy/AASL_infographic_strongstudents-2013.pdf
"American Public Libraries & Community Internet Access"	http://www.webjunction.org/content/dam/WebJunction/Documents/webJunction/USLP_FINAL-Print.pdf

Step-by-Step Example: Promoting Services Raises Funds for Public Libraries

"A picture is worth a thousand words" is an often-spoken phrase. Photos are a great way to share your library's story—pictures of children's story time, rows of computers with every seat filled, teen gaming tournaments, and senior small-group instruction. But what if the information you need to share is numbers? Statistics about your library programs and services are also very important, especially to those interested in how your library's funding is used. They want to know how many adult summer reading program participants you had, what your circulation statistics are, and how many people came to your computer training classes. They want to see what the return on their investment (ROI) is. But numbers are boring. You can put them into a bar graph or pie chart that will make them easier to grasp. However, if you could combine the importance of your statistics with the power of visuals, think how much more interesting your story would be. Infographics represent an exciting new storytelling avenue for libraries, enabling them to share important data stories, visually.

Promoting the Public Library to Garner Funds

At the height of the recession, the American Library Association (ALA, 2012) created an infographic to illustrate libraries' financial struggles since the recession began. The ALA infographic "U.S. Public Libraries Weather the Storm," shown in figure 6.1, encompasses FY2011–2012 and promotes the public library's services, personnel, and collections in order to show the value the library offers the community. Emphasizing the benefits the library provides its patrons engages and inspires the audience and makes fundraising more palatable. It also conveys a main message about your library. Analyzing the step by-step process used to create this infographic provides you with a guide to use as you think about creating your own infographic to help raise funds for your library. Although the example illustrates a public library, the process can be used for fundraising at an academic, special, or school library.

Analyzing the Sample Infographic

Producing an infographic is divided into two phases covering seven steps. First, you will look at a general description of what each step entails. Next, you will analyze parts of the public library infographic "U.S. Public Libraries Weather the Storm" to see how the infographic incorporates important points for an effective infographic in each step.

Phase 1: Planning

Planning the infographic is most important and also can be the most time consuming. You must consider several points even before you actually jump into creating the infographic.

Find a story worth telling. Not everything that happens in your library is worth sharing. One key to great library storytelling lies in knowing what you should write about—an important service, people you've helped, a volunteer who went above and beyond, a special training event, or new additions to your collection, to name some. You can tell stories that evoke emotion, celebrate changed lives, and illustrate your mission. These stories inspire people to support your library.

As you select the story, think about the following: Who is the target audience? What are their interests and what inspires them? What is the main goal? What is the desired outcome, and what do you want to achieve? For example, it may be twofold as in this infographic—promoting the library to raise funds in figure 6.3.

You can see from a quick view that the ALA infographic "U.S. Public Libraries Weather the Storm" (shown in figure 6.1 earlier) focuses on an important service of the library—the technology it provides for its users. Throughout, it also uses comparison and contrast, a popular type of infographic described in chapter 2.

At the top the infographic states the audience—public libraries. The goal is spelled out in a concise statement directly below the title. The reader immediately recognizes the story theme, its goal, and the target audience.

Select a topic. To select the most appropriate topic for your infographic, there are certain measures to consider: operations, usage, satisfaction, and value.

- Librarians have long tracked usage statistics, but what is the data really showing? Identify who needs to see the statistics and whether the data is telling a story that will dramatically affect your audience.
- Customer satisfaction tends to focus on existing products and services. Surveys are typical measurement tools that are used so much the audience often tunes them out. Think whether you are measuring the importance of your product or service in an engaging format.

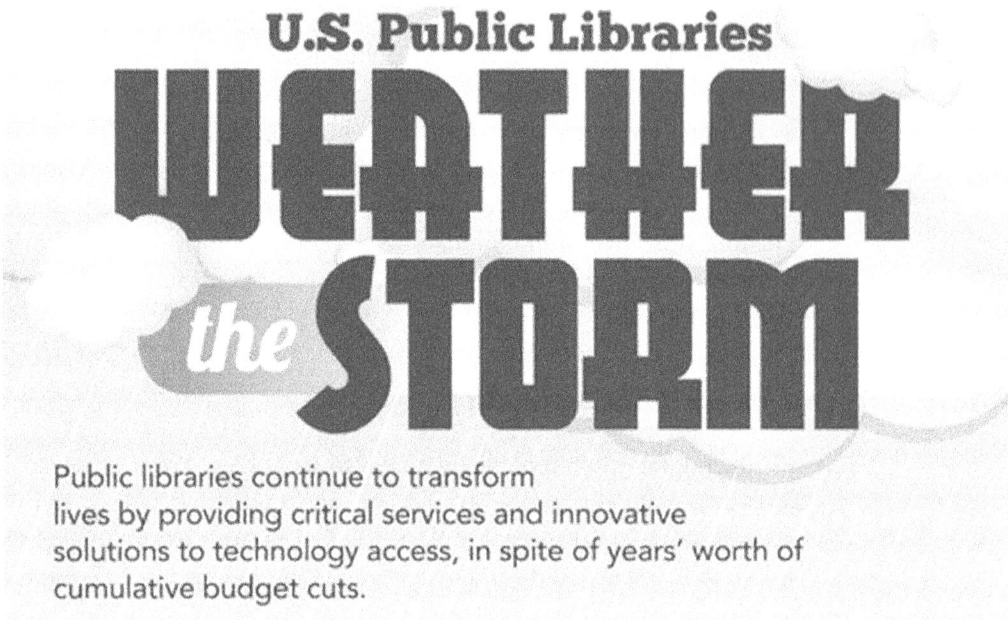

Figure 6.3. Top of Infographic. Used with permission from the American Library Association. "Weathering the Storm Infographic, a Supplement to Libraries Connect Communities: Public Library Funding & Technology Access Study 2011–2012," http://www.ala.org/research/plftas/2011_2012/weatheringthestorm.

- When it comes to value—are you adding value and making a difference? What is the impact of your services and programs and are they adding value to patrons' lives? How has your audience changed as a result of your programs and services (e.g., behavior, skills, knowledge, attitude, awareness, or motivation)?

The ALA example infographic uses data to describe three subtopics, divided visually with dotted lines. It tells the story using statistics and by relating customer satisfaction to technology service. The impact of the service emphasizes value to patrons' personal and work lives.

- Statistics in figure 6.4 point out the increase in technology use in contrast to continued declining budgets necessary to fund technology. According to the infographic (ALA, 2012), Wi-Fi and computer usage have both increased at the same time funding has decreased significantly. In addition, 62 percent of libraries report being the only location offering free public access to the Internet in their communities. These statistics indicate value to patrons.
- A map of the United States shows the states where funding for public libraries has decreased. This visual emphasizes how widespread the problem is.
- Again statistics restate the problem—the percentage of homes without Internet access—and makes the point that public libraries offer the only free access.
- A visual summary reemphasizes the problem: decreased budgets mean decreased services and states two other problems due to funding decline—insufficient Internet connection speeds and number of public computers.

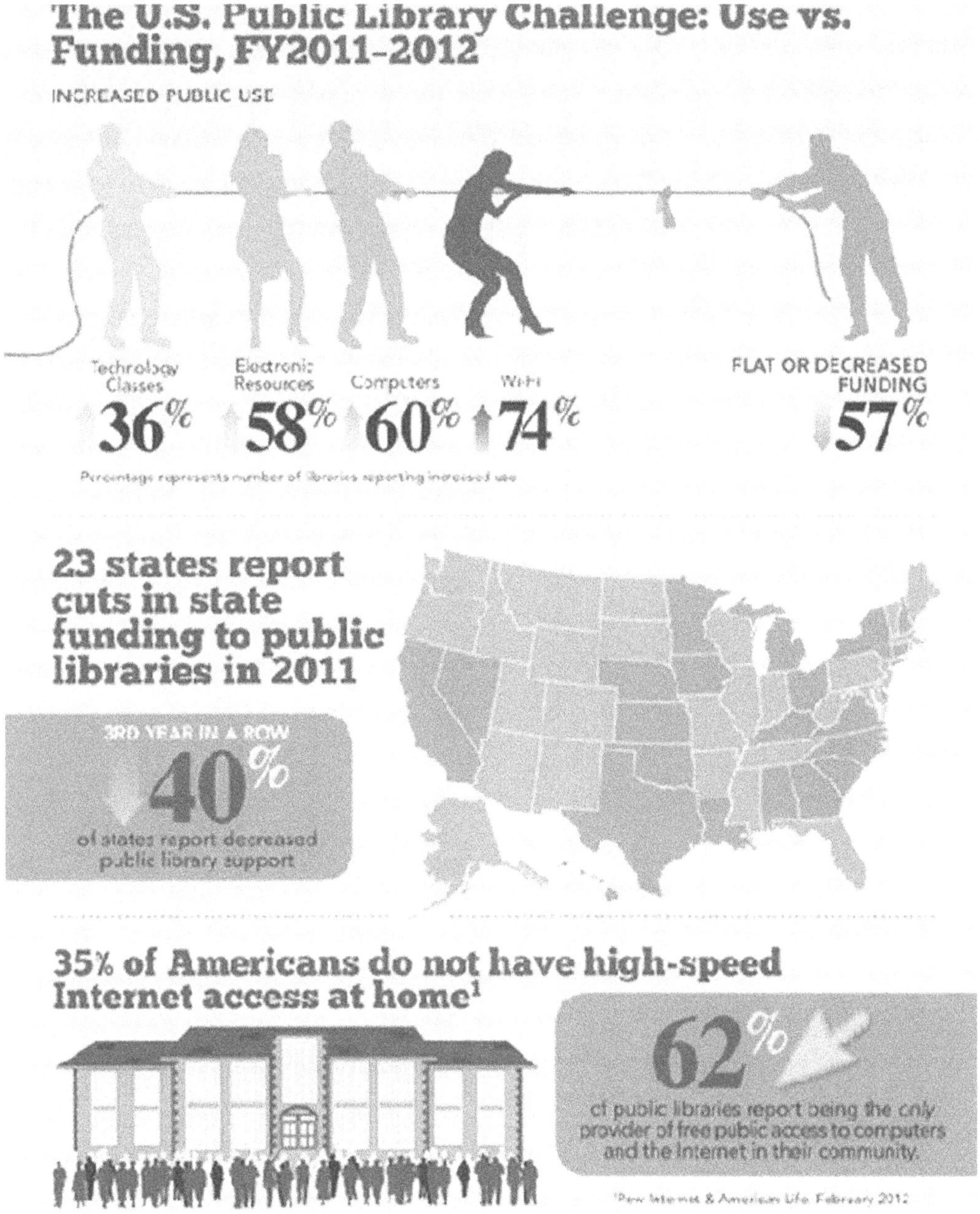

Figure 6.4. Middle of the Infographic: U.S. Public Library Challenge. Used with permission from the American Library Association. "Weathering the Storm Infographic, a Supplement to Libraries Connect Communities: Public Library Funding & Technology Access Study 2011–2012," http://www.ala.org/research/plftas/2011_2012/weatheringthestorm.

Collect data. Collect data through research (see figure 6.5) and decide upon design aspects.

- Identify the problem to spotlight and address the solution to the problem. Data can come from public sources such as Google Public Data or your own data from surveys, polls, or user input. Appropriate comparisons are the context that makes numbers meaningful in a way that allows the reader to form judgments, make decisions, and take action.
- Make the design simple. Seamlessly, weave figures with the text that describes them.
- Find accurate and referenced sources for the information you include.

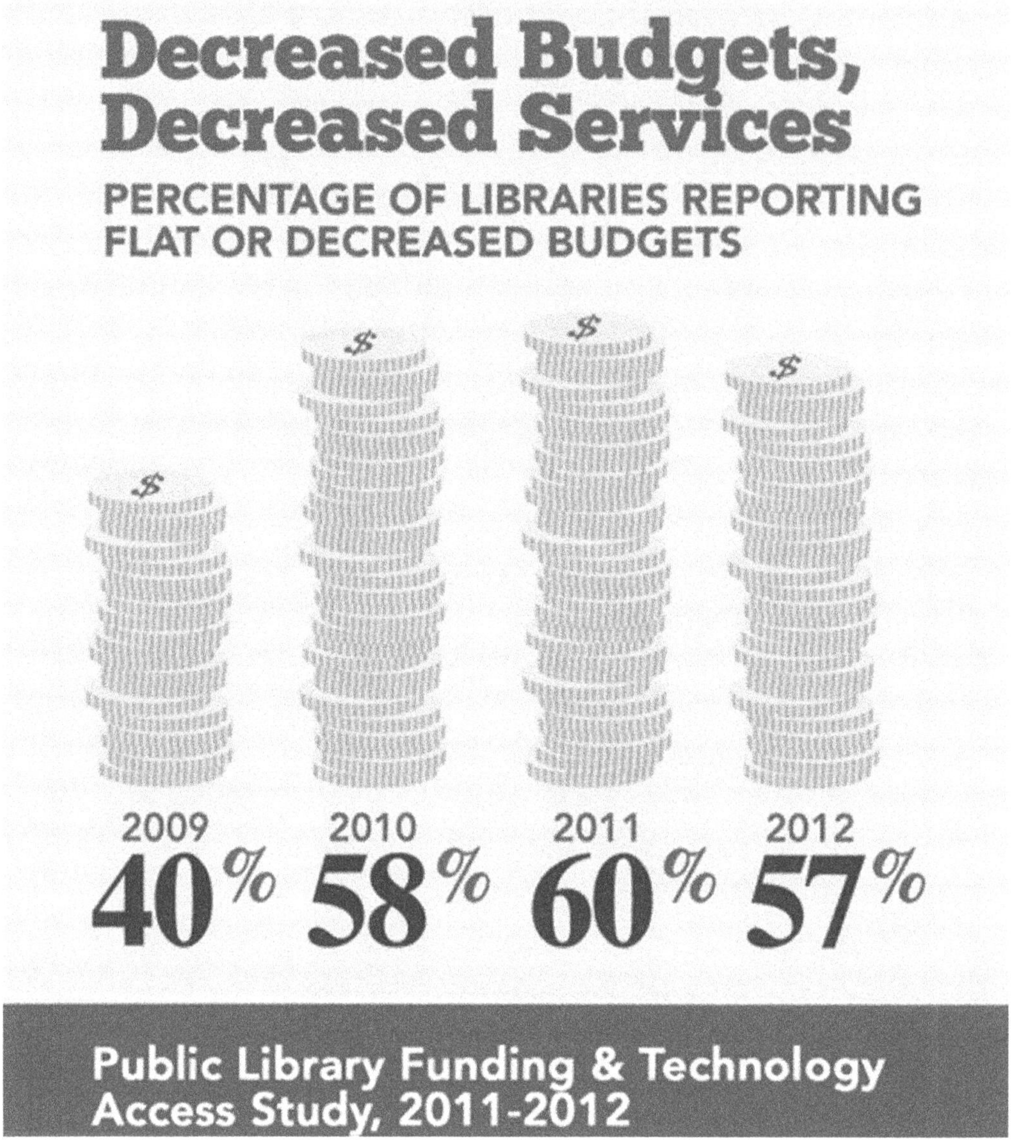

Figure 6.5. Middle of the Infographic: Data Collection. Used with permission from the American Library Association. "Weathering the Storm Infographic, a Supplement to Libraries Connect Communities: Public Library Funding & Technology Access Study 2011–2012," http://www.ala.org/research/plftas/2011_2012/weatheringthestorm.

At the bottom of the ALA infographic, authoritative sources are listed: an access study, covering fiscal years 2011 to 2012 (Hoffman, Bertot, and Davis, 2012), conducted by the American Library Association, in partnership with the Information Policy & Access Center at the University of Maryland. The Pew Internet and American Life organization is also credited for statistics about public libraries providing the only free Internet in their communities. These statistics emphasize that large numbers of patrons are using the technology at public libraries and that lack of funding is having a dramatic effect on the ability of public libraries to continue to support technology use by their patrons. These sources lend credibility to the facts presented in the infographic and have greater impact on the audience (see figure 6.6).

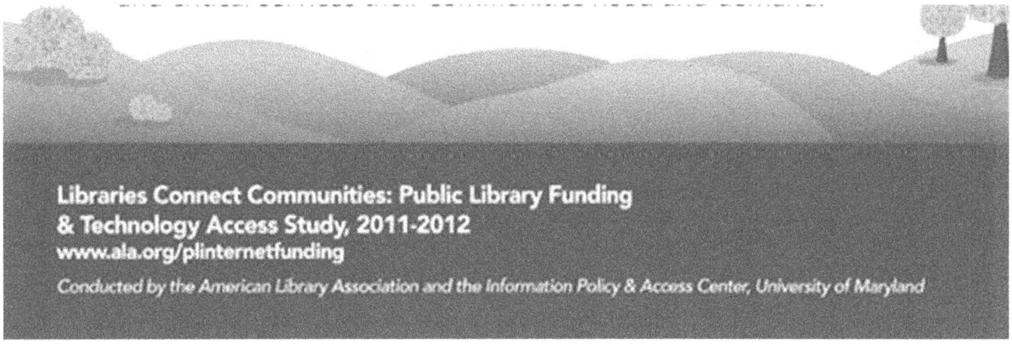

Figure 6.6. End of the Infographic: Sources. Used with permission from the American Library Association. "Weathering the Storm Infographic, a Supplement to Libraries Connect Communities: Public Library Funding & Technology Access Study 2011–2012," http://www.ala.org/research/plftas/2011_2012/weatheringthestorm.

Phase 2: Draft

In this phase, all the planning comes together in a visual presentation. Various design elements emphasize the title and key points, visualize the data, and let the story flow with a beginning, middle, and end.

Create the infographic. As you create the rough draft of the infographic, you will incorporate all of your planning into the wireframe using a variety of design elements.

- Write the headline. Keep it short and concise, approximately fifty words to ensure search visibility; use specific headlines that match content; aim to have approximately six words in your headlines; avoid words that have multiple meanings; and include power verbs and interesting adjectives. The title of the infographic—"U.S. Public Libraries Weather the Storm"—uses a metaphor of a storm to indicate the problem—lack of funding. The largest, thickest, black font is used to emphasize the title and set the tone of a storm.
- Identify key points—what are the compelling and appealing aspects?
- Text is short and concise to state each subpoint. A medium-sized font is used. To direct the eye, points are separated by dotted lines.
- Visualize the data. Selecting a design is a crucial step in the creation process. The design will take your data and transform it into a visually friendly piece of content—a data visualization. Incorporate a background, images, graphs, and photos. Select a color scheme, graphs for statistics, and fonts that appeal to your audience. The layout also needs to be well organized and free of clutter.

In the example, the color palette contains shades of two complementary colors, blue and orange. At the beginning, blue, a cool color, along with the rain falling from the cloud images, gives the feeling of a stormy sky and a despairing atmosphere. In section 2, all words are in orange, including title words in the same large font, to depict a promising, brighter future. Technology images are used; surprising statistics are placed in boxes of the opposite section color to make them stand out. Each of the design elements emphasizes a particular aspect of the message the infographic wants to convey.

Draft a story that flows from the beginning to a call for action at the end. Write about things that are bad, like budget cuts; share patron successes such as how the library has helped them; and highlight new services, products, or programs. Ask, what's in it for the reader? What is something your viewers can take away? Show potential donors some value. Good content increases e-newsletter subscribers, webinar attendees, website visitors, and downloads.

- Generate your infographic and assemble it. Create a wireframe or sketch visual layout. Similar to other forms of content creation, you must analyze content and design elements and put the infographic through an extensive editing.
- Assess the final infographic. Look back at the process and ask yourself what you learned from the process so that you can apply it to the next infographic. Did your infographic meet its goals? What is the typical size of an infographic—is yours too long or too short? What colors go together? What fonts are used on the best-looking infographics? What graphics? How are other wireframes laid out? Can you find one that looks close to what you are trying to accomplish?

In the example ALA infographic, the story is divided into two parts. It has a beginning, the statement of the problem; and a middle with two parts and subpoints with supporting statistics. The end states the call to action and outlines consequences if the action is not fulfilled. A two-color palette emphasizes the contrasting elements: benefits of the library versus decreased funding. Font size, color, and graphics help to move the reader's eye from top to bottom, and boxed statistics highlight special data. Summary text and statistics end part 1 of the infographic. A change in color transitions the reader from showing the problem in part 1 to part 2 highlighting resources the library can provide with adequate funding. Text enclosed in a box at the end leaves the reader with a bonus users can obtain with more funding. The source data also indicates the authority behind the statistics that are included throughout the infographic. As you analyze the final infographic, you can see that the finished product shows a great deal of thought, research, and design skill.

Promote your infographic. Determine locations, people, and media that can convey your infographic to prior and new donors and donors with the most potential. The following are possibilities:

- Outreach to local media
- Calls to influential supporters
- Flyers or posters in key places
- Events
- Everywhere online (e.g., post to websites, e-mail, e-newsletters, social media)
- Your biggest fans—ask your most loyal supporters to spread the word to their networks on your behalf
- Make sure your infographic can be easily shared on social media—Facebook, Twitter, LinkedIn, Pinterest. Have an embed code available with the infographic.

For the ALA infographic, an embed code is available at the American Library Association website so libraries and others can share the infographic. Individual sections of the infographic are also available to be shared at http://www.ala.org/research/plftas/2011_2012/plftasgraphics. In addition to using the embed code, you can also share the link to this infographic by clicking social media icons for Twitter, Facebook, Pinterest, and more next to the infographic.

Analyze, engage, and build relationships. Analyzing the process you went through to create your infographic and its contribution to fundraising is important as you select venues for future fundraising.

- Study data to see results.
- Get feedback from staff, sponsors, and patrons to assess what worked and what didn't. Record and share this information within your library.
- Reengage participants from sponsors to volunteers to donors and attendees at events.
- Make selected "thank you" phone calls and extend a follow-up invitation to patrons and donors to get involved with the library and its services.
- Reach out to new donors with organizational information and future invitations.
- Report back to everyone on the impact of the infographic on your key issue and goal.

As you contemplate your own infographic, remember to keep the process simple. Your information should be easy to read and not confusing. Make sure it can be used on different platforms (e.g., laptop, tablet, phone). Table 6.2 lists additional sites related to fundraising.

Table 6.2. Related Funding Sites and Infographics

DESCRIPTION	URL
"Library Budget Cuts Threaten Community Services across the Country" (11/16/2011)	http://www.huffingtonpost.com/2011/11/16/can-the-american-library-_n_1096484.html?ref=libraries-in-crisis
"Why It's Time to Speak Up for Our Libraries" (11/16/2011)	http://www.huffingtonpost.com/andrew-losowsky/libraries-in-crisis-introduction_b_1096030.html?ref=libraries-in-crisis
State of American Libraries: A Report from the American Library Association (2014)	http://www.ala.org/tools/libfactsheets/alalibraryfactsheet06#usagelibs
"ALA Releases 2014 State of America's Libraries Report: Libraries Continue to Transform to Meet Society's Needs, but School Libraries Feel the Pain of Tight Budgets"	http://www.ala.org/news/press-releases/2014/04/ala-releases-2014-state-america-s-libraries-report
"Infographics Are a Powerful Tool in Non-profit Marketing and Fundraising"	http://www.theagitator.net/communications/infographics-produce-fundraising-results/
Report provides statistics, graphs, and tables on correlation between librarians and reading test scores	http://www.lrs.org/documents/closer_look/CO4_2012_Closer_Look_Report.pdf
"End-of-Year Fundraising"	https://www.salsalabs.com/why-salsa/strategic-best-practices/end-year-fundraising

Libraries need to be more proactive in conveying their value to the public. There are thousands of people out there who have never been encouraged to use the library or who think it is just for scholars and computer users. The library may not be on many people's radar, and they often don't know what the library offers. Without knowing the value the library brings to patrons' lives, raising funds will continue to be a problem. Lack of communication is one of the biggest problems.

More librarians are now creating their own infographics using tools available to visualize data. Infographics can reach a wide range of the public and make the library come alive for those who do not yet know its value. When more people know what the library has to offer and how it can enrich their lives, they are more likely to donate to this worthy institution.

Key Points

This chapter presented information on the importance of fundraising for libraries. Numerous examples and a detailed analysis of an infographic illustrate the importance infographics can play in this vital role.

- Research suggests that libraries need to do a better job of demonstrating the library's value to their patrons and users, as well as to those who do not frequent the library.
- Specific examples illustrate how school, public, academic, and special libraries are using infographics to illustrate uses, services, and expertise libraries can offer.
- Models provide steps libraries can take to follow in the footsteps of libraries already using infographics.
- By following seven steps provided in a detailed analysis of an infographic, you can plan, create, and share your own infographic to promote fundraising at your library.

When library patrons and nonpatrons know more about the programs, services, events, products, and expertise the library has to offer, they are more likely to visit the library and open their wallets to give to it. When elected officials and administrators see the value of the library through a visualization as infographics can provide, they are more likely to commit tax dollars and government funds for libraries. The main emphasis of this chapter is to take advantage of the benefits of infographics to forward this cause.

Exercises for Chapter 6

To reinforce what you learned in this chapter, try the following:

1. If you are working in a library, create your own infographic to promote fundraising, either alone or divide up the tasks with a small group. (If not, work together with your local library to create an infographic to promote or fundraise for the library. They'll appreciate your help!)
2. Select your topic either about the library as a whole or one service or program, such as technology or e-books.
3. Divide the tasks so one person is writing text, another is collecting appropriate images, another is researching the topic (e.g., talking to patrons, collecting data, or listing sources), and another works on a design and elements to use.
4. Decide on a tool to use to create the infographic (e.g., PowerPoint, Infogr.am, Piktochart).

a. Regroup and discuss the material each person has brought to the table. Decide what content and images to include and how it will be arranged in a draft infographic. Select one or two individuals to create it.
b. Review the infographic and analyze it using the questions discussed in this chapter (e.g., audience, purpose).
c. Create a blog post and embed your infographic into the post to publicize it. List other groups or venues to promote your infographic.
d. Write about your experience: What did you like/dislike about the process? The tool(s) you used? How easy or difficult it was to create the infographic? The data collection process?

References

ALA (American Library Association). 2012. "U.S. Public Libraries Weather the Storm." *Huff Post Books* (blog). June 26. http://www.huffingtonpost.com/2012/06/26/library-infographic_n_1627784.html.

Hoffman, Judy, John Carlo Bertot, and Denise M. Davis. 2012. "Libraries Connect Communities: Public Library Funding & Technology Access Study 2011–2012." http://www.ala.org/research/plftas/2011_2012.

LRS (Library Research Service). 2013. "School Libraries & Student Achievement." http://www.lrs.org/data-tools/school-libraries/impact-studies/.

Zickuhr, Kathryn, Kristen Purcell, and Lee Rainie. 2014. "From Distant Admirers to Library Lovers—and Beyond." Pew Research Center. March 13. http://www.pewinternet.org/2014/03/13/library-engagement-typology/.

Zickuhr, Kathryn, Lee Rainie, and Kristen Purcell. 2013. "Library Services in the Digital Age." Pew Research Center (Pew Internet & American Life Project). January 22. http://libraries.pewinternet.org/2013/01/22/library-services/.

Zickuhr, Kathryn, Lee Rainie, Kristen Purcell, and Maeve Duggan. 2013. "How Americans Value Public Libraries in Their Communities." Pew Research Center (Pew Internet & American Life Project). December 11. http://libraries.pewinternet.org/2013/12/11/libraries-in-communities/.

CHAPTER 7

Library Partnerships
A Win-Win Combination

IN THIS CHAPTER

- ▷ Research related to advantages of librarian partnerships
- ▷ The importance of collaborations and partnerships between libraries and other organizations
- ▷ Examples of libraries that use infographics to illustrate different types of partnerships
- ▷ Ways infographics can help foster partnerships
- ▷ Important aspects of infographics designed to teach information literacy
- ▷ A step-by-step infographic for the purpose of improving partnering between academic libraries and faculty

NUMEROUS PARTNERSHIPS OCCUR in the library community—between libraries, local organizations and the library, between librarians and faculty and teachers to educate students, the library and government organizations, and many more. The purposes and goals of these partnerships are many. This chapter addresses the importance of partnerships as librarian roles continue to evolve. It also illustrates how infographics can enhance the effort both as a teaching tool and by giving the library more visibility. Numerous examples in this chapter describe libraries that already use infographics in their collaborations and partnering efforts. Library partnerships are a trend for the future. The popularity of infographics offers the librarian a visible way to showcase these partnerships.

Teacher-Librarian Partnerships: A Bit of Background

As described in a post on the *Edutopia* blog, "libraries are reinventing themselves as content becomes more accessible online and their role becomes less about housing books and more about connecting learners and constructing knowledge" (Holland, 2015). Students and teachers no longer need a library simply for access. Instead, they require a place that encourages participatory learning and allows for co-construction of understanding from a variety of sources. For example, Loertscher, Koechlin, and Zwaan describe the contemporary school library as a learning commons, "the hub of the school, where exemplary learning and teaching are showcased, where professional development, teaching and learning experimentation, and action research happen" (quoted in Zmuda and Harada, 2008: 4). Teacher-librarians, once primarily managers of school resources, can now become instructional leaders, supporting and collaborating with every teacher in the school, promoting inquiry-based learning and fostering a thriving reading culture.

According to Paige Jaeger, librarian and coauthor of *Think Tank Library: Brain-Based Learning Plans for New Standards*, librarians were some of the first educators to realize that the Internet made finding information much easier (Jaeger and Ratzer, 2014). They recognized that students would need help synthesizing and analyzing the vast amounts of information available to them. Jaeger emphasized that librarians, using an inquiry-based approach, should focus on teaching students how to assess and use information and not just find it. This is an ideal role to form the basis of a partnership between teachers and librarians.

Librarians in school, academic, public, and special libraries are expanding partnering opportunities. School libraries are collaborating with teachers and partnering with public libraries and online organizations. Academic and special librarians are becoming an integral part of faculty course work and research.

Models of Infographics Illustrating Library Partnerships

During the collaboration process, where do infographics make sense? The next examples illustrate how infographics again can be helpful to engage public, school, academic, and special libraries with partners for a wide range of purposes. They may give you ideas for fostering collaboration between your library and organizations with which you wish to partner. Go to the URL of each example to see the complete infographics in color, one of the important design elements.

The following partnerships have the materials—images, text, and a story to tell—that could form the basis of infographics for the purpose of promoting their partnerships, providing awareness of the work being completed by the partners, and creating new partnerships, to name just a few.

Example 1: Public Libraries and Workforce Development Partnerships

When the public library builds partnerships, it strengthens the ties to its community, shares resources, and builds positive relationships with diverse stakeholders. Reaching out to initiate community partnerships begins with identifying both traditional and nontraditional partners and exploring new ways to work together. Effective collaborations are sustained through a shared commitment to serving the ever-changing needs of the community.

In the example in figure 7.1, the State Library of North Carolina and the North Carolina Department of Cultural Resources used infographics to highlight partnerships between North Carolina public libraries and numerous other agencies. These collaborations provided programs and services to the public, especially on workforce development, during 2012 and 2013.

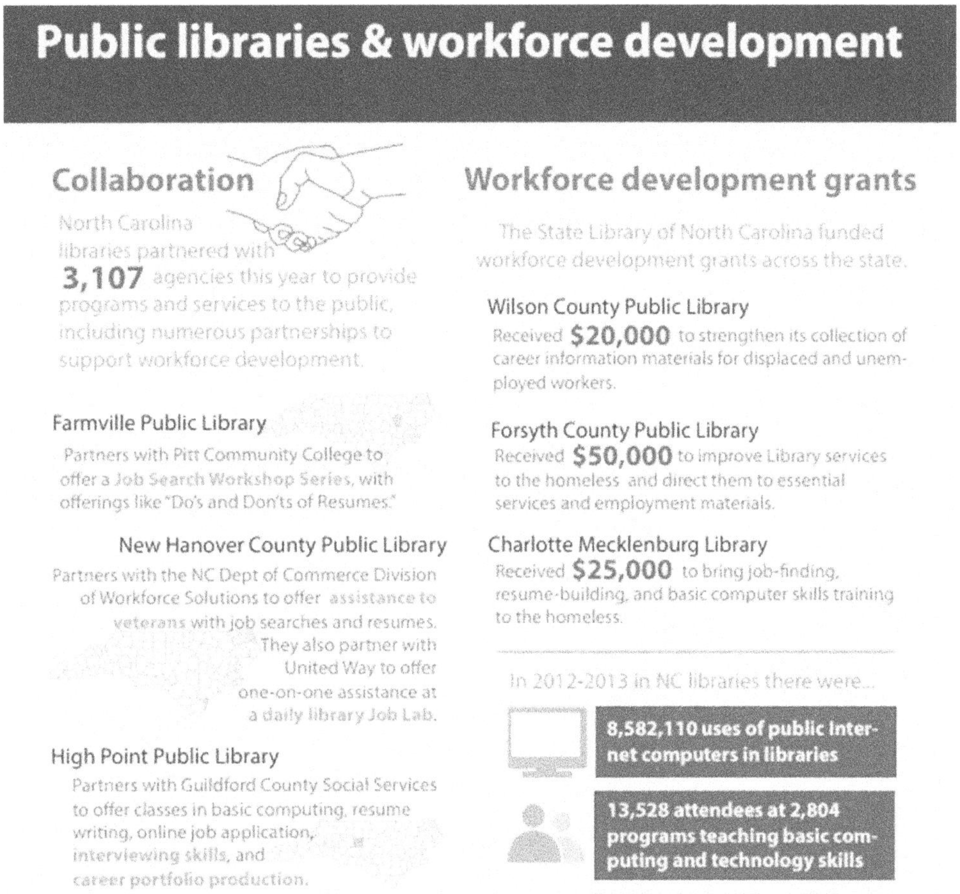

Figure 7.1. Public Libraries and Workforce Development Partnerships. Designed by the State Library of North Carolina and the North Carolina Department of Cultural Resources, http://plstats.nclive.org/infographics/LibLegDay_workforcedev_2014.pdf.

In just two pages of statistics, short text with color for emphasis, maps to locate the libraries, and images, the infographic is able to concisely describe diverse library partnerships in North Carolina. For example, short, colorful text explains three partnerships:

- the Farmville Public Library collaboration with the Pitt Community College to offer job search workshops,
- the New Hanover County Public Library and the North Carolina Department of Commerce Division of Workforce Solutions partnership to offer assistance to veterans with job searches and resumes, and
- the High Point Public Library partnership with Guildford County Social Services to provide classes in computer applications and interviewing skills.

Maps pinpoint the library locations. Statistics emphasize numbers of patrons participating in the programs.

These types of social services are an important collaboration provided by public libraries nationwide. Using infographics, the North Carolina State Library was able to inform the public about its services and promote partnerships with organizations throughout North Carolina.

Example 2: Academic Embedded Librarianship

In the infographic in figure 7.2, the academic library at King University explains and promotes the online embedded librarian program, a collaboration between faculty and librarians, and the course offered at King University.

The infographic begins with two photos contrasting a traditional library lined with shelves of books with a student at a computer involved in embedded library instruction. Text explains what online embedded librarianship is; images and text show three main parts of the program, along with other services offered. At the end of the infographic, a call for action provides contact information about the embedded library program. This program is a tailored instructional online experience. The infographic offers a way for the library to describe and promote its program to university faculty, the audience for the infographic.

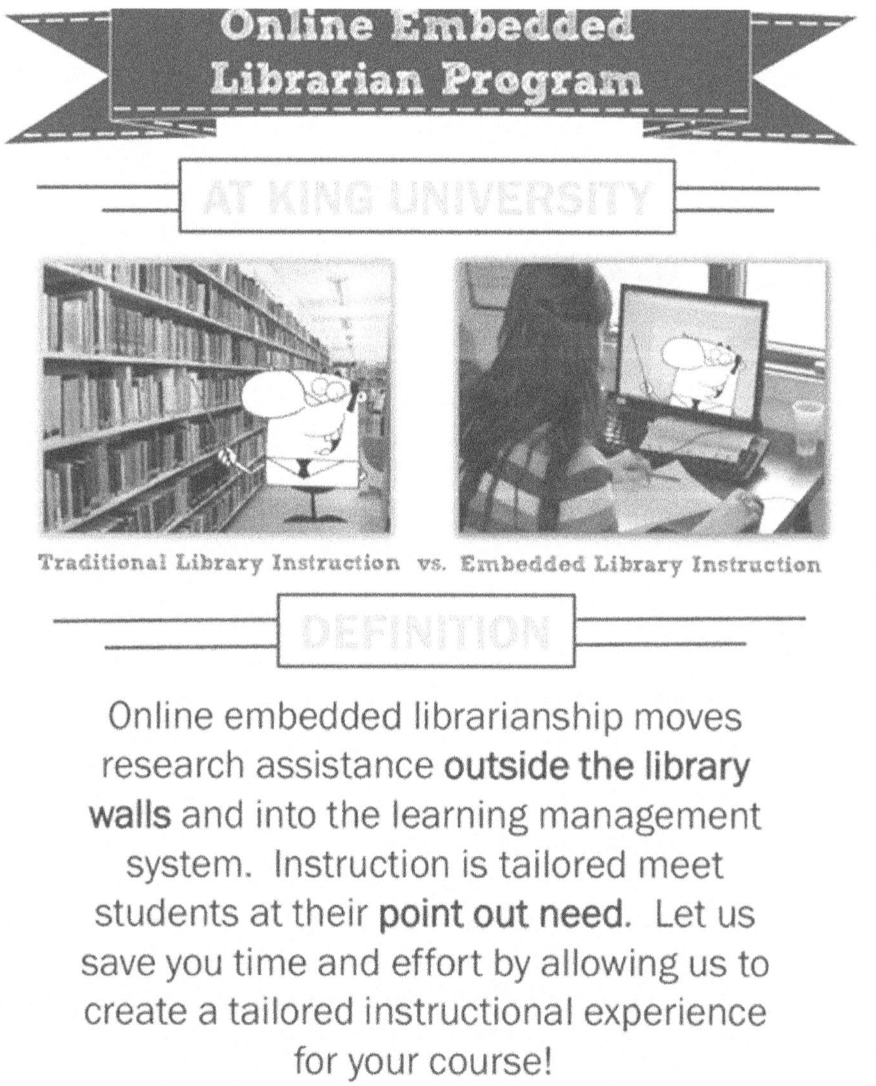

Figure 7.2. Embedded Librarianship. Created by Seth Allen, King University Library, http://www.slideshare.net/sethallen26/online-embedded-librarianship-at-king-university.

Example 3: Partnering in a Health Care Special Library

The staff at the MD Anderson Center Medical Library created an infographic, shown in figure 7.3, to demonstrate the library's role in assisting faculty to publish their research. The library staff's goal in creating the infographic was to show faculty the expertise and resources provided by the library and how librarians can help faculty in their publishing efforts.

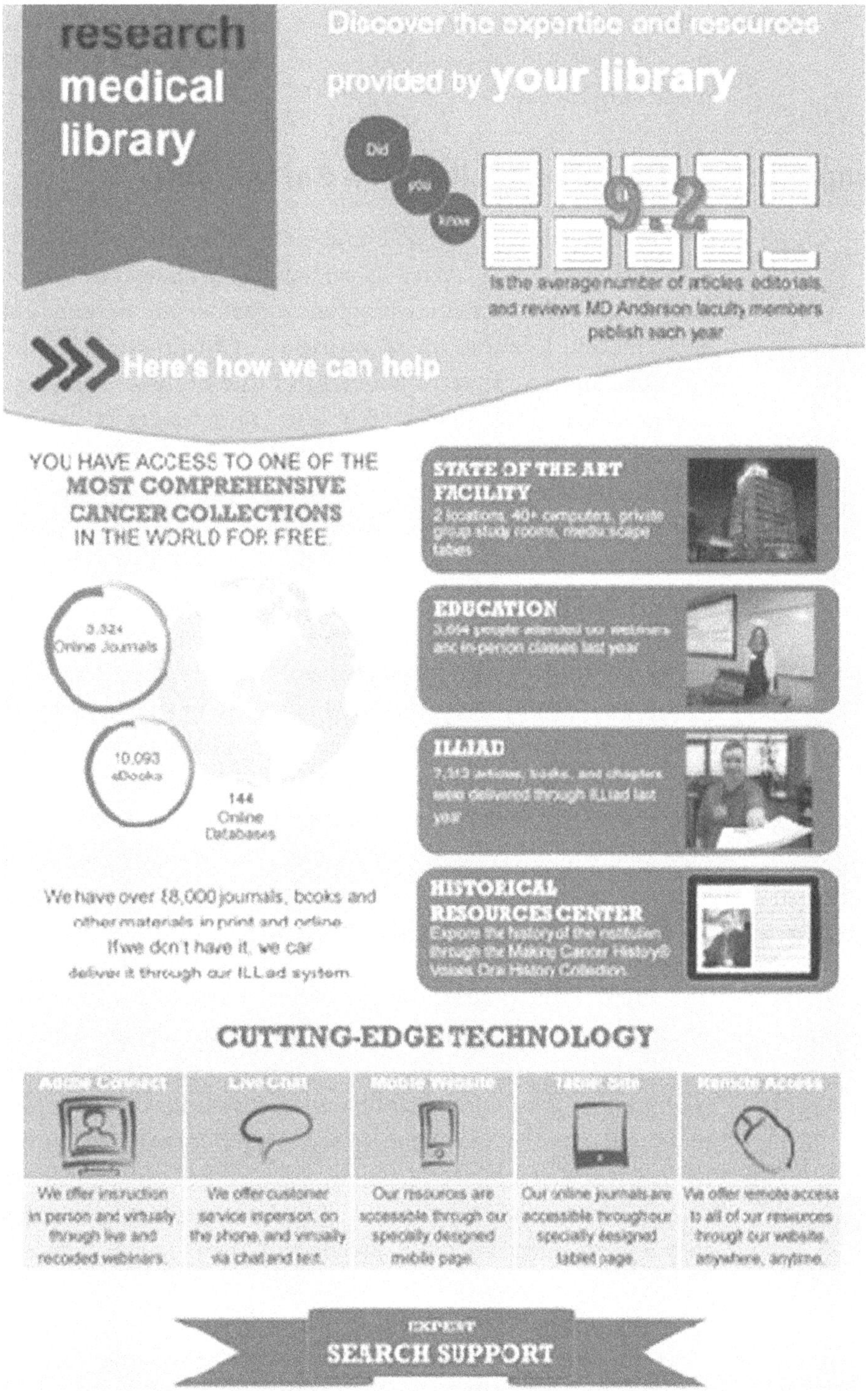

Figure 7.3. MD Anderson Center Medical Library. Created by April Aultman Becker and Laurissa Gann at the Research Medical Library at the MD Anderson Center, http://librari-andesignshare.org/2012/12/12/infographic-how-our-library-helps-faculty-publish/.

Using statistics and images, the infographic describes the library's comprehensive cancer publication collection. Also highlighted in individual boxes, the infographic uses different elements—pictures, short text, and statistics—to describe the state-of-the-art facility; numbers of people who attended webinars; resources available from the ILLiad, the interlibrary publication delivery system; and the historical resources center. Next, the cutting-edge technology available at the library is listed, as well as mention of remote access availability. Statistics emphasize the superb search expertise by indicating the number of searches completed and in what type of publication. This infographic tells a story designed to let faculty know the advantages of partnering with librarians in their publishing endeavors.

Example 4: Faculty-Special Librarian Partnership

The infographic at https://librariandesignshare.files.wordpress.com/2014/06/aia-poster-draft-small.png was created as part of the Assessment in Action (AIA): Academic Libraries and Student Success program, a partnership between the Association of College and Research Libraries, the Association of Institutional Research, and the Association of Public and Land-Grant Universities. The St. Mary's College of Maryland team that also participated was interested in learning if faculty-librarian collaboration had an impact on students' information literacy (IL) skill development in the First Year Seminar (FYS), a required course for all first-year students. Assessment included student, faculty, and librarian surveys, rubric-based assessment of student essays, and faculty interviews. Displaying the research in a format that made sense of so much information they wanted to share was particularly challenging. The infographic proved to be the ideal vehicle.

The librarian used Adobe Photoshop to create the infographic. A timeline format visualized the methods used for assessment. She used short text to state the research question, statistics to identify the participants in the study, and an image to reveal the results of the faculty-librarian collaboration. A second graphic shows where collaboration fell short and where there was no correlation. A call to action to emphasize expert search support available to faculty completes the infographic. Review the entire infographic in color at https://librariandesignshare.files.wordpress.com/2014/06/aia-poster-draft-small.png.

Example 5: The Hobbit Infographic Project

The Hobbit Infographic Project is an interesting collaboration between fifth-grade teacher Janelle Thompson and school librarian Shannon Miller that incorporates the use of infographics as a teaching tool. These two educators worked together from the very beginning of the project deciding on curriculum, ways to infuse technology, the assignment, and other technology tools necessary. Because the class was reading *The Hobbit* and the newly released movie version would soon be available, they decided *The Hobbit* would provide ideal content for the unit and cover aspects of both reading and language arts. As they implemented the lesson, Janelle and Shannon collaborated to

- outline the topic and create the assignment
- explain what should be included in the infographic. A sample assignment sheet is available at http://vanmeterlibraryvoice.blogspot.com/2012/12/the-hobbit-infographic-projecta-great.html.
- keep track of project goals and tasks in Google Docs

- select a tool Piktochart to create the infographics
- create an example infographic template based on Hobbit characters to illustrate the process to students (see figure 7.4)
- design a rubric for assessment

Students received copies of the assignment sheets to use to gather information for their infographics.

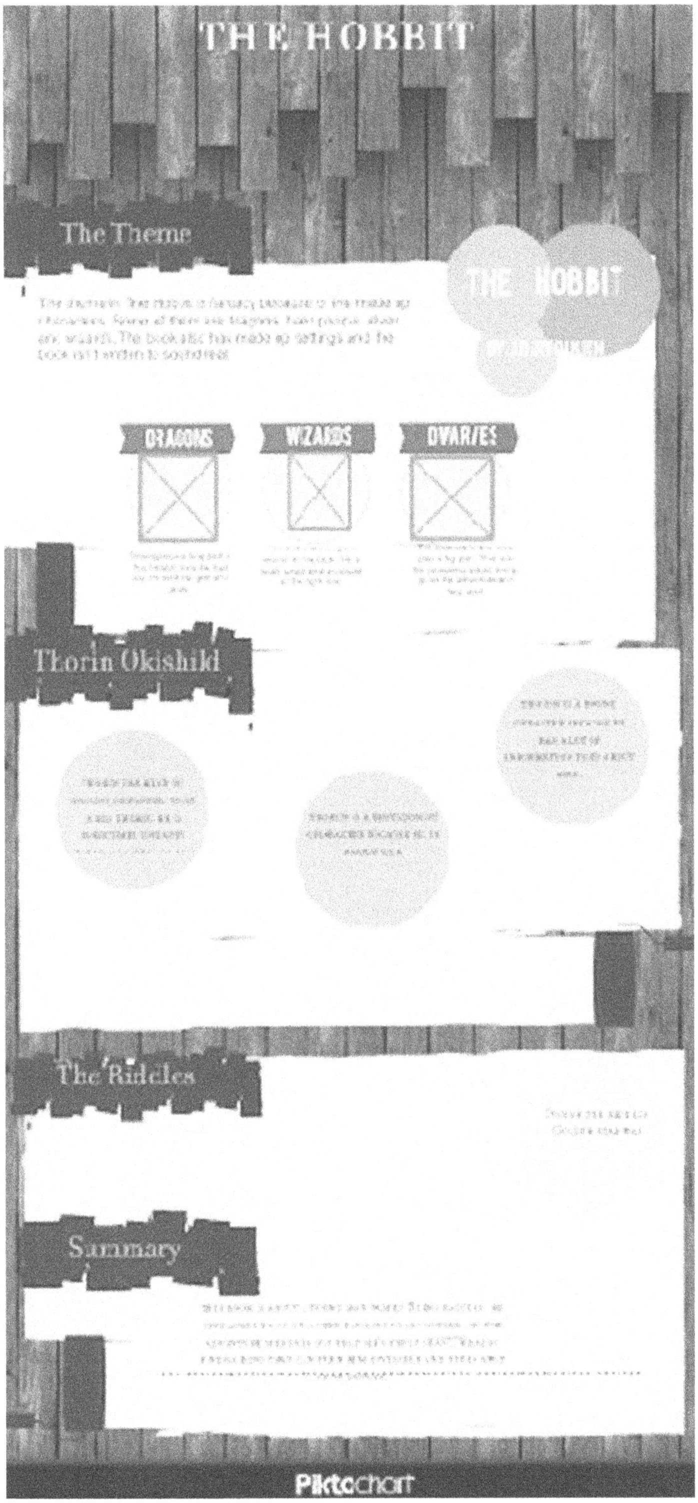

Figure 7.4. Sample Template for Hobbit Infographic. Created by Janelle Thompson and Shannon Miller, Van Meter Elementary School, http://vanmeterlibraryvoice.blogspot.com/2012/12/the-hobbit-infographic-projecta-great.html.

At the beginning of the two-week project, Janelle explained the project requirements during a library period, and Shannon spoke about what research students would do and how to find information online. Together they demonstrated Piktochart, showing students the features and ways to design their infographics. Students then used laptops in the library to start collecting data.

Students also needed to design their infographics in Piktochart. The template used has three parts—the header with the title, subtitle, and facts about the book. Figure 7.5

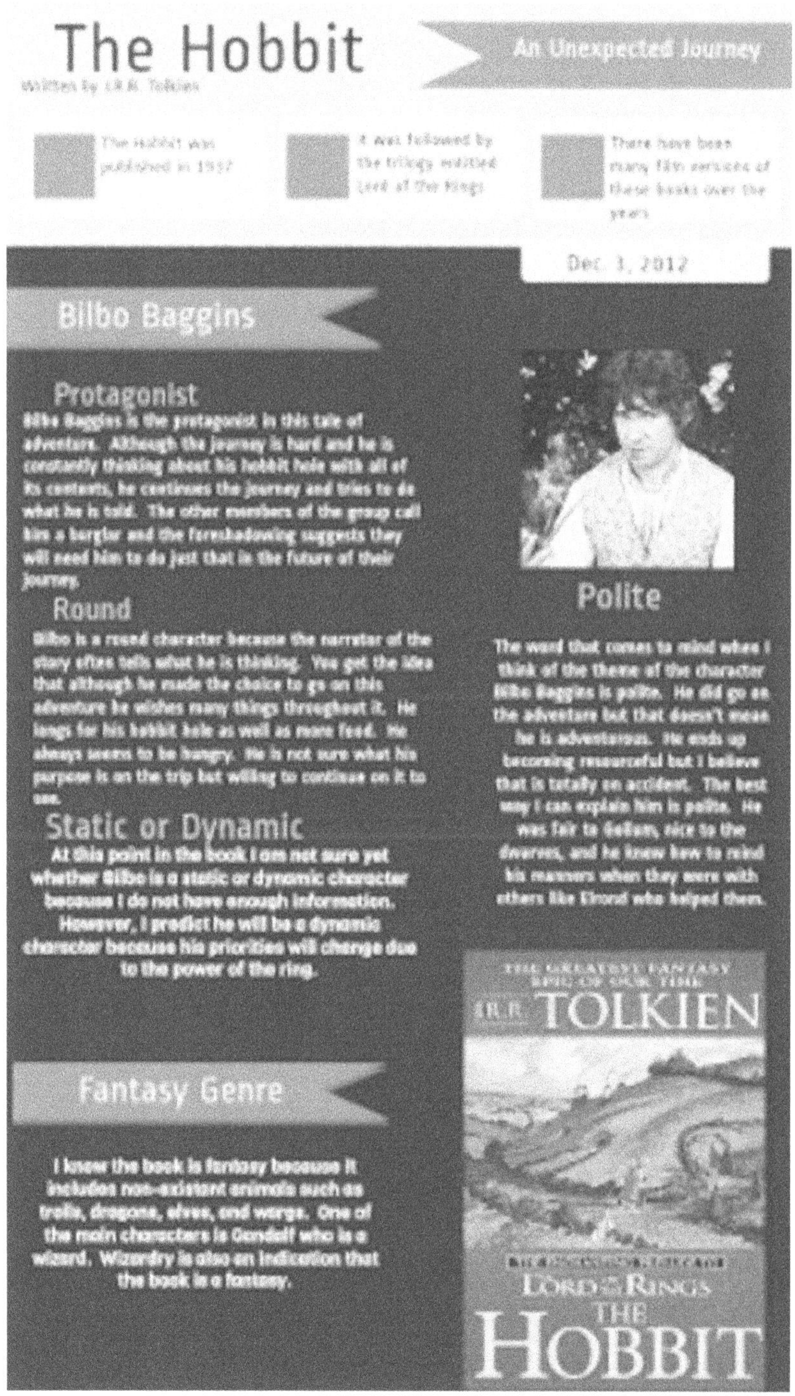

Figure 7.5. Top of Sample Hobbit Infographic. Created by Janelle Thompson and Shannon Miller, Van Meter Elementary School, http://vanmeterlibraryvoice.blogspot.com/2012/12/the-hobbit-infographic-projecta-great.html.

shows the header and top part of the example infographic. Note the color palette uses two complementary colors (red and green). Red banners highlight the subtitle, "An Unexpected Journey," and the titles of the first main section, describing the character Bilbo Baggins. Images of the character and the book add interest and break up the short text.

In figure 7.6, the second half of the infographic, you see the other main sections—the genre and point of view. To maintain consistency, the red banners continue to direct the reader's eye from point to point. A poem emphasizes the subtitle about an unexpected journey to complete the infographic.

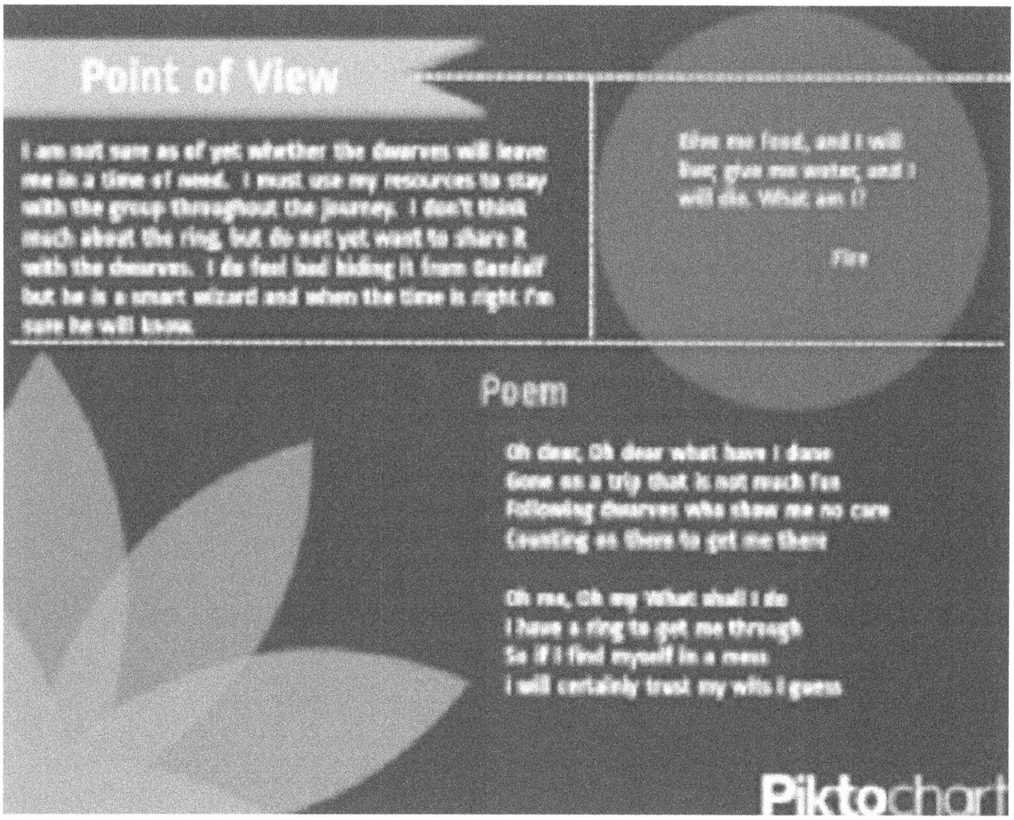

Figure 7.6. Bottom of Sample Hobbit Infographic. Created by Janelle Thompson and Shannon Miller, Van Meter Elementary School, http://vanmeterlibraryvoice.blogspot.com/2012/12/the-hobbit-infographic-projecta-great.html.

Students were very excited as they worked on this project. They especially liked the idea that their infographics would be shared in the school and online to the world. Figure 7.7 shows one of the fifth-grade students' infographics. More are available at http://vanmeterlibraryvoice.blogspot.com/2013/01/couldnt-wait-to-share-hobbit.html.

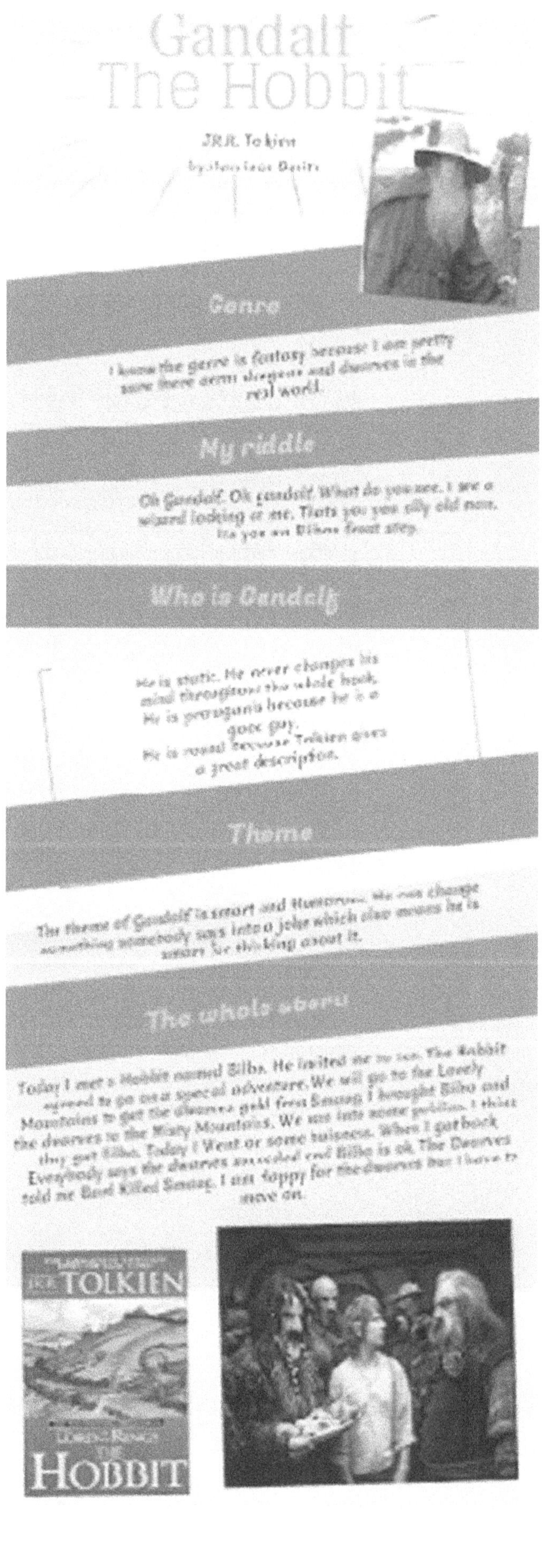

Figure 7.7. Student Hobbit Infographic. Created by a fifth-grade student, Van Meter Elementary School, http://vanmeterlibraryvoice.blogspot.com/2013/01/couldnt-wait-to-share-hobbit.html.

Example 6: "Working Together Is Working Smarter"

Created by the American Association of School Librarians (AASL) Research & Statistics Committee, the infographic "Working Together Is Working Smarter" at http://www.ala.org/aasl/research/ncle-infographic describes key findings from a nationwide survey of educators from all grade levels and subject areas. The resulting report by the National Center for Literacy Education (NCLE) found that school librarians are highly involved leaders who play a critical role in their schools through consistent and sustained collaboration with other educators, and in their professional learning communities both inside and outside of the school. The report investigated the connection between professional learning, educator collaboration, and student learning.

The infographic's title—"Working Together Is Working Smarter"—immediately calls the reader's attention to the partnership/collaboration theme. Using statistics, a bar graph, and images, each of the three main sections—"Internal Collaborative Teams," "External Professional Networks," and "Professional Development"—shows high rates of school librarian participation in collaborative teams, professional collaboration with colleagues and peers, and professional development outside of school. A two-color palette (orange and gray) and a hierarchy of font size direct the reader's eye through the infographic. At the end, authoritative sources are listed prominently to provide credibility to the information. Review the entire infographic in color at the URL listed in the previous paragraph.

Example 7: Partnering to Achieve Common Core State Standards

With the advent of the Common Core State Standards (CCSS), it is imperative that school librarians play an active role that encompasses a total partnership with other school leaders to successfully implement CCSS in their schools. Because school librarians work across grade levels and across disciplines, they are uniquely positioned to influence and implement many of the school-wide goals and initiatives to ensure that all students are college and career ready. With CCSS, explicit literacy instruction is now a shared responsibility of all teachers, librarians, reading specialists, and technology integration specialists throughout the school.

An action plan created by the American Association of School Librarians (AASL) and Achieve (2013) at http://www.ala.org/aasl/sites/ala.org.aasl/files/content/externalrelations/CCSSLibrariansBrief_FINAL.pdf describes the Common Core State Standards and provides examples of ways K–12 librarians have collaborated with classroom teachers, specialists, and administrators to raise student achievement.

In this example, one of many examples described in the action plan, fourth-grade social studies teachers and the librarian collaborated to create a research project about the fifty states to determine what makes a state a desirable place to live. The librarian and teachers brainstormed together to determine the guiding questions on which state is the best to live in, worked together to guide students through the research process, and determined the assessment, an oral report supported by either an interactive digital poster or a web page. Together the teachers and librarian led a joint discussion.

The content in the infographic at http://www.ala.org/aasl/sites/ala.org.aasl/files/content/aaslissues/toolkits/Six_Shift_Infographic_Final.pdf depicts the collaborative role the school librarian can take in implementing CCSS. The title, enclosed in a sweeping green bar, catches the reader's attention by using the word "Star" to characterize the school librarian. The first two sections of the infographic also point out the importance of collaboration between the classroom teacher and librarian in planning and teaching the CCSS. Section 2 identifies specifics of the collaboration and introduces inquiry-based learning. Sections 3 and 4 suggest ways the librarian and classroom teacher can coteach inquiry skills.

The infographic's design uses two pairs of complementary colors—red/green and purple/yellow. The color red emphasizes main words in the text so they can be seen quickly. Yellow lines divide sections for easy scanning. The star-shaped Wordle image appears twice to emphasize the collaborative nature of the topic and tie the sections together. A trail of stars from each image is a directional cue to guide the reader's eye from point to point down the page. Links at the end of the infographic provide sources.

This infographic provides a succinct visual representation to emphasize the collaborative role of librarians in the implementation of the Common Core State Standards, an important nationwide K–12 educational initiative. It issues a call to action challenging school librarians to collaborate with classroom teachers to integrate the CCSS into instruction, to provide leadership in implementing them, and to promote the role of the school library program in student achievement. Review this entire infographic in color at the above URL. AASL has also added two other infographics—one on reading comprehension and CCSS and the other on six instructional shifts to help librarians promote their critical role in student achievement.

Faculty-Librarian Partnership

Infographics might take a little more effort to produce than a blog post, but they can be a powerful link in an instructional partnership between the librarian and faculty when it comes to teaching students about the important topic of information literacy (IL).

Research Study Results

A study conducted at the University of Minnesota (Head, 2013) describes the vital need for these faculty-librarian partnerships. Results showed the following:

- Students entering college were often unfamiliar with the expectations of college research, such as defining a topic, identifying keywords, and selecting sources.
- Most freshmen interviewed for the study said they were "overwhelmed" at the prospect of digging for research sources using a campus library that could have nineteen times as many library databases as their high school library.
- Students indicated that coming up with keywords for searching a scholarly database like LexisNexis had very little in common with the Google searches they executed many times before.
- Others said they had little practice with choosing credible and trusted sources and extracting the passages they needed.
- Often students had no idea they might need to reresearch a topic as their discovery process unfolded and they formulated their thesis. They struggled with evaluating, selecting, and putting trusted information to good use once they found it.

These are the core information competencies that are critically important to the college-level research process. They are also the forte of the librarian's instructional knowledge.

Results also indicated that the greatest gains may occur by focusing on teaching freshmen because this is the time when students are new to higher learning and most excited about discovering more about topics that interest them. Another conclusion stated the need for coordinated efforts between librarians and educators, so that information literacy is taught in a progressive and contextual manner.

Because school libraries have been widely impacted by the recession both in declining numbers of credentialed teacher-librarians and current books on the shelves (AASL and Achieve, 2013), many freshmen are new to library research and have limited understanding of what the research process entails and how the library can best help them. Therefore, it is important that higher education librarians and faculty recognize the effect underfunding is having on school libraries and take the lead to teach information literacy collaboratively.

Recommendations from the Minnesota study (Head, 2013), presented to librarians, faculty, and administrators who worked with freshmen, emphasize the following points:

- Expand partnerships between librarians, faculty, and academic assessment people to more clearly state what they want students to learn, how they are going to make sure that happens, how they are going to assess if they learned the information, and what they are going to do if they didn't learn.
- Increase collaborative efforts through dialogue and formal relationships between school, college, and university librarians, faculty, and staff, especially those who teach first-year students.

A finding of the study pointed out the need to integrate the teaching of information concepts in both lower- and upper-division courses, and that the embedded librarian has more opportunity to form a real partnership with faculty and other staff on campus. As a result, librarians should become more extensively integrated into the teaching of first-year students as faculty and instructor.

Example Collaboration Project

The previous research shows that today's college students must develop keen research competencies and strategies to develop a research question and sort through and evaluate the myriad of information sources available to them. According to a Pew Internet Research report, more than 50 percent of Internet users post pictures online and more than 45 percent repost them (Duggan, 2013). Images are as much, if not more, a means of communication as text. The current generation of students uses all forms of media—Pinterest, Instagram, YouTube, Flickr, Facebook to name some—to communicate their ideas and thoughts using images.

What better way to communicate information literacy (IL), an important topic for the twenty-first-century learner, than through the graphics and stories of infographics. Infographics can provide the tool for presenting content about information literacy clearly, concisely, and in a manner that today's youth will find interesting and entertaining. Infographics can be skimmed quickly and distill a great deal of complex information into an easily digestible format. When done right, they can also be a great reference resource.

Using infographics can also provide a tool for a full collaboration between librarians and faculty. This project on information literacy at the University of Minnesota illustrates a collaborative project between a faculty member and librarian who used infographics in a step-by-step process to teach IL.

The Electronic Library for Minnesota (ELM) and Minitex (http://www.minitex.umn.edu/Communications/RefNotes/2014/05May.pdf) created a series called College Research Guides to explain steps in the research process. The guides were written as infographics, making it easy for students to understand the process that has become more complex as the information landscape has shifted in the past years from one of scarcity to one of overabundance. Online information resources, available through subscription-based online library databases (e.g., InfoTrac, JSTOR, PubMed) and on the open web (e.g., government sites, *Wikipedia*, Google Scholar), have significantly changed college-level research. Today's college students need to develop keen research competencies and strategies for evaluating and sorting through the myriad of information sources now available to them.

The following infographics illustrate a step-by-step research process. They emphasize how to create the content for your infographics to enable students to understand the challenging task of deciding on a topic, finding sources, and analyzing the information.

Step 1. Write a research question. Figure 7.8 outlines the procedure to write a thought-provoking question:

a. Choose a topic. In order to select a thought-provoking question, it is necessary to conduct some preliminary research in encyclopedias, databases, or online.
b. Find an interesting aspect of the topic. This may entail asking questions that answer "who" the people involved are, the time period "when," and the place "where."
c. Learn more about a specific aspect of the topic by asking "how" and "why" questions.

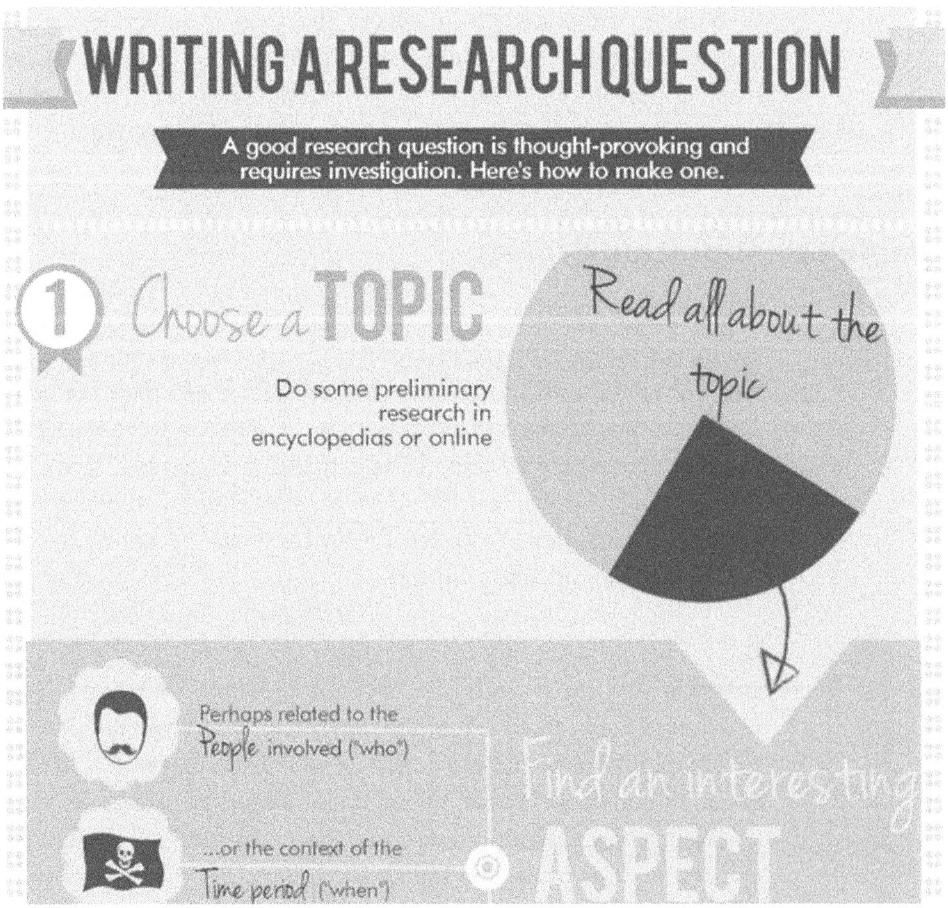

Figure 7.8. Identify a Topic. Created by Matt Lee, Minitex, http://referencenotes.minitex.umn.edu/wp-content/uploads/2014/04/ResearchQuestion-CRG-2014.png.

d. Determine if the scope of the question is focused. A complex question will take more than one sentence to answer and will include specifics that require more than a Google search for the investigation.
e. Evaluate the question you plan to research. The infographic lists three questions: is it interesting, is it researchable, and what information is needed to answer the question.
f. The final comment in the infographic points out that a well-thought-out research question has been created. It also provides a call to action to use the library to find the information needed to answer the question.

Step 2. Determine where to look. Once you have a research question, you are ready to find appropriate information in your library. Based on your topic, you will want to check out scholarly journals, magazines, newspapers, and encyclopedias to locate research findings, current events, and topic overviews. The infographic in figure 7.9 illustrates how to determine where to look for sources that support your topic and how to gather the data.

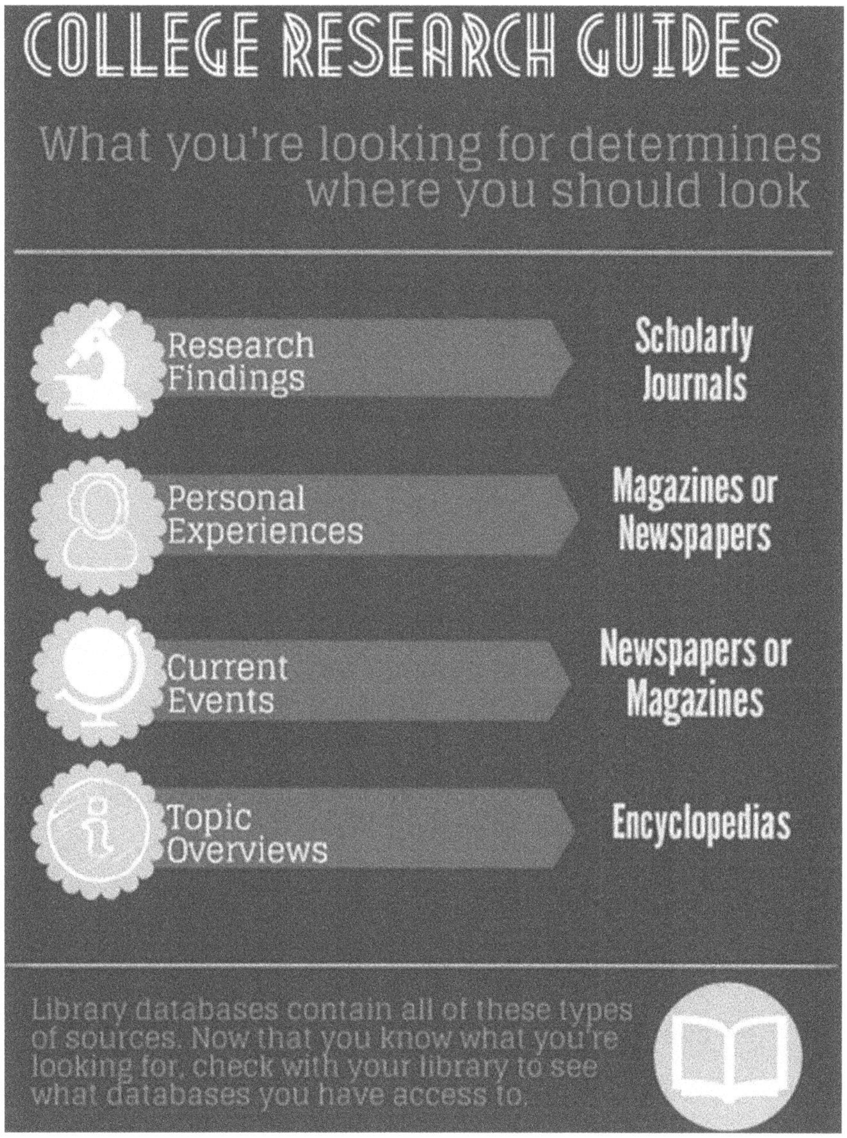

Figure 7.9. What Are You Looking For? Created by Matt Lee, Minitex, http://referencenotes.minitex.umn.edu/wp-content/uploads/2014/04/WhatYoureLookingFor-CRG-2014.png.

The infographic in figure 7.10 identifies sources that contain specific types of information to provide details, context, and background. It also indicates how to find the sources on the library website in databases, such as EBSCO, ProQuest, SIRS, CENGAGE Learning, and more. Note that you can also use tools, such as SurveyMonkey and Google Forms, to create surveys and polls to gather data about your own library.

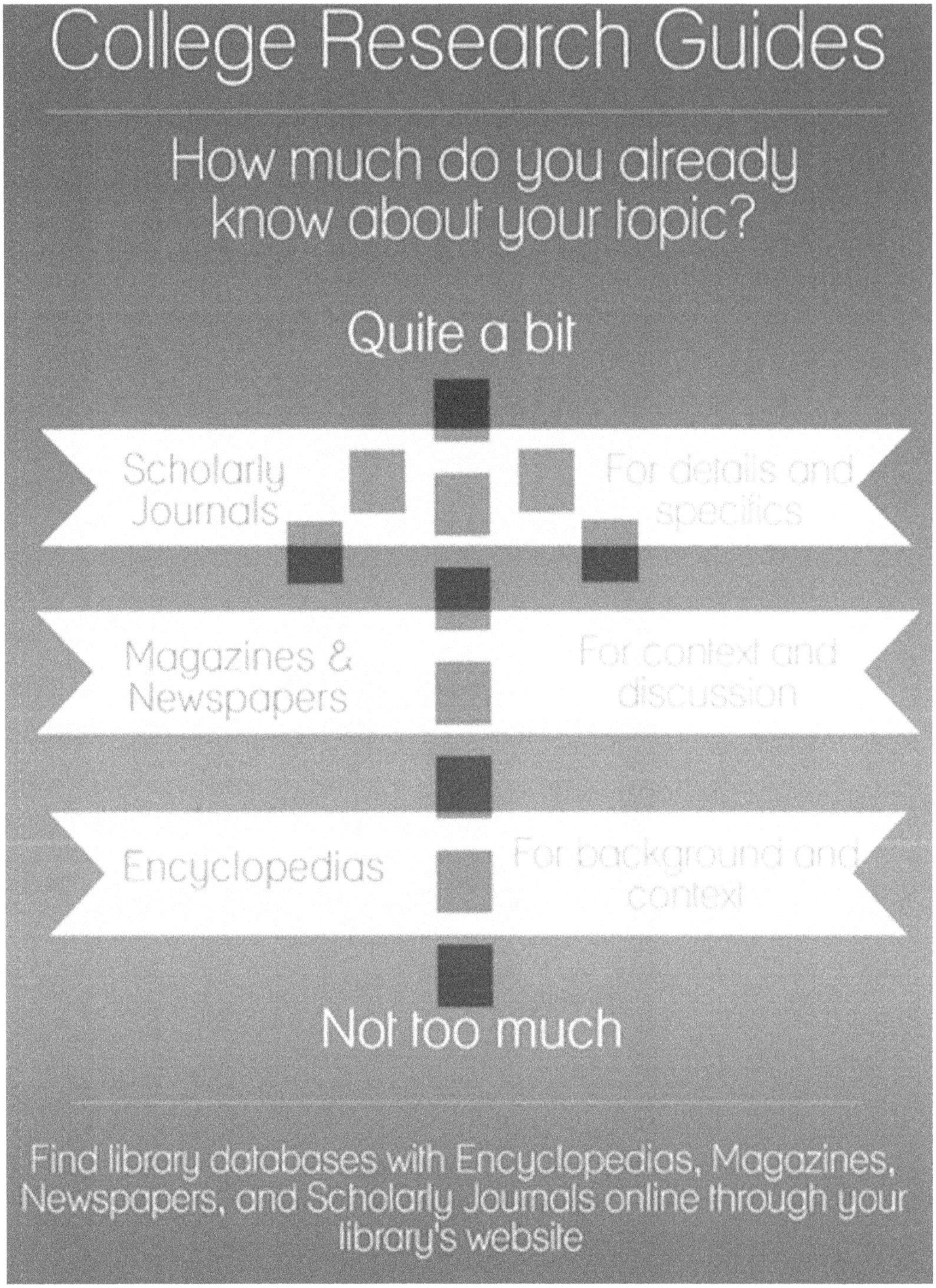

Figure 7.10. How Much Do You Know about Your Topic? Created by Matt Lee, Minitex, http://referencenotes.minitex.umn.edu/wp-content/uploads/2014/04/HowMuchDoYouAlreadyKnow-CRG-2014.png.

Step 3. Analyze the data. Once you have collected data from authoritative sources, it's time to organize the information. You may also analyze statistics using charts and graphs. One way to do so is to tell a story with the data.

a. The story provides context and includes character, obstacles, and outcome. It also makes the data memorable. Decide whether the data informs or persuades your audience.
b. You are using your infographic as a way to present data in a visual way. Because people are visually wired, infographics provide a new way of seeing things. They offer an informed conversation. Their organization shows the big picture and divides it into smaller parts to make the story more understandable. It can also show the potential future and lead to action.
c. Develop your story using best practices.

    - Know your audience.
    - State the thesis and objectives.
    - Create a narrative or metaphor.
    - Select two to three key points.
    - Write an objective narrative.
    - Cite your sources.

Questions about the way students conduct research have always been interesting to librarians. Today's college students need to develop keen research competencies and strategies to find, evaluate, and sort through the proliferation of information sources available to them. The previous study presented several recommendations for librarians, faculty, and administrators who work with freshmen to implement.

Collaboration efforts—dialogue and formal relationships—between school, college, and university librarians, faculty, and staff, especially those who teach first-year students, is important. Another finding of the study pointed out the need to integrate the teaching of information concepts in both lower- and upper-division courses. The embedded librarian has more opportunity to form a real partnership with faculty and other staff on campus. As a result, librarians should become more extensively integrated into the teaching of first-year students as faculty and instructor.

To advance this effort, creating modules, such as the infographics shown earlier, helps students learn about research as they are conducting it. Study findings recommend that librarians take charge of this initiative on campus, as well as promote their services to faculty and staff working with first-year students. In both efforts, infographics can provide the vehicle so librarians can be more involved. Review more examples of infographics in table 7.1.

TIPS WHEN PLANNING CONTENT FOR THE INFOGRAPHIC

A typical setup of an infographic that's trying to motivate your viewers must include (1) an introduction that contains the thesis; (2) a few key data information pieces that are compelling; and (3) a conclusion with a hook to get the audience to act. To create content for an effective infographic, consider the following tips:

- Brainstorm to formulate a solid idea. Work with your partners. What type of information do you have? Is it spatial, chronological, quantitative, or a combination? This will help you decide on the type of infographic to design.
- Identify your goal or purpose. Do you want to inform or persuade? What's the point of the infographic?
- Who is your audience? How much do they know about the topic?
- Create a core story with a central idea. You want to tell something new in short, simple blocks.
- Research well to find relevant information and data. How much data do you have? Find infographics you like to serve as models to help you create a visual style that fits the purpose of the infographic.
- Grab the reader's attention with a persuasive header and an eye-catching design. Conclude with a summary and call to action. Identify basic elements you want to use—diagrams, maps, charts, images.
- Cite sources to improve credibility.
- Publish and go viral.

Considering these points provides the greatest opportunity for your infographic to be successful enough to go viral. Figure 7.11 uses these tips as the content to describe an effective infographic.

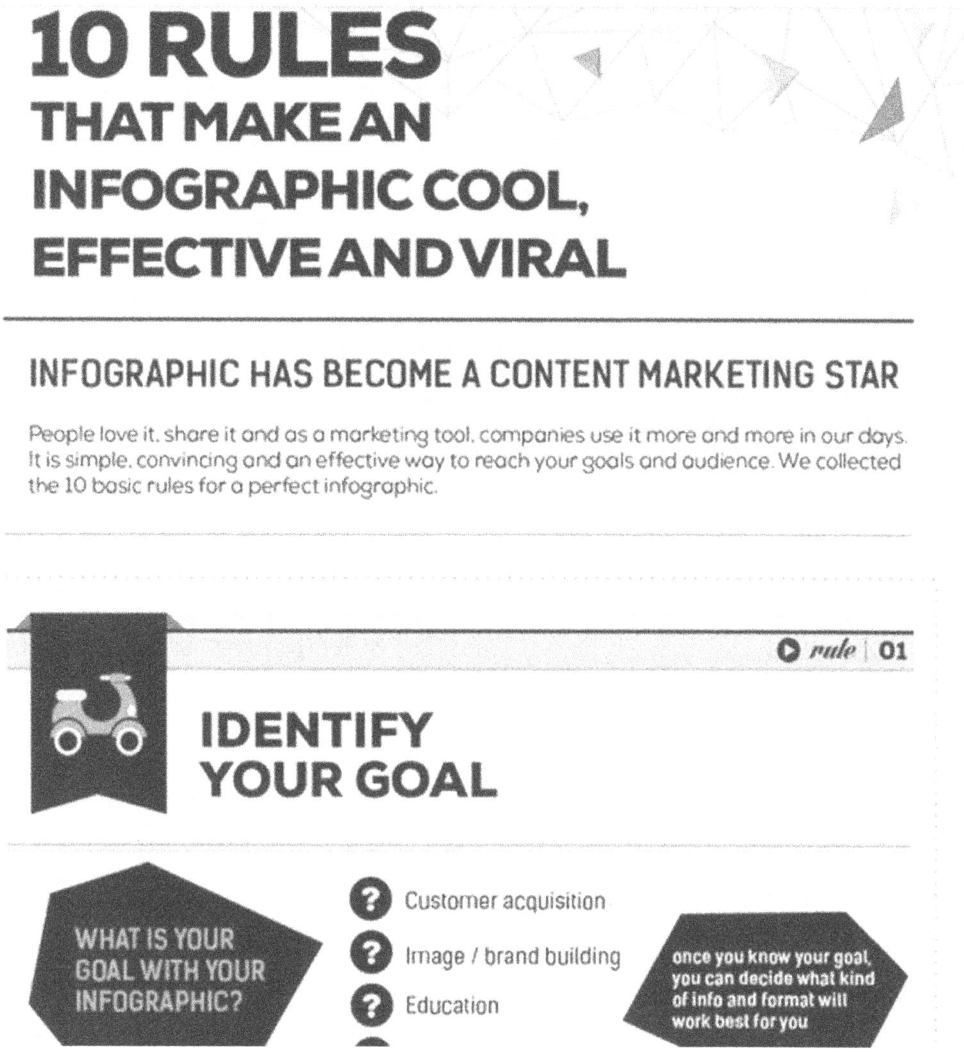

Figure 7.11. Tips to Create an Effective Infographic. Created by Avalanche Infographics, https://www.pinterest.com/pin/569846159071672543/.

Table 7.1. Infographic Examples

DESCRIPTION	URL
Tutorial for infographic design	http://www.asmallbrightidea.com/pages/tutorial.html
Infographic resources from Library Research Services	http://www.lrs.org/webjunctionoclc-webinar-energize-your-base-tips-and-tools-to-raise-awareness-and-build-support-for-library-services/
Infographic showing results of research on librarian collaboration in first-year IL skills at Claremont Colleges	http://scholarship.claremont.edu/cgi/viewcontent.cgi?article=1021&context=library_staff
School Library Impact Studies	http://www.baltimorelibraryproject.org/wp-content/uploads/downloads/2013/09/Library-Impact-Studies.pdf
Page of a variety of infographics	http://www.scoop.it/t/great-infographics-by-john-van-den-brink
"10 Rules That Make an Infographic Cool, Effective and Viral"	https://www.pinterest.com/pin/569846159071672543/

One starting point could be to initiate a campus dialogue to increase awareness about the information practices of today's freshmen, including both the strengths and weaknesses they bring to college. Informed dialogue may give rise to new collaborative efforts that would better prepare freshmen to succeed as information users in their course work and after graduation. Infographics can be an important way to create and publicize strategies to increase awareness and recognition of library contributions to college and university campuses.

Key Points

When using infographics in partnerships, you should keep in mind several important points:

- Equal collaborations between librarians and faculty, staff, and departments in the academic environment can benefit all parties whether teaching students or helping faculty with their research.
- When public libraries establish partnerships with organizations in the community, they can accomplish more.
- Examples in school, academic, special, and public libraries illustrate ways infographics are used to promote, inform, and enhance partnerships.
- Creating infographics is a step-by-step process that incorporates identifying a research question, locating authoritative sources, and analyzing data to answer the question.

Research indicates that infographics can be an integral part of any collaborative effort. Libraries need to take advantage of this popular venue that library patrons will find useful as well as interesting.

Exercises for Chapter 7

To reinforce and practice what you learned in chapter 7, try the following:

1. Use the sites listed next to look for two or three infographics you think might be good models to use in a collaborative endeavor.
   - Library Connect at Elsevier—http://libraryconnect.elsevier.com/articles/2014-03/download-infographic-research-data-starter-steps-libraries or http://libraryconnect.elsevier.com/sites/default/files/RDM_5_steps_for_libraries.png
   - Daily Infographics—http://dailyinfographic.com/
   - Cool Infographics—http://www.coolinfographics.com/
   - 40 Useful and Creative Infographics—http://sixrevisions.com/graphics-design/40-useful-and-creative-infographics/
2. From the infographics you reviewed, select and analyze one infographic using the following criteria to determine its effectiveness.

- Purpose
    - Is the purpose clear?
    - What is the thesis or question to be answered?
    - Who is the audience?
    - How does it use data, visuals, and limited text to tell a story?
    - Is the text succinct? How does it support the message?
- Data
    - Is it well chosen for the purpose and why is it compelling?
    - How was it collected? What, if any, are its limitations?
    - What analysis was done of data?
    - Are sources cited? Are they authoritative?
    - Is data current? Complete? Accurate?
    - Is it at an appropriate level of detail—or too much or oversimplified?
    - What does the data not cover? How is this important for the thesis?
    - Does the data need to be analyzed further? Why?

3. Identify a group or organization (e.g., PTA, faculty, public service group) that you are thinking of partnering with.
    - How would you use an infographic to aid the partnership or collaboration—as a teaching tool, for communication, to promote critical thinking?
    - How could you use an infographic to further or promote the collaboration?
    - What would be the purpose of the infographic?

References

AASL (American Association of School Librarians) and Achieve. 2013. "Implementing the Common Core State Standards: The Role of the Librarian." November. http://www.ala.org/aasl/sites/ala.org.aasl/files/content/externalrelations/CCSSLibrarians Brief_FINAL.pdf.

Duggan, Maeve. 2013. "Photo and Video Sharing Grow Online." Pew Research Center. October 28. http://www.pewinternet.org/2013/10/28/photo-and-video-sharing-grow-online/.

Head, Alison J. 2013. *Learning the Ropes: How Freshmen Conduct Course Research Once They Enter College.* Project Information Literacy Research Report. December 5. http://projectinfolit.org/images/pdfs/pil_2013_freshmenstudy_fullreport.pdf.

Holland, Beth. 2015. "21st-Century Libraries: The Learning Commons." *Edutopia* (blog). January 14. http://www.edutopia.org/blog/21st-century-libraries-learning-commons-beth-holland.

Jaeger, Paige, and Mary Boyd Ratzer. 2014. *Think Tank Library: Brain-Based Learning Plans for New Standards.* Santa Barbara, CA: Libraries Unlimited.

Zmuda, Allison, and Violet H. Harada. 2008. *Librarians as Learning Specialists: Meeting the Learning Imperative for the 21st Century.* Westport, CT: Libraries Unlimited.

Further Reading

ALA (American Library Association). 2013. "School Librarians Bear the Brunt of Staff Reductions." *State of America's Libraries Report 2013.* http://www.ala.org/news/state-americas-libraries-report-2013.

Head, Allison J., and Michael B. Eisenberg. 2010. *Truth Be Told: How College Students Evaluate and Use Information in the Digital Age.* Project Information Literacy Progress Report. November 1. http://projectinfolit.org/pdfs/PIL_Fall2010_Survey_FullReport1.pdf.

Lee, Matthew. 2014. "New Infographics on the Research Process." Minitex Reference Notes. April 30. http://referencenotes.minitex.umn.edu/new-infographics-on-the-research-process/ and http://www.minitex.umn.edu/Communications/RefNotes/2014/05May.pdf.

Schwartz, Katrina. 2015. "How Can Your Librarian Help Bolster Brain-Based Teaching Practices?" Mind Shift. December 19. http://ww2.kqed.org/mindshift/2015/01/19/how-can-your-librarian-help-bolster-brain-based-teaching-practices.

CHAPTER 8

Increasing Awareness of Underutilized and New Library Services

IN THIS CHAPTER

- ▷ The problem libraries face regarding awareness of library services and resources
- ▷ Examples of existing and new programs and services that public, academic, special, and school libraries offer inside the library and online
- ▷ How infographics can help solve the library services awareness problem
- ▷ Methods to increase awareness of current and new library offerings

LIBRARIES OFFER MANY SERVICES to their patrons, the traditional ones—borrowing books, free computer and Internet use, and availability of reference material and resources—and new services especially designed for twenty-first-century learners and their needs. A problem exists, however—that of awareness of what the library has to offer.

A survey from the Pew Research Center's Internet & American Life Project (Zickuhr, Rainie, and Purcell, 2013) explored activities at libraries and those that citizens would like to see if they could make changes. In the survey respondents declared overwhelmingly that public libraries are important to them, their families, and communities. Despite their stated importance, however, very few had a complete view of the library's offerings. They think of libraries in terms of their traditional services like borrowing books, free access to computers and the Internet, and requesting reference services.

Clearly, users don't know about newer services that libraries have available, such as makerspaces, the Ask a Librarian service, lending programs for book readers, and much more. Only about a fifth of those asked said they know most or all of the services available; and almost a third said they knew little or nothing about their library's services.

Overall, there is a general lack of knowledge about what libraries offer both at the library itself and services that are remotely accessible.

The study also shows that the people surveyed are open to new services. Review a full color infographic at http://libraries.pewinternet.org/2013/01/25/public-library-resources-infographic/ for services users are interested in. Putting effort into developing programs and services, however, doesn't necessarily mean potential users know about them, use them, and keep on using them regularly. Patrons have no chance to use services they don't know about. If libraries don't do better at getting the word out, services suffer, and if services are not used, funding sources will dry up. Libraries must keep offering services that are new, especially those relating to technology, as well as many of the services that have been around for a long time because these services are going to be new to many in the community.

Many of the librarians surveyed in the study's focus groups indicated that it is difficult to reach patrons and tell them about the services offered. Often it is word of mouth when someone comes to the library for a traditional service that gives the librarian the opportunity to mention a new service. Infographics can help with this necessary awareness campaign.

Examples of Current Programs That Need Revisiting

As the Pew survey pointed out, the fact that there is a lack of awareness about library services can translate into lack of use and also lack of funding to continue current services and develop new ones. Some services that have been a mainstay in libraries are reading programs for all levels, reference services, and explaining issues such as copyright. The examples that follow discuss promoting these current services and introducing new innovations for the twenty-first-century user in school, special, academic, and public libraries.

Example 1: Improving Literacy

Literacy instruction and instilling a love of reading have long been a goal of all libraries. The library's role, however, is more than supplying books and highlighting best sellers and classic literature. Many librarians are striving to connect patrons with books that help them develop a love for reading and encourage them to want to read more, as well as provide them with opportunities to make reading a regular part of their daily lives. Yet students, parents, and community leaders do not know about programs offered by libraries, such as children's story time, teen and adult book clubs, classes for non-English speakers, and more. Along with providing these programs, libraries must make sure that their clientele knows about these free services. Again, infographics can highlight the services in a visual way for all from a seven-year-old child to an immigrant struggling to learn English.

The Shepaug Valley School Library in Connecticut has comprehensive LibGuides on "Tech Tools for Teaching and Learning." Their Infographics tab explains what infographics are, lists tools to create them, and provides numerous examples. One example they call their librarian's favorite, created as part of the Canadian National Reading Campaign, is titled "Readers Save the World!"—a title that encourages the reader to ask the question "how" will this happen? Created in shades of red and blue, the infographic in figure 8.1 (see the complete infographic at http://www.cbc.ca/books/2013/10/infographic-readers

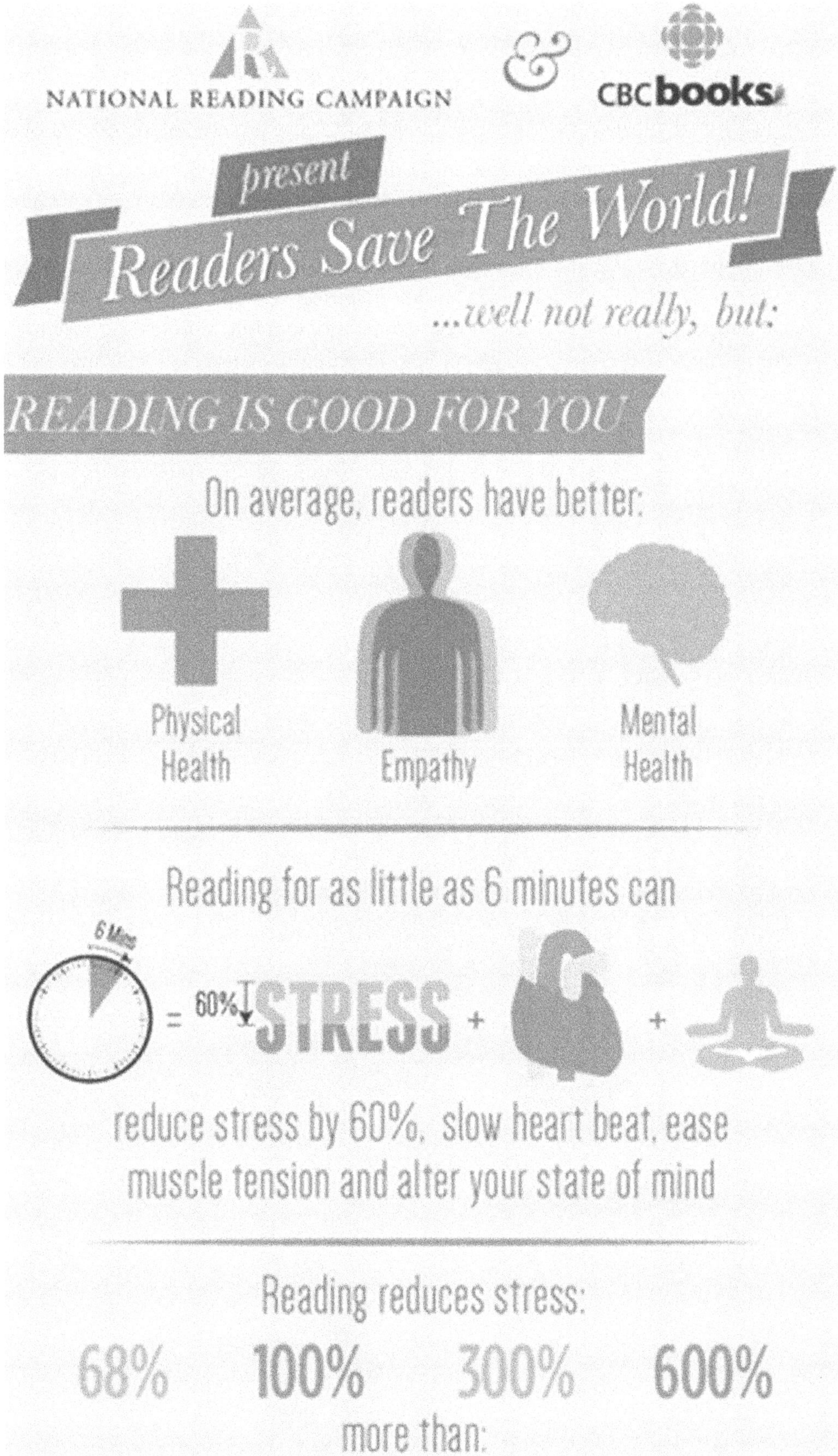

Figure 8.1. Reading Campaign. Design created by Ferheng Ghajar, information from National Reading Campaign, "Reading Can Save the World," http://www.nationalreadingcampaign.ca.

-can-save-the-world.html) has three subpoints—numbers of Canadians who use libraries; reasons reading is good for you—physically, mentally, and through empathy—noting specifically how it reduces stress; and that it is good for others who then donate time and money. The call to action is to "get reading" to become a better person and make the world better as a result. This last line ties together with the title. Statistics compiled by the National Reading Campaign lend authority to the claims in the infographic.

In addition to traditional reading programs, the e-reader, a relatively new innovation, is proving to be an aid to increase reading. An infographic "Teaching Us to Read Again," shown in figures 8.2 and 8.3, uses a stark visual contrast to compare the "old days" with today to illustrate how new e-readers are inspiring Americans to increase their reading. The images in figure 8.2 in an old sepia-toned photograph, representing yesterday, depict the problem of the past: lack of reading, resulting in nonreaders who may not succeed later in life. The title is also unique in demonstrating the lack of reading skill.

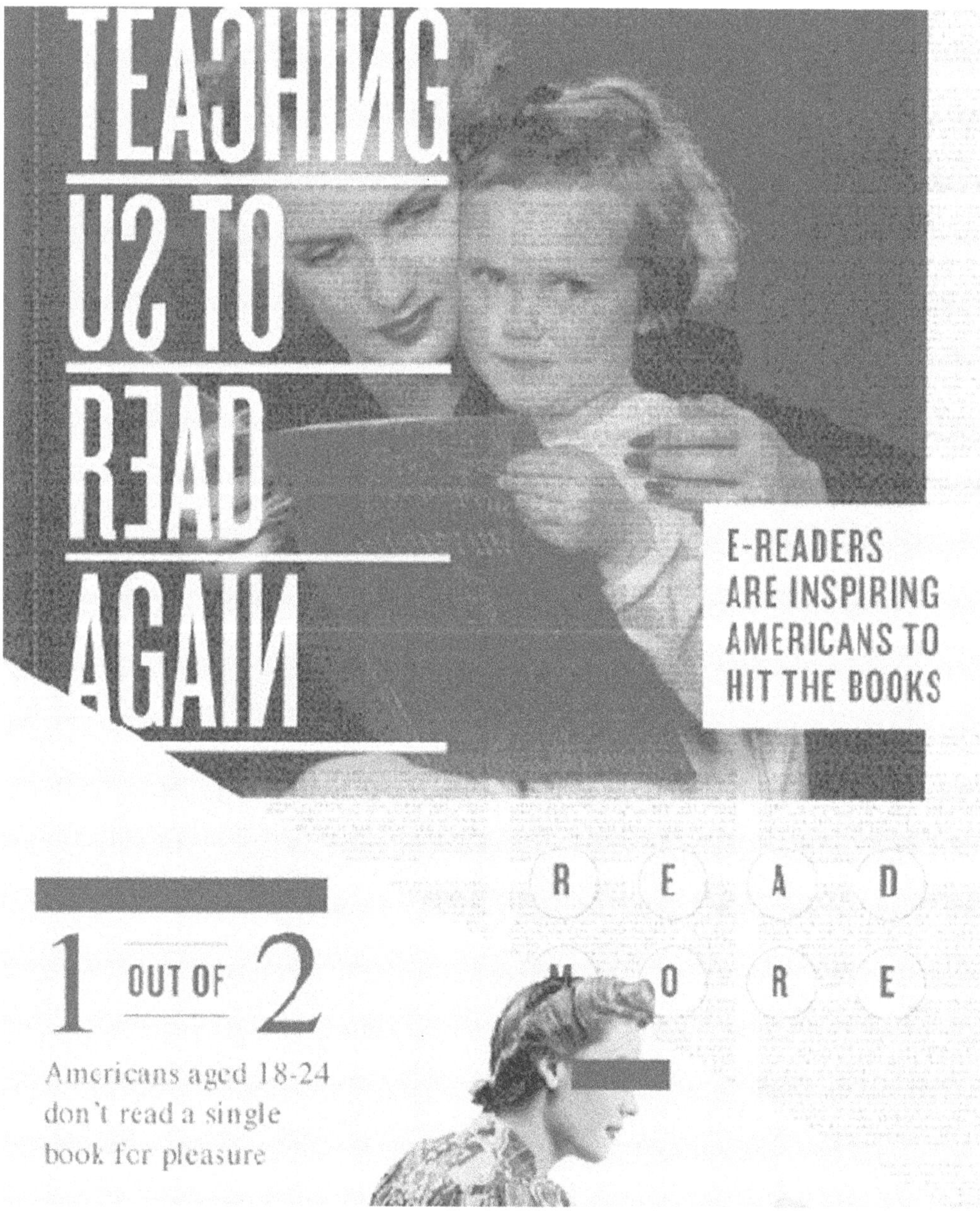

Figure 8.2. Traditional Reading. Created by OnlineTeachingDegree.com, licensed under Creative Commons, http://the-digital-reader.com/2012/07/09/teaching-us-to-read-again/.

The second half of the infographic in figure 8.3 represents today and introduces the e-reader, a new technology. The design now includes color, a modern design, and statistics that tell the story of patrons who use an e-reader and emphasizes the increased amount of reading. A list of sources supports the conclusion. This infographic uses design in a unique way to illustrate positive changes to reading habits as a result of e-readers. This is just one of many infographics that illustrates e-readers.

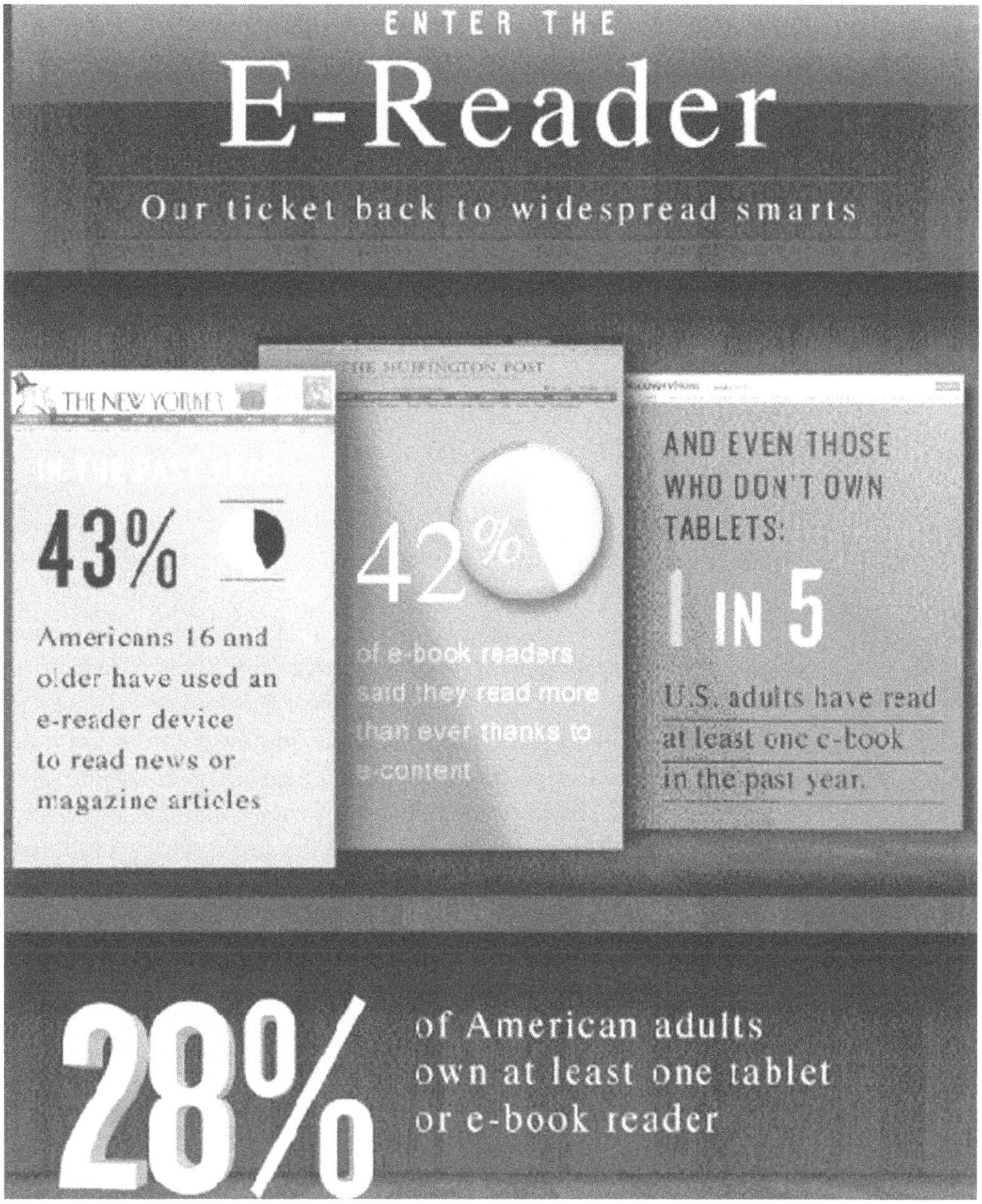

Figure 8.3. E-readers. Created by OnlineTeachingDegree.com, licensed under Creative Commons, http://the-digital-reader.com/2012/07/09/teaching-us-to-read-again/.

Example 2: Changes in Copyright—Fair Use and Creative Commons

The digital age has changed the way information and creations are shared. It has also opened new discussion on copyright issues. The Internet provides a way to collaborate with others and thus creates the need for work to be shared and yet those articles, books, photographs, and music must be protected from misuse. Copyright law often affects the work of academic and research librarians because so much of these librarians' work deals with accessing, storing, exhibiting, and providing access to copyrighted material. Librarians must also address aspects of copyright, including fair use and now creative commons. Fair use is the right to use copyrighted material without permission or payment under some circumstances and often affects teaching faculty and researchers. The fair use doctrine is described only generally in the law, and it is not tailored to the mission of any particular community. Ultimately, determining whether any use is likely to be considered "fair" requires a thoughtful evaluation of the facts and the law of the relevant community.

The Terry P. McMahan Library at Hodges University has compiled several infographics to support faculty. "Know Your Copyrights" (http://library.hodges.edu/faculty/copyright/infographics) illustrates what instructors can and cannot use in their teaching. The infographic "You Want to Know about Copyright in Education" (https://www.pinterest.com/pin/144467100523168624/) is more detailed, pointing out the different types of copyright. It uses a flowchart to show decision points you would need to consider if you wanted to create your own media and stay true to copyright restrictions.

In January 2012, the Association of Research Libraries (ARL, 2012) in collaboration with the Washington College of Law at American University in Washington, D.C., developed a document, titled *Code of Best Practices in Fair Use for Academic and Research Libraries*, to assist academic and research librarians in their discussions about fair use. This thirty-three-page code states what fair use is and isn't and outlines eight sets of current practices in the use of copyrighted materials in academic and research libraries to which fair use can be applied. Each principle includes limitations and enhancements when considering fair use.

To assist librarians in using this document, an infographic, shown in figure 8.4, was also created. This visual document contains five sections that fit on an 8½ x 11 sheet of paper. It discusses libraries' need for fair use, bulleted guidelines and best practices, the eight principles, how it was created, and how it can be used. Yellow banners introduce each section, and shades of its complementary color purple explain major points of each part. Statistics accompanied by images highlight the need; interlocking circles identify each principle; and an image in the shape of a pyramid describes each phase of development. The "How You Can Use It" banner gives the call to action—use the new fair use guidelines. The final banner at the bottom of the infographic indicates where you can find more resources about fair use. The infographic distills a thirty-three-page report into an easy-to-read sheet that patrons and librarians alike can review as they grapple with copyright issues.

Creative Commons, a nonprofit organization, offers free Creative Commons (CC) copyright licenses for anyone to use that enables sharing and use of creativity and knowledge. Six types of CC licenses (Libatique, 2013), at http://creativecommons.org/licenses/, give the public permission to share and use creative work under certain conditions of their choice and have become quite commonplace in the educational community. A CC license is not a substitute for a copyright; rather, licensors retain copyright but allow others to copy, distribute, and make some use of their work noncommercially. Most licenses can be used or adapted for educational purposes, as long as the author is cited. For example, instructors often use information under creative commons for course handouts. The infographic in figure 8.5 is part of a longer infographic that covers copyright, Creative Commons, fair use, and open educational resources all in one. This interactive infographic contains a video explaining Creative Commons, and by clicking

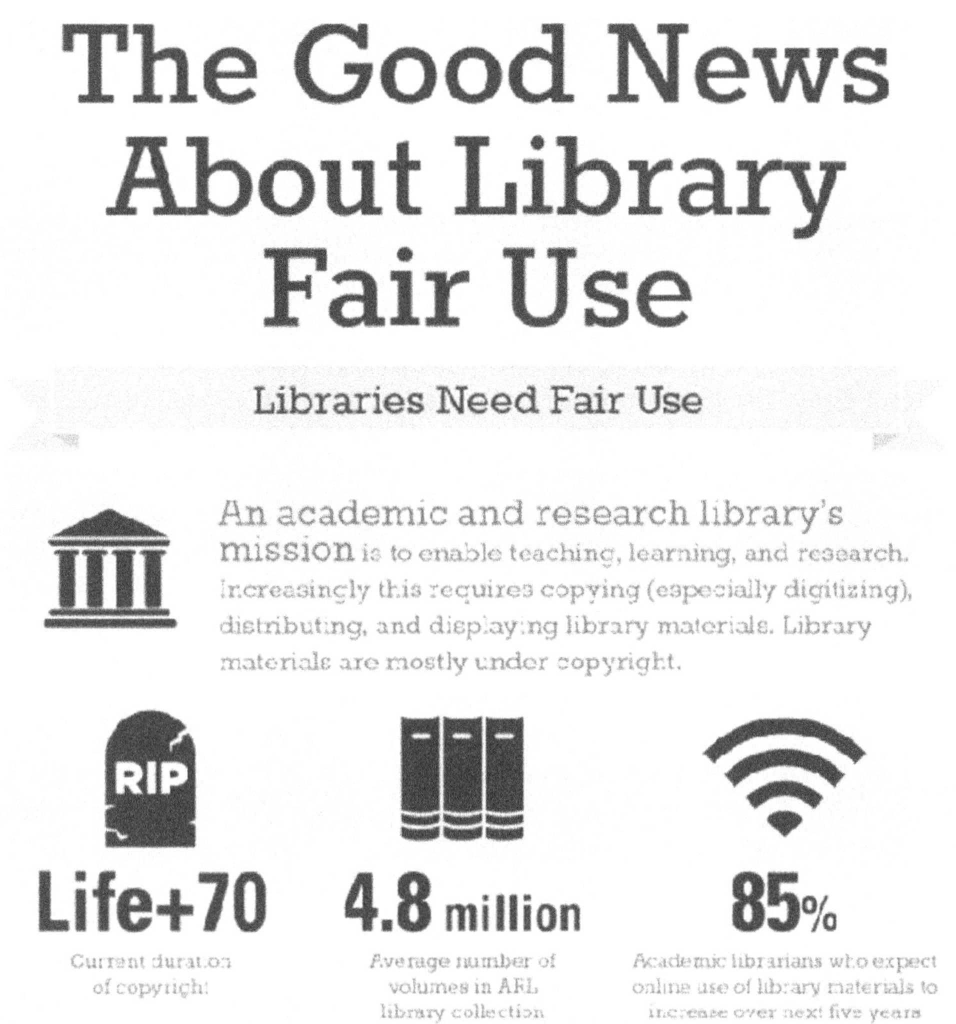

Figure 8.4. Library Fair Use. Design created by Yippa, licensed under Creative Commons, http://www.arl.org/storage/documents/publications/fair-use-infographic-aug2013.pdf.

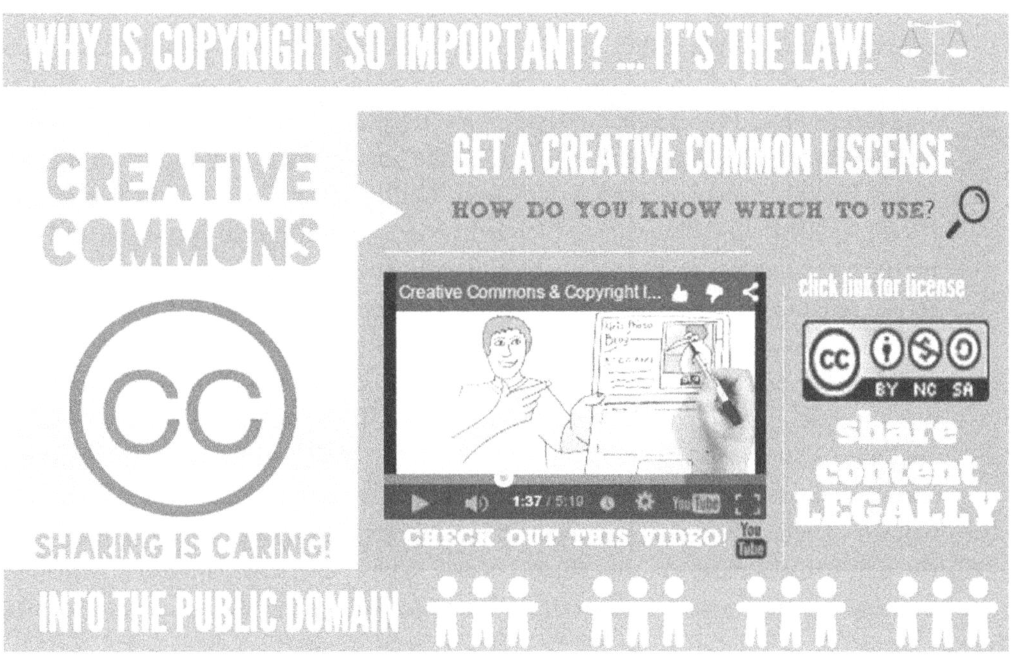

Figure 8.5. Creative Commons License. Created by @annkozma723, licensed under Creative Commons, https://magic.piktochart.com/output/2363961-copyright-creative-commons-oers.

an image of a CC license, you can see descriptions of differences among the licenses. The links also take the reader to other information about Creative Commons. This infographic is a complete compilation of all major copyright issues and is an especially useful guide that concisely points out all the differences.

Example 3: Reference Services—Old and New

What methods do you employ for reference today? What works? What doesn't? How does social media play a role? Libraries still provide unparalleled reference service to patrons using traditional methods and materials; however, reference services continue to evolve with changing patron needs, a variety of information resources, and new delivery formats. Librarians are exploring new methods of undertaking the reference role, and both public and academic libraries are reviewing and refining their reference functions.

In addition to new methods, much of traditional practice remains important to providing quality information services to patrons. In a traditional sense, the reference desk is framed around the "reference interview" where skilled librarians identify patrons' questions and information needs. They explore topics such as information literacy and Internet resources. They answer health and legal questions for patrons, and incorporate innovations in digital and virtual reference.

At the Arlington Heights Memorial Library (AHML), a pilot call center was formed with the goal to connect patrons as easily as possible with the materials and information they want. In addition to the reference desk, all library staff members are encouraged to answer any question of which they are capable. Because the reference desk has its own area, no phones are constantly ringing in the public area of the library. Staff at the information desk is free to assist people without interruption and work with the public in a collaborative learning environment. While roving with an iPad or tablet, staff can confirm the availability of materials, place holds on an item, and demonstrate how to use the catalog, databases, or e-materials. This approach encourages those patrons to ask for help who are reluctant to "bother" the librarian. The staff also uses walkie-talkies connected to headsets to communicate with each other and shift smoothly between the call center and the public service area, based on customer needs.

Reaching out to the community and fulfilling information needs with virtual reference methods is now a reality. The goal at AHML was to communicate with users in ways they knew and used themselves, primarily electronically. Each month, the staff answers an average of 4,700 reference questions by telephone and three hundred online chats, making AHML the most active Illinois public library in the QuestionPoint network, the virtual reference management system from Online Computer Library Center (OCLC) (Phillips, 2014). The library uses blended services, a call center approach, and roving librarians to meet the diverse needs of its user population. This new model of information services that is unique in its delivery is based on the library's size, physical layout, and the community it serves.

Another example at the University of Illinois at Urbana-Champaign Libraries illustrates a different approach to handling reference. The staff conducts online reference via chat with instant messages coming in through the "Ask a Librarian" widget on the website. They answer all kinds of questions including basic questions on holdings, as well as helping conduct research. Chat is a single service staffed by a group of people from across the university libraries. If a question needs a subject specialist, a referral is made, sometimes in real time online. If a specialist is not available, a response is sent to the patron by e-mail or phone, or an appointment is set up. The patron does not have to decide where to go to ask—the chat system determines it automatically. The undergraduate library tried combining circulation with reference, but switched to separate reference services at café tables with scheduled roving. Even with the new online services, the library continues to offer courses on the reference interview, which are always filled—indicating there is still a need for traditional services. The model was particular to the Urbana library and their patrons, but draws on many of the trends and practices that all types of libraries, large and small, are developing.

In this next example, the infographic discusses the Ask a Librarian service at Ontario Council of University Libraries that encompasses nine libraries (Schwartz, 2013). The graphic reviews a year of service emphasizing the number of chats to answer patron questions, length of chats, and wait time. Other sections of the infographic mention the number of users at each library and the main questions they asked. It also points out the excellent service rating and user preference for virtual reference. Review the entire infographic in color at http://www.infodocket.com/2012/06/27/infographic-ontario-council-of-universtiy-libraries-ask-a-librarian-usage-statistics-2011-2012/.

In rethinking reference service, it is important to be aware of what other libraries are doing nationally but also to do what works for your own library. The methods of supplying reference may differ, but the goal remains the same: find and fill information needs of students, researchers, other patrons, and the community. Review table 8.1 for more infographics and articles about underused library resources.

Table 8.1. Underused Library Resources and Services

DESCRIPTION	URL
Infographic on interest in new public library services	http://libraries.pewinternet.org/2013/01/25/public-library-resources-infographic/
"Summer Reading Flowchart: What Should You Read on Your Break?"	http://teach.com/great-educational-resources/summer-reading-flowchart/
"The DNA of a Successful Book"	http://voices.nationalgeographic.com/2012/08/28/the-dna-of-a-successful-book
Infographic on how to obtain a Creative Commons license	http://homegrown.ph/wp-content/uploads/2013/12/2013_December_BusinessBasics_HowToObtainCreativeCommonsLicense_Infographic.jpg

New Library Services

Libraries aren't just warehouses for documents anymore; they're places to exchange and analyze information. Librarians are often considered quite traditional, but in reality they are leaders in adapting to new information tools of the digital age. Libraries embrace change. They are adding services such as wireless Internet, e-readers and tablets, and virtual reference. Libraries are looking for opportunities to incorporate these and other new and emerging technologies into their service efforts. The next examples illustrate how some public, academic, special, and school libraries are already incorporating new services, many of which respondents in the Pew survey had requested. They also point out how libraries are using infographics to increase awareness of these resources, a problem also pointed out in the survey.

Example 1: New Online and Print Collections—Law Library Research Series

Infographics & Law is a research series at the Brian Dickson Law Library at the University of Ottawa that showcases available online and print collections related to a current affairs topic of interest. This initiative presents data such as photos, videos, graphs, maps, and timelines in an infographic format. To engage library users, these visual interactive presentations describe current incidents, such as the 2014 Ebola outbreak and the mysterious disappearance of the Malaysia Airlines jetliner (https://infogr.am/bdbuottawa_1401201014), as well as important issues like the emerging carbon market, and the unique challenge climate change presents for economics (https://magic.piktochart.com/output/5489474-vista-grande-public-library-co).

To get the word out about their collections, the law library has created interactive infographics that highlight online and print sources related to specific topics. In one example, the library created an infographic about the 2014 Ebola outbreak. First, staff researched situation reports from the World Health Organization (http://apps.who.int/ebola/current-situation/ebola-situation-report-1-april-2015-0). These reports contain a range of current and historic data from different countries to explain the Ebola crisis in detail. Next, the law librarians analyzed the data to determine the geographic area and time frame to cover in the infographic. Using Infogr.am, a free infographics program, they compiled data from the reports into the interactive infographic, shown in figure 8.6, to explain the scope and location of cases in countries involved in the Ebola outbreak. Statistics emphasized case fatalities and the countries where they occurred. Clicking the radio buttons for each country displays the percentage of fatalities. Clicking country maps in North America and Africa depicts the number of cases in each country. This part of the infographic illustrates the magnitude of the epidemic. Clicking each section of the pie chart below the maps shows subject headings and the number of sources related to law on this topic. A sample list of recommended books and articles from the law library highlights individual sources related to the subject of health and infectious disease. These sources provide a starting point for articles on the topic, including international law, global governance, policy, and regulatory questions. Infographics for Brian Dickson Law Library have proved to be a viable way to publicize their collections for faculty and students.

Example 2: Literacy Skill Training Online

One of the most important roles the library and librarians encounter today and will face to a greater degree in the future is teaching and training communities to improve essential and constantly changing digital literacy skills. The librarian has often provided one-on-one assistance to patrons and students on what the library contains and how to find books, articles, and reference materials. However, with an abundance of information available and Google being the most popular way to find it, users more than ever need to know how to evaluate a wealth of sources and select those most appropriate. E-learning is now a hot topic in libraries from massive open online courses (MOOCs) to the development of small e-learning modules. In academic libraries, the focus is more on support

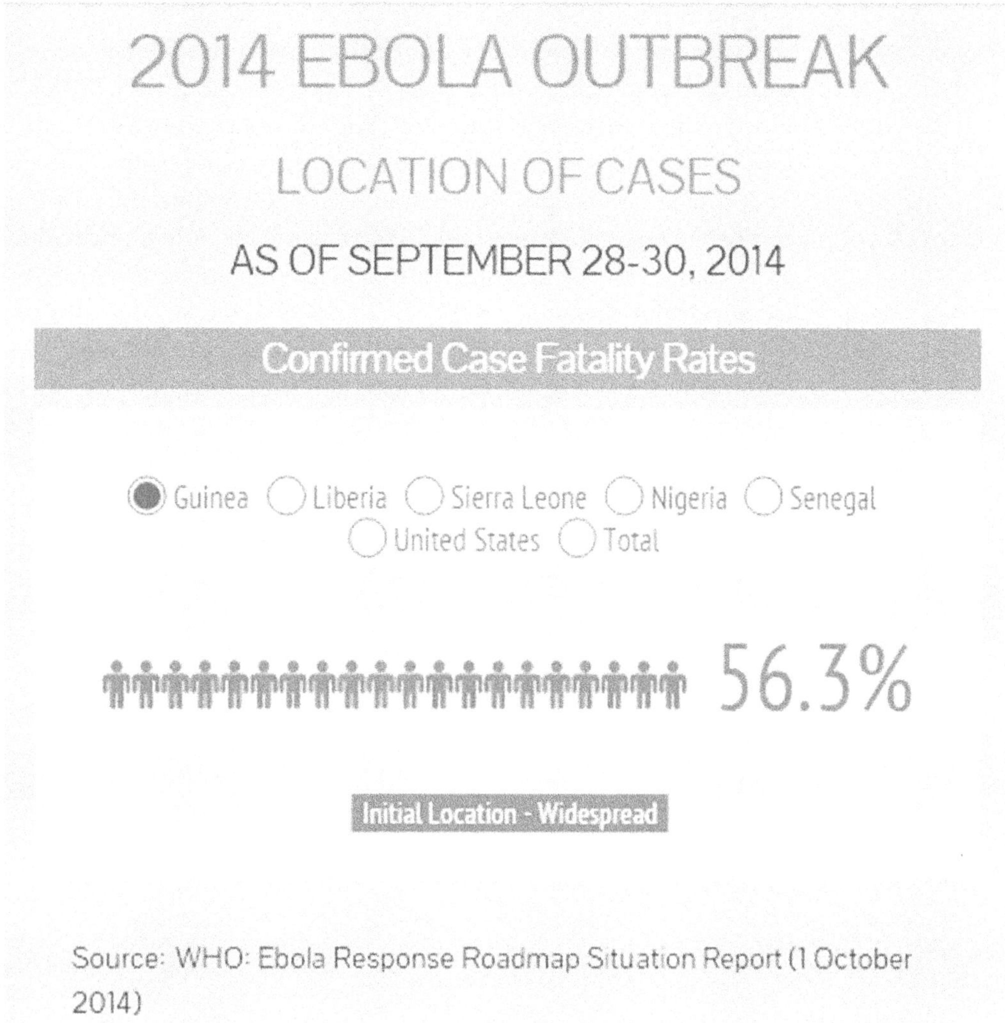

Figure 8.6. 2014 Ebola Outbreak. Created by the Brian Dickson Law Library, https://infogr.am/2014-ebola-outbreak.

of the curriculum and in public libraries as a gateway to lifelong learning. To that end, librarians are being called upon to provide their own instruction, often as partners in an embedded library program with faculty in academic institutions (see chapter 7 for additional information) and collaborating with teachers in K–12 schools.

There are numerous ways that infographics can help in this endeavor. From describing the rise and history of MOOCs to MOOC 101 to identifying the major providers and courses to following trends, infographics are being used in numerous ways with this new educational delivery method. Created by Top10OnlineColleges.org, the infographic at http://elearninginfographics.com/the-rising-power-of-moocs-infographic/ offers a visual overview of MOOCs—what they are, student demographics, why they are popular, information about the schools offering them, and their pros and cons. A statistic at the beginning of this infographic indicates that only about one-fourth of Americans know what a MOOC is. This comprehensive infographic provides a factual background that can be absorbed quickly and easily by the uninitiated.

MOOCs have many advocates, as well as those who see major challenges ahead. As the field of higher education changes to incorporate more e-learning, it appears that MOOCs will play a major role. Librarians foresee challenges, specifically on helping participants with information literacy, aiding faculty to support their resource needs, and understanding copyright. The open format of the courses necessitates using content with open copyright, a topic discussed in more detail later in this chapter. Faculty can incorporate infographics into their MOOC courses as search aids, copyright information sheets, and ways to highlight projects, to name some. The infographic MOOCs.com provides a comprehensive view of MOOCs from the definition to providers and common courses to demographics of students, including prior education level, to types of MOOCs. Check this one out at http://moocs.com/index.php/mooc-infographic/ for more information.

E-learning is also growing globally. Libraries and e-learning are now woven together into teaching and learning for students and educators. Infographics have been created for uses from steps to create an e-learning storyboard to advantages of e-learning to strategies to transition to e-learning and even to demonstrate ways to add humor in e-learning courses. Figure 8.7 provides a good example of an infographic that explains an important topic for libraries. It focuses on digital research and points out students' weak research areas and where librarians must play a role.

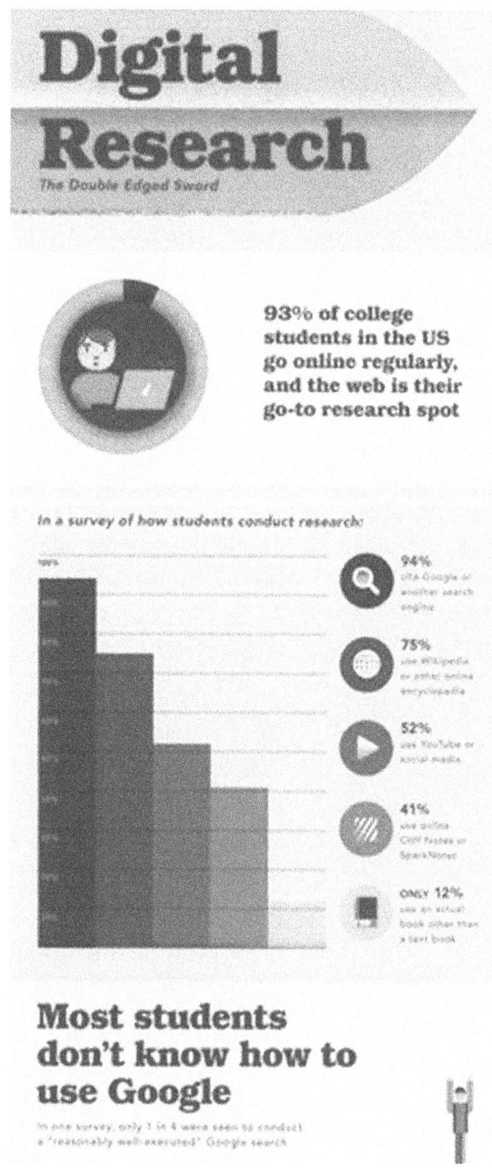

Figure 8.7. Digital Research. Created by OnlineEducation.net, "Digital Research," licensed under Creative Commons, https://www.pinterest.com/pin/366621225891855049/.

Example 3: Makerspaces

Another new opportunity for libraries is a fast-growing makerspace community. Makerspaces provide a place where people can learn to use tools and materials and develop creative projects. It can be embedded within an existing space or stand alone. It can be shaped to meet educational goals, as well as individuals' creative interests. Libraries are becoming more involved with makerspaces because they foster exploration, support opportunities for learning, encourage peer-to-peer learning, and develop a culture of creating. Today's library has expanded from an institution that holds books and materials to one that also promotes lifelong learning and knowledge creation in the community. Projects completed in makerspaces help users increase skills of inquiry and questioning, problem solving, networked social learning, and construction of knowledge. Programs for all ages are possible from 3D printing to LEGO clubs to digital production of content to promoting science, technology, engineering, and math (STEM) and the arts (STEAM) programs vital to the K–12 Common Core. 3D printing will be discussed in more detail in example 4 next.

Infographics can be integral to makerspaces at your library. Beginning with the planning process, they can illustrate what makerspaces are, how they benefit library patrons, and set out a plan to create a makerspace. As projects unfold, infographics can be used as instruction sheets. They can then visually display completed projects and tell stories about the activities and services to market and publicize the makerspace, contributing to community excitement and expertise. See the infographic about makerspaces in figure 8.8.

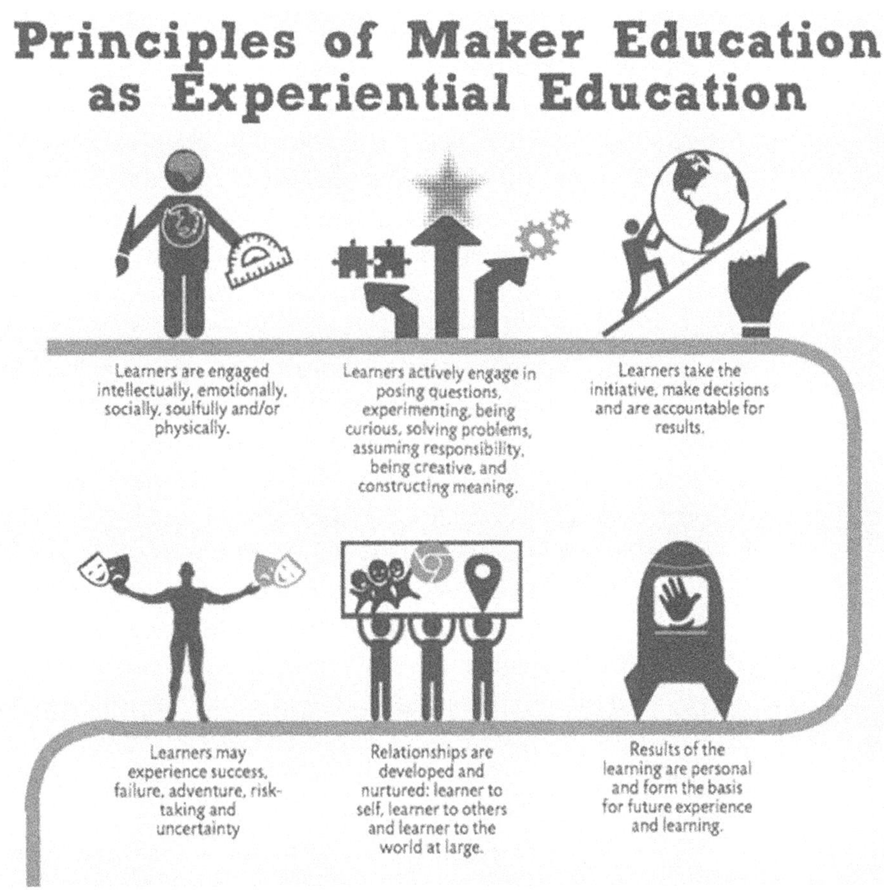

Figure 8.8. What Are Makerspaces? Created by Jackie Gerstein, adapted from the Association of Experiential Education, licensed under Creative Commons, https://www.pinterest.com/pin/244953667208735449.

Some examples illustrate these goals. In the Chattanooga Public Library (Thompson, 2014) at http://www.wired.com/2014/09/makerspace/, you can find the usual rows of books, magazines, and computers. However, the fourth floor has something unusual about it—a makerspace. The fourth floor has transformed the Chattanooga Public Library into an open, collaborative, creative, flexible, participatory system. Through the interaction with 3D printers, homemade electronic objects, and a diverse mix of people at work, the space fosters an environment of learning by doing. The revamped floor gives patrons access to new forms of literacy: design, programming, video editing, book writing, and website building. This new makerspace turns the library into a place not just to absorb knowledge but to create it—physically. Innovative activities bring in people who normally shun libraries, typically men and people with limited education.

The Cleveland Public Library has a similar space. Librarians in this library report that their job is helping with access to knowledge, and they are ready to do this by adapting to new information tools and providing ways for their users to create their own content.

Example 4: 3D Printers

The library community has assumed a leading role in the effort to help people of all ages build skills and competencies they need to thrive in a high-tech world. As a result, university and public libraries and other entities like museums have begun to embrace 3D printing, often as part of a makerspace, and offer it to students and communities, mostly free of charge. Library professionals are now helping to expand the creative, entrepreneurial, and educational applications of 3D printing.

Library 3D printing is empowering people to engage in creative learning, launch business ventures, and solve complex health problems. For example, an inventor at the Chattanooga Library (Cook, 2014) created prostheses for his young adopted son whose arms ended below the elbow. With his newly created limbs, his son can now eat without help. This is one of several examples of ways inventors with the aid of 3D printers are improving the lives of individuals with special needs. By offering access to 3D printing, libraries nationwide are adding the role of labs of experimentation and innovation for aspiring entrepreneurs and at the same time helping advance creativity for everyone.

Because 3D printers have such diverse uses, possible legal ramifications of not only copyright but also patent, design patent, trade secrets, and product liability must be addressed. The American Library Association (ALA) is exploring 3D printing policies for libraries as it is yet to be determined whether libraries could be subject to liability for a product created with a library 3D printer.

For this type of endeavor, libraries will need not only to provide instruction in the basics of these printers, but also to develop best practices to guide patron printing behavior. Infographics can be used for both of these tasks. For example, the infographic "How 3D Printing Will Revolutionize the Classroom" points out what 3D printing is, universities that use 3D printers as part of classroom instruction, step-by-step instructions showing how it works, objects that can be made, and why schools should use it. The part of the infographic displayed in figure 8.9 shows how 3D printing can be used in different subject areas to revolutionize the classroom.

In the design of this infographic, the title immediately portrays the 3D theme with the font used. Logos point out universities incorporating 3D printing into the curriculum. Short text coupled with simple images illustrates the step-by-step instructions indicating the simplicity of using the 3D printer. To reinforce the idea of using a 3D printer in the

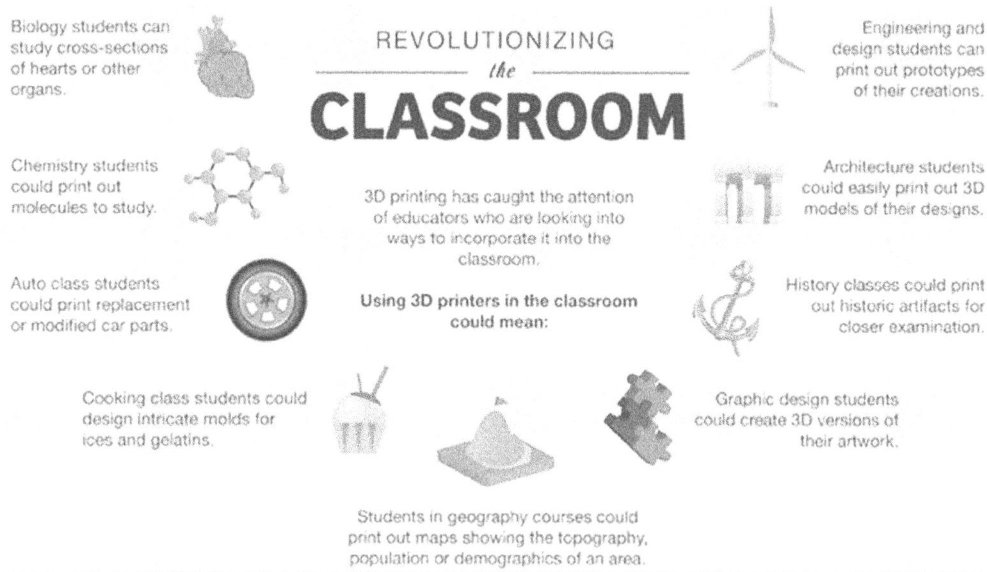

Figure 8.9. How 3D Printing Will Revolutionize the Classroom. Information provided by Online De grees.org, licensed under Creative Commons, https://www.pinterest.com/pin/459507968205744548/.

classroom, text enumerates reasons to use it. In case the faculty is worried about doing so, links to resources, including lesson plans and designs from a major manufacturer of 3D printers, are also mentioned. This infographic has a simple design to reinforce the theme that using a 3D printer as part of classroom instruction will be easy to do.

Infographics can illustrate applications for the library's 3D printer to share with other libraries. A well-placed infographic, outlining a user policy for 3D printer use, can also set guidelines for patron use in the library, and an infographic at https://www.pinterest.com/pin/512917845036515409/ outlines the possible problems that may arise with copyright.

Another example (Millsaps, 2015) describes a partnership between the University of Massachusetts at Amherst and MakerBot, a maker of 3D printers, and how a MakerBot Innovation Center with fifty 3D printers and other technology has been created in the Digital Media Lab in the Du Bois Library on campus. As part of this project, students and faculty will be encouraged to work on 3D printing projects that cross disciplines and majors. In fact, faculty in biology, public health, public policy, and engineering are already working together to offer a makerspace class with 3D printing capabilities.

Of course, setting up a printing lab is only a small part of the challenge. Staff must be trained in the fundamentals of design, 3D scanning and printing, and maintenance of the machines. A program must be implemented to handle potential designers who want to use the equipment, workshops and training sessions must be created, and a way to deal with charges for materials must be maintained. To help in these tasks, librarians can create how-to infographics for training. In addition, creating infographics on library and campus websites, as handouts in appropriate classes, and positioned in local libraries to promote services in the makerspace, can get the word out on campus and involve the community as well.

According to Johan-Till Broer, public relations manager of MakerBot (Millsaps, 2015), "An increasing number of libraries throughout the U.S. offer 3D printing services as a way to foster creativity and entrepreneurship. To date, MakerBot 3D printers and scanners are in an estimated 500 libraries nationwide." 3D printing is on the upswing in libraries, and infographics can aid in many tasks surrounding them.

Example 5: Open Access versus Open Educational Resources

Open access (OA) has increased dramatically in the twenty-first century. Open access resources include online books, articles, images, and other resources that anyone can read or download at no cost, anywhere, anytime, and they are free of most copyright and licensing restrictions (Suber, 2012). OA is made possible because of the Internet and the consent of the author or copyright holder.

Advantages of open access are numerous. One benefit is to increase discovery. With open access to scholarly journals, researchers can now read and build on the findings of others without restriction. Moreover, much scientific and medical research is paid for with public funds. Open access allows taxpayers to see the results of their investment. There are many benefits for education, too. Open access means that teachers and their students can access the latest research findings throughout the world. Students can also continue to use OA resources after they graduate. OA provides reliable access because budget cuts do not jeopardize using these resources. Library collections can continue to grow with OA resources at no cost. Researchers and the public can more easily obtain current, scholarly data, and authors can get their scholarly achievements noticed and cited more frequently (McKinnon and Helge, 2014).

Often, however, in academic institutions, students, faculty, and even administrators are not aware of their OA options. Libraries are ideal advocates for OA resources, but they must face the challenge by facilitating access to these free online sources for faculty, students, and administrators in academic institutions and the community through public libraries. Librarians must help their patrons find sources that are of high quality, and locate resources in particular subject areas.

The next example illustrates just how amazing access to authoritative sources can be. With open access to medical journals, a high school student won the Intel Science and Engineering Fair contest for his project—a new test for attacking pancreatic, ovarian, and lung cancer. Now in clinical studies, his new method would also be able to detect the cancer in its early stages, thus increasing chances of survival. See the interview at https://www.youtube.com/watch?v=G55hlnSD1Ys to learn how this student took advantage of open access (NIH, 2013).

Open access, however, also raises some controversies meaningful to libraries. Different copyright ramifications may arise, as with 3D printing discussed earlier. Copyright and fair use is a consideration as librarians conduct more informal and formal instruction both on-site and online. Librarians also need to be aware of and transmit to students and patrons not only basic copyright information and rules for fair use but Creative Commons licenses and open access considerations.

Using infographics, libraries can help with basic awareness and communication of information about OA. The infographic in figure 8.10 provides an introduction to open access and key issues that can be posted or distributed to faculty, students, and the public to alleviate any misgivings on using open access sources.

Libraries have already helped support the growth of open access research, and they can do the same for free open educational resources (OER), geared specifically to education. "OER are teaching, learning, and research resources that reside in the public domain or have been released under an intellectual property license that permits their free use and re-purposing by others" (William and Flora Hewlett Foundation, 2015). The OER Commons at https://www.oercommons.org/ provides services to help libraries find open educational resources. Their services include training on how to find

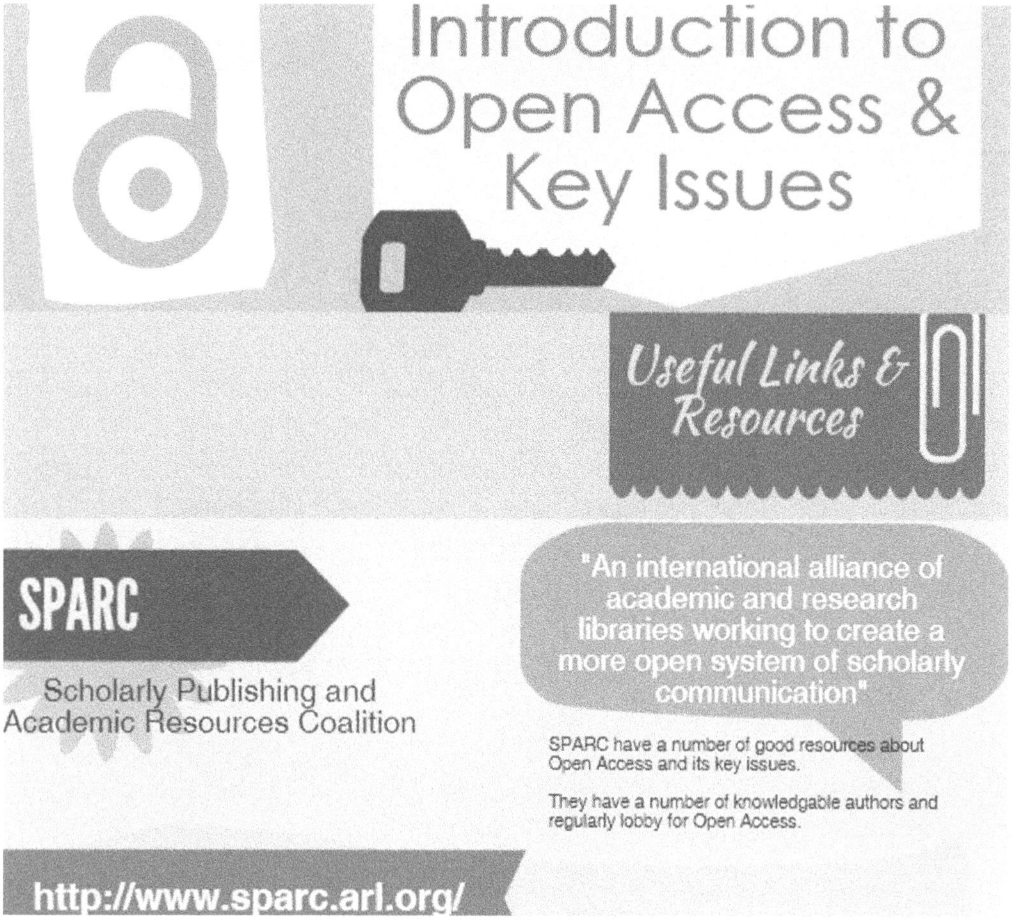

Figure 8.10. Introduction to Open Access & Key Issues. Created by Leah Maughan, Robinson Library, Newcastle University, licensed under Creative Commons, https://magic.piktochart.com/output/2154130-useful-links-for-introduction-to.

OER, tools, and curated topics, ranging from the arts to mathematics and the sciences. Areas of interest include Common Core, primary sources, teachers as makers, flexible and game-based learning, and more. A real difference from OA sources is that with OER, you can edit, remix, save, and share text, pictures, sound files, and video as openly licensed educational resources.

Librarians need to communicate these differences to interested parties, including teaching faculty, students, and the public. The Center for Open Educational Resources and Language Learning at the University of Texas at Austin used the infographic in figure 8.11 to describe how to search for open educational resources.

As you review this infographic, you will see that it is created with shades of orange and blue complementary colors, pleasing to the eye. Go to the URL to see the entire infographic in color. It opens with an introductory section that identifies educational uses of open access resources important to instructors and states the problem—difficulty in finding resources that can be edited and shared without copyright restrictions. Section 2 models the process with an example for foreign languages. It provides step-by-step instructions on how to find resources that fit the audience, for example, students studying German, and the purpose, improving students' vocabulary or pronunciation. After pointing out ways to find and use these materials, the infographic also shows where and how to share the final product and emphasizes the importance of doing so. Because this

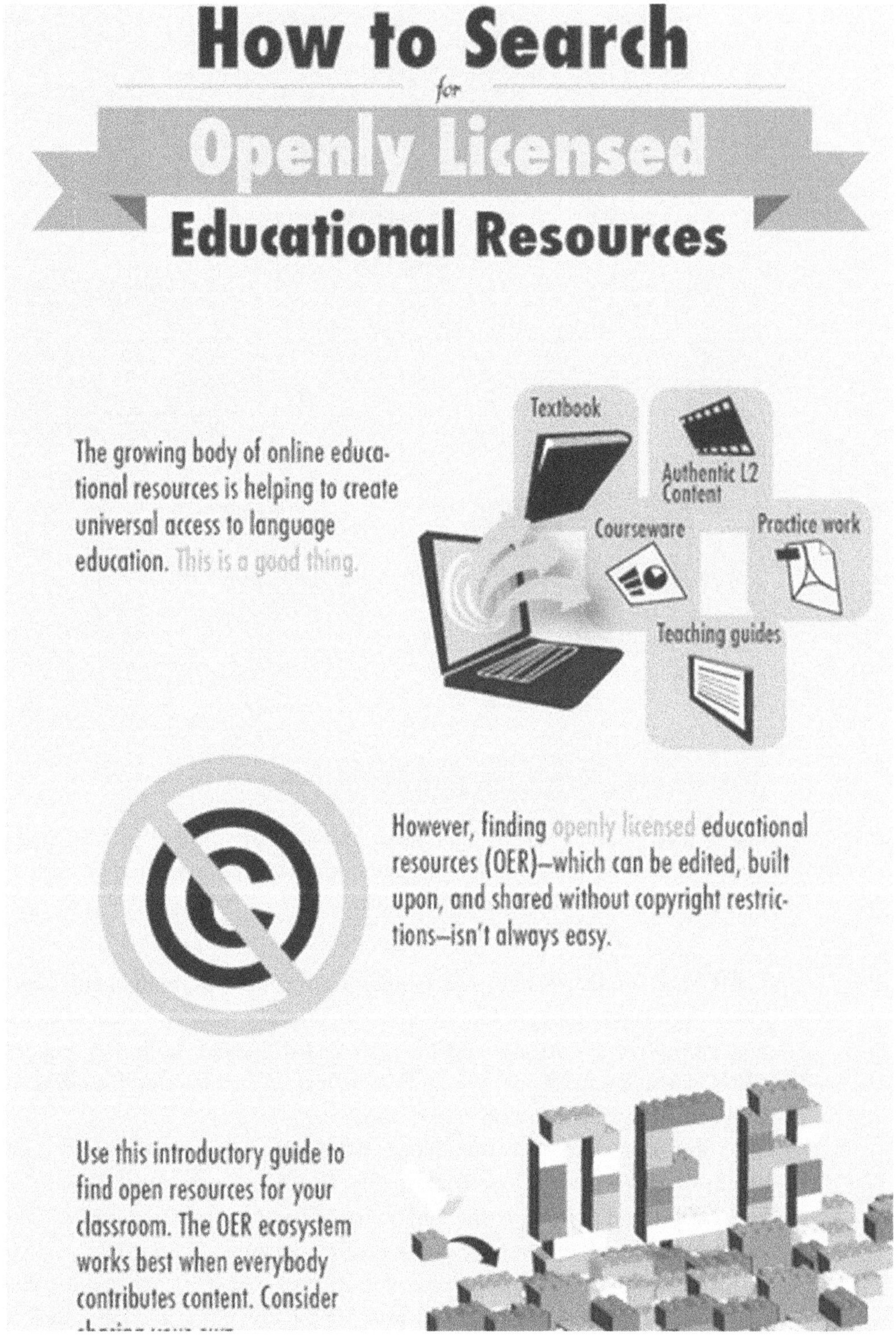

Figure 8.11. How to Search for OER. Created by the Center for Open Educational Resources and Language Learning, Licensed under Creative Commons, https://www.coerll.utexas.edu/coerll/sites/coerll.utexas.edu.coerll/files/finding-oer-infographic.pdf.

infographic has the proper license under Creative Commons, you could adapt the infographic for use with your students as they use open educational materials in your courses.

This next example showcases a new degree program at Tidewater Community College in Virginia, the first college to offer a textbook-free associate degree in business administration. Courses in the program used no textbooks, thus the name Z degree (for zero textbooks). Materials for the courses consisted of open educational resources (OER). All course content was openly licensed and could be used at all campus locations. With the high cost of textbooks, students were now able to save money and obtain immediate access to course materials. To begin the project, the thirteen-member faculty focused on learning outcomes for courses in the curriculum and selected OER content that best achieved the learning outcomes. An advisory board and supporting individuals and organizations, including a library media specialist and the associate vice president for libraries, participated closely in the project.

Along with a comprehensive report on the Z degree, an interactive infographic illustrates the pilot project results and supplies additional resources available to students in this degree program. Review the infographic at http://www.tcc.edu/academics/zdegree/zdegree.html to learn more about this new degree program.

The infographic begins with the benefits of this pilot project for students and faculty. The large "Z" image displays the project name, and the arrow at the bottom of the image directs the reader's eye to the next section that points out program successes. Clicking each image provides a graph of statistics on the subject—student satisfaction, improved retention, and savings. Images, text, color, and different font sizes clearly communicate the message. Again, this infographic can serve as a model for other teachers using OER in their courses and can be modified for specific subjects and audiences.

The bottom of this same infographic displays additional resources available. Clicking each tab displays more open educational resources. Because the infographic is interactive, one page can provide access to a wealth of information—videos, interviews, presentations, news articles about the program, contact and policy information—all materials students and faculty will need for their courses, succinctly packaged in one infographic.

Several other institutions and systems are developing or have developed their own zero-textbook-cost degrees, including Northern Virginia Community College, the Virginia Community College System, the Washington State Community College System, Thomas Edison State College, and the University System of Maryland. These institutions represent models that other schools can adopt or adapt to help their own students lower the costs of higher education while increasing college access and success. The infographics discussed can also be adapted for use by other academic institutions.

Today's libraries use online instruction to teach a multitude of topics to a range of audiences. Academic libraries instruct undergraduates to evaluate the credibility of a website; medical libraries teach future doctors how to search for evidence-based resources, and public libraries teach patrons how to use the online catalog, download e-books, and provide gateways to resources for lifelong learning. Infographics provide that visual representation of OER and their benefits and where academic institutions who want to try such a program can go for models and advice.

Spreading the word will become ever more important. Infographics can be an integral part of teaching about, promoting, and sharing underused and new services to any audience in any library. Table 8.2 provides descriptions and links for additional infographics and articles about all of these new library services.

Table 8.2. New Library Services and Technology

DESCRIPTION	URL
"Rise of the MOOCs"	http://visual.ly/rise-moocs
MOOC overview	http://elearninginfographics.com/massive-open-online-courses-infographic-2/
The Makerspace Playbook—a comprehensive guide to makerspaces	http://makered.org/wp-content/uploads/2014/09/Makerspace-Playbook-Feb-2013.pdf
"3D Printer Cheat Sheet"	https://www.pinterest.com/pin/94716398388469239/
"What Is 3D Printing?"	https://www.pinterest.com/pin/94716398388594135/
What's the Deal with Copyright and 3D Printing?	https://www.publicknowledge.org/files/What's%20the%20Deal%20with%20Copyright_%20Final%20version2.pdf
Infographics related to e-learning	https://www.pinterest.com/vparham007/elearning-tips/
"3D Printing: The Future Is Now"	https://www.pinterest.com/pin/572520171355393661/
"3D Printing: How Long till the Revolution?"	https://www.pinterest.com/pin/512917845036515409/
Open Educational Resources Commons	https://www.oercommons.org/
Open Educational Resources: The Basics	https://www.coerll.utexas.edu/coerll/sites/coerll.utexas.edu.coerll/files/oer-handout_0.pdf
The "Z" Degree—report on the Tidewater Community College OER project	http://www.tcc.edu/academics/zdegree/docs/Z-Degree%20Booklet%20for%20Hewlett.pdf
The Curriculum of the Future: How Digital Content Is Changing Education—research report on OER and delivery methods, etc.	http://www.centerdigitaled.com/paper/Curriculum-of-the-Future-How-Digital-Content-is-Changing-Education.html?promo_code=Newsletter_BannerAd_300x250_Centerdigitaled

Key Points

Through various research studies and by listening to their patrons, libraries have gotten the message: "We don't do enough self-promoting."

- Despite the good impression and exemplary comments about libraries, patrons and nonpatrons are not familiar with many current programs, services, and technology offered by academic, public, special, and school libraries. Infographics can provide that necessary communication.
- With numbers of users of current services in some libraries decreasing, infographics can help libraries get the word out to patrons and other potential users.
- Infographics can promote the change in the library's image by making patrons and nonpatrons aware of new services, such as makerspaces, 3D printers, digital reference services, and more.
- As open access (OA) and open educational resources (OER) become more available, infographics can be used to provide awareness and as instructional materials on how to use them in college courses.

- Infographics fit the profile to increase awareness of library services because of their visual quality, concise messaging, and interesting format.

Libraries are finding innovative ways to engage users and meet their twenty-first-century needs. As infographics continue to evolve and grow in popularity, so do the different ways users can view them. Patrons of all ages are often making mobile phones their technology of choice. As a result, infographic-specific apps have begun showing up on these devices. The functions of these apps include viewing world statistics, infographic design portfolios, company dashboards, and creating mind maps. Spreading the word about libraries and their services is becoming ever more important, and infographics are making that communication easier.

Exercises for Chapter 8

1. Analyze your current library services. Determine which one(s) are being underutilized and why you think that is the case. Select one service where you think you can create more usage using an infographic. Outline the main theme for your infographic and at least three subpoints for the story you think will help increase usage.
2. Review the following infographics for content and design:

   a. https://www.pinterest.com/pin/81627811965903371/—"Traditional Books vs. Digital Readers"
   b. https://www.pinterest.com/pin/522487994238994002/—"E-book Nation"

   Think about purpose, audience, and communicating the message. Ask yourself the following questions:

   a. Is one better than the other, and why?
   b. Does one have a more appealing design to convey your message, and why?
   c. How do the message and design contribute to each other?
   d. What would you change in each one, and why?

3. Select one service you want to promote (e.g., makerspace, 3D printing, Ask a Librarian, OER) and create a draft of an infographic.

   a. In your planning, identify your audience and consider the purpose.
   b. Decide what type of infographic you will create (e.g., comparison, timeline). See chapter 2 for types of infographics.
   c. Do a quick outline of your design that includes color scheme, font, and images.
   d. Review with colleagues and select where you will promote the infographic.

References

ARL (Association of Research Libraries). 2012. "Code of Best Practices in Fair Use for Academic and Research Libraries." January. http://www.arl.org/storage/documents/publications/code-of-best-practices-fair-use.pdf.

Cook, David. 2014. "Cook: The Father of Invention." Timesfreepress.com. March 16. http://www.timesfreepress.com/news/opinion/columns/story/2014/mar/16/the-father-of-invention/134435/.

Libatique, Melanie. 2013. "Share and Use Creative Work Using a Creative Commons License." *Homegrown, Cultivating Success* (blog). December. http://homegrown.ph/share-and-use-creative-work-using-a-creative-commons-license/.

McKinnon, Laura Fargo, and Kris S. Helge. 2014. "Copyright, Open Access and Library Instruction." *Library Hi Tech News* 31, no. 10 (November/December). http://www.emeraldgrouppublishing.com/newsletters/proimg/nt/pdfs/LHTN_31_10.pdf?PHPSESSID=1t219ml3sr3pc1r0amr6mddjr3.

Millsaps, Bridget Butler. 2015. "MakerBot and UMass Amherst Team for 50-Printer Innovation Center in Library." *3D Printer & 3D Printing News*, March 24. http://3dprint.com/53386/umass-amherst-makerbot/.

NIH (National Institutes of Health). 2013. "How Open Access Empowered a 16-Year-Old to Make Cancer Breakthrough." The Right to Research Coalition. YouTube video, 3:59. June 11. https://www.youtube.com/watch?v=G55hlnSD1Ys.

Phillips, Nancy. 2014. "Reference Renovation." *ILA Reporter*, April. http://www.ila.org/Reporter/April%202014/pg_12-15.pdf.

Schwartz, Meredith. 2013. "Report Summary: Pew Internet Releases New Report on Library Services." *Library Journal*, January 22. http://www.infodocket.com/2013/01/22/pew-internet-releases-new-report-on-library-services-plus-commentary/.

Suber, Peter. 2012. "Open Access Overview." June. http://legacy.earlham.edu/~peters/fos/overview.htm.

Thompson, Clive. 2014. "Why Your Library May Soon Have Laser Cutters and 3-D Printers." Wired.com. September 2. http://www.wired.com/2014/09/makerspace/.

William and Flora Hewlett Foundation. 2015. "Open Educational Resources." Accessed September 17. http://www.hewlett.org/programs/education/open-educational-resources.

Zickuhr, Kathryn, Lee Rainie, and Kristen Purcell. 2013. "Summary of Findings: Library Services in the Digital Age." Pew Research Center (Pew Internet & American Life Project). January 22. http://libraries.pewinternet.org/2013/01/22/Library-services/.

CHAPTER 9

Speaking Out

Creating Your Own Story to Advocate for Your Library

IN THIS CHAPTER

- ▷ The importance of advocacy for your library
- ▷ Methods libraries use to advocate
- ▷ Ways to use infographics in your advocacy efforts
- ▷ Your library's story via infographics
- ▷ A script for an infographic to advocate for your library

CHAPTER 9 FOCUSES ON ADVOCATING for the library—what it means, who does it, how you get started, and much more. Advocacy has been defined as "the process of turning passive support into educated action by stakeholders" (ALA, 2015). Simply put, advocacy is voicing your support for libraries and encouraging others to do the same.

An excellent way to advocate for your library is to tell its story—a story that makes the listener feel emotion that is truthful, heartfelt, and sincere (Cruz, 2013). This chapter outlines effective ways to communicate your message and things to avoid. It highlights infographics, an ideal storytelling venue, one that transmits the message without bogging down the reader in voluminous text but rather creates interest and excitement in a concise, visual format. You will see examples that illustrate advocating for libraries and learn more about partnerships built to advocate.

A Bit about Library Advocacy

Whether you are a school, public, academic, or special librarian, part of your job is to advocate for your library. How do you do it? What do you say? Whom do you contact? These are all valid questions that must be answered. Organizations, such as the American Library Association (ALA), the Public Library Association (PLA), and the American Association of School Librarians (AASL), realize the importance of advocating for your library and provide you with tools to facilitate the process, including ready-made brochures, templates to customize your own story, message boxes to help you write a script, and more. See table 9.1 for more tools.

Table 9.1. Advocacy Tools

DESCRIPTION	URL
Advocacy brochures from AASL	http://www.ala.org/aasl/advocacy/tools/brochures
K–12 advocacy messages	http://www.ala.org/aasl/sites/ala.org.aasl/files/content/aaslissues/slm/Message_Box_and_Tips_FINAL.pdf
Guidelines and template for creating a K–12 story	http://www.ala.org/aasl/sites/ala.org.aasl/files/content/aaslissues/slm/CreateYourOwnStory_Guidelines.pdf
Infographic of skills and resources for twenty-first-century K–12 students	http://www.alastore.ala.org/CloseUp.aspx?uid=
Tips from Alaska Snapshot Day to advocate for school libraries	http://akasl.org/wp-content/uploads/2012/03/20-Easy-Ways-1.pdf
School library PALS in Utah—Parents Advocating for Libraries in Schools	http://schoollibrarypals.wikispaces.com/
District Dispatch, ALA Washington Office blog	http://www.districtdispatch.org/
State advocacy information	http://yalsa.ala.org/blog/2009/02/09/28-days-of-advocacy-9-state-advocacy-where-it-all-begins/
Speaking Up for Library Services to Teens (guide)	http://www.ala.org/yalsa/sites/ala.org.yalsa/files/content/advocacy_final.pdf

With continuing budget shortfalls and more groups and services vying for decreasing funds, it is more important than ever to increase advocacy for public, school, academic, and special libraries. You can tell your story in so many different ways—showcasing electronic resources; promoting the virtual library; highlighting special collections; promoting library staff; providing outreach to students, faculty, and patrons; and promoting the library as a place where numerous activities, technology, and events are available, to name a few. When library users know about and value what the library has to offer, they too become advocates for libraries.

There are many ways to advocate for your library, and you are probably using some of these already. This chapter focuses on using infographics as the means to communicate your story—your successes and value. An infographic provides the means to take dense, confusing information that your target audience has little interest in nor time to read and present it in an easy-to-understand, interesting way. Whether your message is about data to influence or drive decision making or motivate action, these popular infographics are a quick way to visually present the library's story. In addition, you can use infographics on your website, social media, or in print materials to reinforce other ways you are advocating for your library.

Organizations use infographics to convey important information to generate awareness about the library. For example, in chapter 6, figure 6.1, the infographic "U.S. Public Libraries Weather the Storm" was designed to bring attention to the increased use and reliance on public libraries despite decreasing budgets. To advocate for an issue, such as support for teens at the library, you can share some interesting data about the topic with an infographic.

Library advocates must make their voices heard these days beyond the local school or community. Thus, legislative advocacy is also important. Library advocates reach out by e-mail to their representatives, send action alerts via text messages, blog to raise awareness within communities, and even call a senator's office. At the local level, public libraries usually present an annual report to their library board. Telling the story of the library with an infographic that summarizes main points or contains an anecdote that highlights a specific function or program of the library is more interesting and much more likely to be read than that typical long, rather boring, report. The ALA has its own Legislative Action Center (http://cqrcengage.com/ala/) so you can find out what's happening on issues nationwide. Toolkits on the site can help you make your case. State libraries are also knowledgeable about state and local issues. For example, a coalition of more than twenty education businesses, associations, and media groups—including Scholastic Inc., EBSCO Information Services, and the Association of American Publishers—is asking the U.S. Congress to support dedicated school library funding in the reauthorization of the Elementary and Secondary Education Act (ESEA), which provides federal funding for national K–12 education programs (Sheketoff, 2015). Advocacy is only limited by imagination. The infographics you will see next should spark your creativity to advocate for your library.

Examples of Libraries That Use Infographics to Advocate

Infographics are a way to inform your library community about what you do and why you do it. They have been around for quite a while. For example, in the spring of 2011, a high school librarian used Microsoft PowerPoint, a program with which most librarians are familiar, to create the infographic http://yalsa.ala.org/blog/?s=infographic&submit=-Search to demonstrate the uses of her library (Braun, 2011).

Reading about other libraries' advocacy successes can inspire your own efforts. The following examples illustrate ways libraries are integrating infographics into their advocacy programs in public, academic, school, and special libraries. Each example addresses the content and ways the design enhances the message. Go to links in the examples that follow to view entire infographics in color.

Example 1: Academic Library Survey Shows Value

The infographic in figure 9.1 uses statistics from a LibQual survey, conducted by the library at Paul Smith's College, to tell the library's story. LibQual provides services that

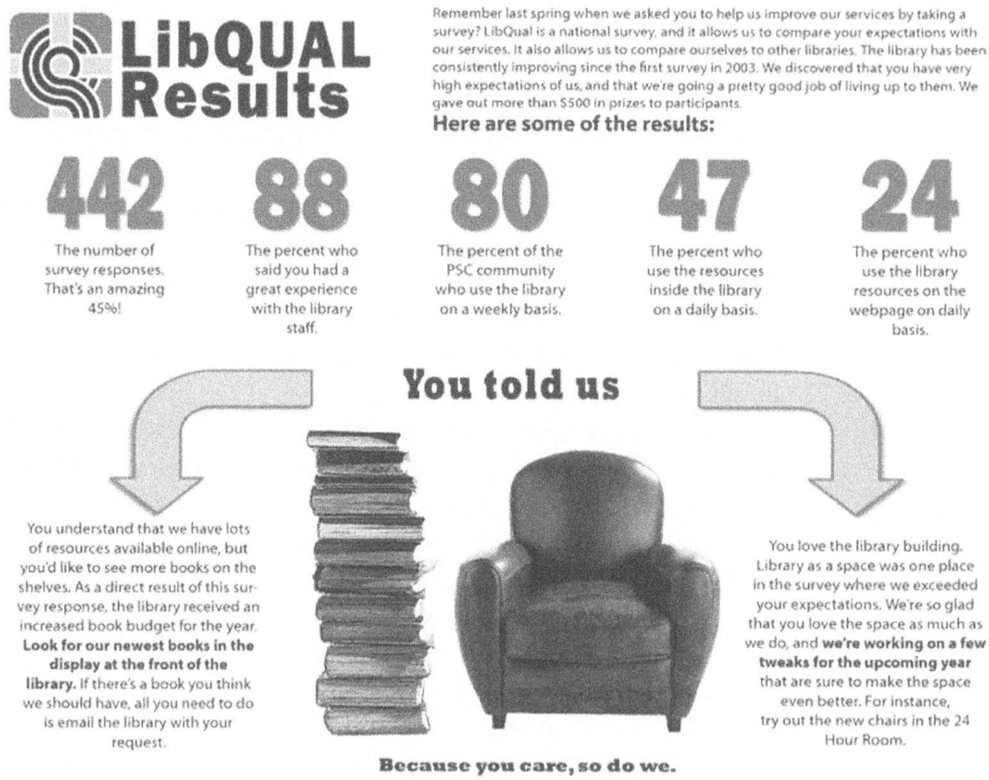

Figure 9.1. LibQual Infographic: Data Reimagined. Created by Meggan Frost, 2013, Joan Weill Adirondack Library, Paul Smith's College, http://librariandesignshare.org/2013/03/15/libqual-infographic-data-reimagined/.

libraries use to solicit, track, understand, and act upon users' opinions of their service quality. Rather than provide patrons with a long report, this infographic is a good example of visually representing data gathered through the library assessment. The infographic was then displayed at the front of the library to share with the campus community.

The beginning of the infographic states the purpose of the survey—to help improve library services. Next, statistics portray results, also emphasizing the large number of survey responses. Using images and text, the infographic visually shows two major results, one where the library exceeded expectations and the other where improvements were needed.

A two-color palette, arrows to direct the reader's eye, and images to represent each result makes the infographic easy to read and understand the large amount of information collected in the survey. The data adds credibility to the results. The final text summarizes the reason for the survey and lists changes the library plans as a result.

Example 2: "Colorado School Librarians: Improving Student Achievement"

The Colorado State Library in collaboration with the Colorado Department of Education (CDE) created an infographic, shown in figure 9.2, to advocate for school librarians in Colorado. This is an informative infographic, designed to show the value of the school librarian. If the audience's opinion was already positive, the story reinforces that mind-set with statistics from credible sources listed at the bottom. For those who had no opinion or one that was not so positive, the goal is to change their minds.

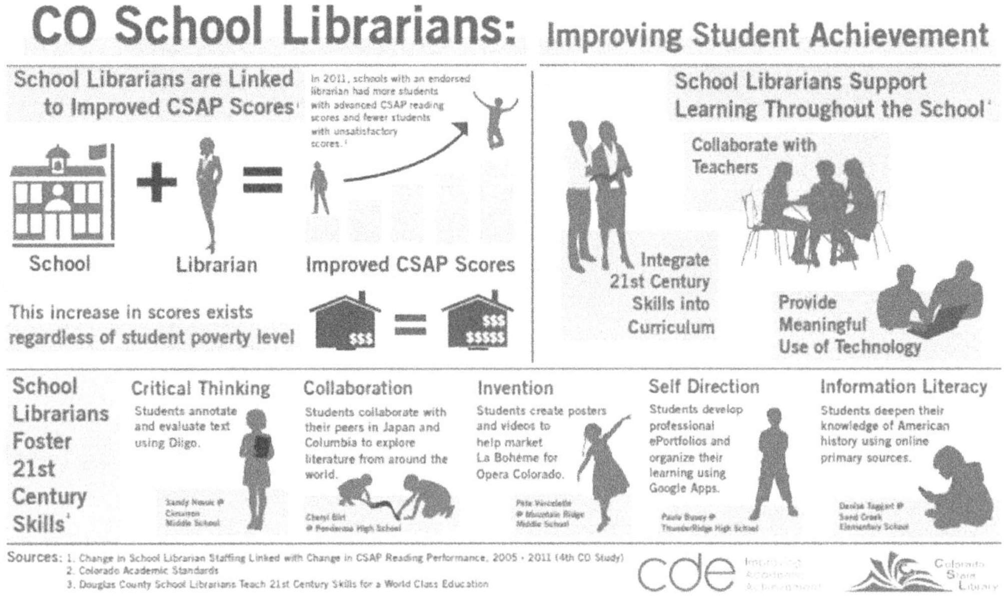

Figure 9.2. Colorado School Librarians: Improving Student Achievement. Created by Library Research Service (LRS) staff at the Colorado State Library, https://docs.google.com/file/d/0B7270S224HtMRVNpY2prdmcyY3M/edit?pli=1.

The story focuses on how school librarians improve student achievement, important to all parents, school board members, and voters in the state of Colorado. Three subpoints support the theme of achievement: improved Colorado assessment test scores, support for school-wide learning, and librarians' ability to foster students' twenty-first-century skills. A blue-gray palette and blue boxes highlight the text to emphasize the main points to advocate for the importance of school librarians. Images provide a visual picture of twenty-first-century skills, such as use of technology, collaboration, information literacy, and more. Concise text summarizes main and subpoints in limited space, ideal for today's reader.

Example 3: Advocating for Library Programs

Not only can you advocate for the library and its personnel but also for a particular program or user group, such as teens, within the library. For example, in a public library, you might advocate for a dedicated teen space, bigger and better young adult collections, a young adult specialist, more staff, more and better computers, and faster connections. The infographic in figure 9.3, "The Future of Library Services For and With Teens: A Call to Action," is based on a report by the Young Adult Library Services Association (YALSA) (Braun et al., 2014). The executive summary of the report outlines main and subpoints based on statistics and provides a nice summary of the information for the infographic. The infographic looks at the teen population and its effect in today's world on both public and school libraries. Designed to persuade the audience to take action, the infographic describes teens as library users and presents issues they face. It then shifts to what teens need from libraries and whether libraries are ready to handle changes affecting this population. A call to action at the end emphasizes the goal for public and school libraries to join with other stakeholders to advocate for this group at their own libraries and in their community.

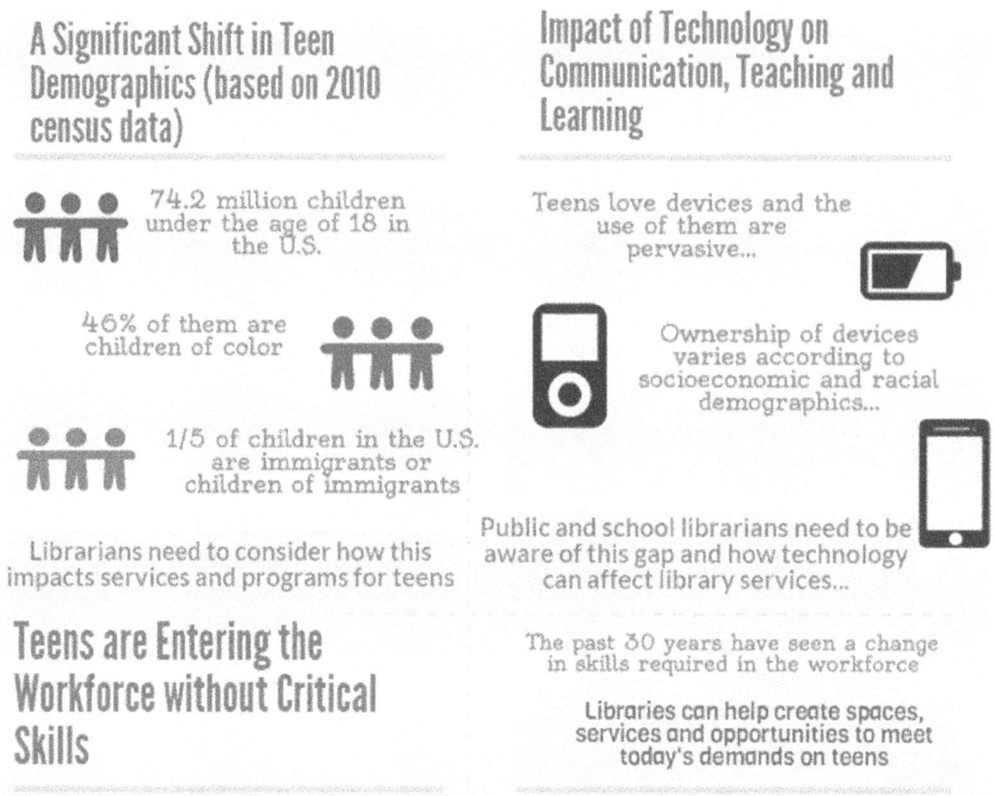

Figure 9.3. The Future of Library Services For and With Teens: A Call to Action. Created by Naomi Bates, Northwest High School Library, https://magic.piktochart.com/output/1326505-yalsa-teen-and-library-report.

The infographic is divided into parts by blue bars. Part 1 identifies three things: the action wanted as stated in the title, the credible source, and short sentences that highlight the main points of the fifty-plus-page report. The statistic of forty million teens points out that this is not a small problem that only one library faces and leads directly to the next section, which describes the problem for this significant population of library users. Again, statistics illustrate the changing demographics, the impact of technology, and how this will change library services needed. Part 3 explains how libraries are affected by these changes and asks a provocative question: Are libraries ready? The infographic outlines what teens need from libraries and implications for libraries. At the end, an emotional call to action addresses both public and school libraries to help these teens.

Created by a high school librarian using a template in Piktochart, the infographic uses shades of red and blue primary colors to create a simple, straightforward design. A combination of simple graphics, hierarchical text, and different font types directs the reader from one point to the next in an easy-to-read format. By the end, the story has been told, and the message is clear. Review the entire infographic in color.

Several other libraries have used infographics where the focus has been on teens and teen issues. Review table 9.2 near the end of this chapter for links to more advocacy resources.

Example 4: Library Value-Added Events

Library Snapshot Day provides a way for libraries of all types across a state, region, system, or community to show what happens in a single day in their libraries. For example, a public library might gather the following information: How many books are checked out? How many people receive help finding a job, doing their taxes, working on their homework? This initiative provides an easy means to collect statistics, photos, and stories that will enable library advocates to prove the value of their libraries to decision makers and increase public awareness.

The Texas Association of School Librarians at http://www.tcxaslibrarysnapshotday.org/ advocates for libraries each year with the Texas Snapshot Day. Each library across the state collects data, stories, activities, and photographs of patrons on that day and submits it to the state library. See https://www.flickr.com/groups/librarysnapshotday for pictures and statistics from Texas Snapshot Day. Libraries can then use the information in their own promotions, review what other libraries are doing, and get a sense of statewide library usage. Some data from Texas Libraries Snapshot Day (TLA, 2014) include:

- Librarians at academic institutions are collaborating on at least twenty support and collaborative class efforts with faculty.
- The average public library building sees about 225 kids every day for story time, and more than 270 people attend other programs.
- The average school library hosts over 230 students participating in non-class-related activities, such as book clubs and individual study, and approximately 405 students receive instructional assistance from librarians.
- Other statistics include circulation; Internet and computer use; and number of children, teens, and adults participating in programs.

Comments from patrons also make a good value story highlighting some of the libraries' services, personnel, and technology: "I am learning English at the library, and this helps me to help my daughter with her homework." "Without the library, I would never have learned how to use a computer." "I use the library to work remotely and take online classes." "The librarians are very helpful. The computer tutorials are very educational, and the librarians will try to help you any way they can to find a solution" (TLA, 2014).

The data collected on a Snapshot Day is ideal for inclusion in an infographic to advocate for any type of library. Created by a high school librarian, the infographic at http://ecisd-libraries.blogspot.com/2013/05/ shows the typical day in one of the East Central libraries in Texas on Library Snapshot Day. Statistics included daily student visits, resources checked out, and students served through instruction. Very simple and straightforward, this two-color infographic provides statistics from the school library that will be meaningful to the local community, parents, and the school board (TLA, 2014). An example from Carstairs Public Library in Canada (http://carstairspublic.prl.ab.ca/files/SnapshotDay2012Powerpoint_0.pdf) shows an infographic using statistics and pictures to illustrate results obtained at that library on Library Snapshot Day.

Example 5: Advocating for Libraries Using Personal Stories

Unlike data that creates no empathy, stories provide context and make data memorable. They draw people in on an emotional level. Stories may show how a library helped you through a difficult situation; taught you something important; or contributed to your education, employment, or entrepreneurship. They may tell about a time the library provided you with a needed space to just laugh or think. Stories may show how your life would be different if your library didn't exist.

To tell their stories, North Carolina Library Association created a Library Advocacy Taskforce, an ad hoc group of the state association. With the assistance of various library associations across the state, they created a website to advocate for libraries. Because they wanted legislators and community members to see the emotional connection people have with libraries, they collected personal stories and comments from library patrons from each congressional district on why libraries were important to them. For National Legislative Day, ambassadors compiled the results into videos (https://nclibraryadvocacy.wordpress.com/nc-libraries/ncla-student-ambassador-program/ncla-2014-student-ambassadors/ and https://nclibraryadvocacy.wordpress.com/nc-libraries/north-carolina-leads-national-rally-for-libraries-in-washington/nlld-student-ambassador-video-why-we-love-libraries/). The video in figure 9.4 shows a middle school boy dressed as his grandfather might have, relating the virtues of the library in his grandpa's words and voice.

The content emphasized patrons' feelings about libraries and how the library and librarians contributed to work goals, camaraderie, learning, love of reading and books, and so much more. North Carolina students ranging from second graders to middle and high school students made comments and told their library stories. One library patron told her success story about attending a writing workshop given by an author at the library. Following the author's advice, she wrote her own story, which became a best seller.

Using infographics as a way to inform the library community about what libraries do and why they do it is one method to communicate a library's story to others. A one-page, interactive infographic could be used to promote the personal stories just reviewed. Clickable videos embedded in sections of an infographic identifying the different ways the library helped patrons would visually and quickly share the libraries' stories so readers can feel patrons' emotional connections with libraries.

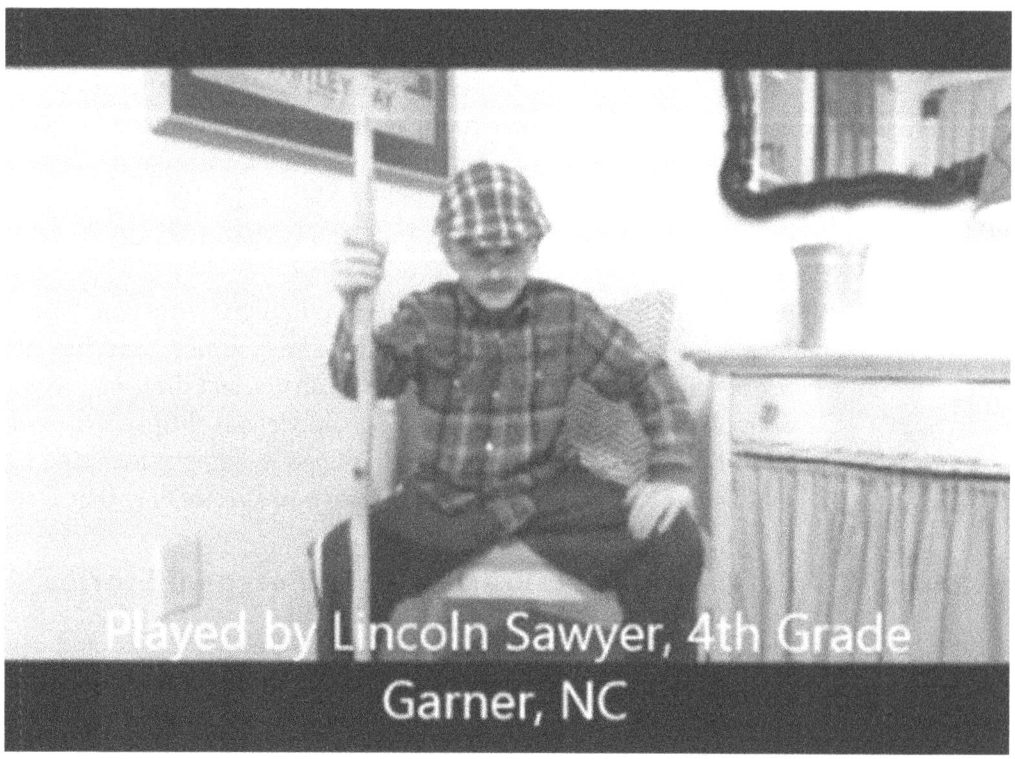

Figure 9.4. Personal Library Advocacy Stories. Credit: North Carolina Library Association, National Library Legislative Day Student Ambassadors video, https://nclibraryadvocacy.wordpress.com/nc-libraries/ncla-student-ambassador-program/ncla-2014-student-ambassadors/.

Example 6: Advocating for Librarians

The Claremont Colleges Library's Research, Teaching & Learning Department offers information literacy (IL) instruction to help prepare both undergraduate and graduate students to become confident researchers and critical thinkers. Librarians and faculty worked together as partners consulting on what should be included in the syllabus, creating online research tutorials and guides, and librarian-led workshops. Librarians also conducted one-to-one student appointments oriented toward specific research assignments, including papers and annotated bibliographies, on which faculty and librarians had collaborated.

Figure 9.5 shows an interesting outcome—an infographic titled "Librarians Matter." The infographic visually describes the results of a study that librarians conducted on the level of collaboration in their first-year seminars.

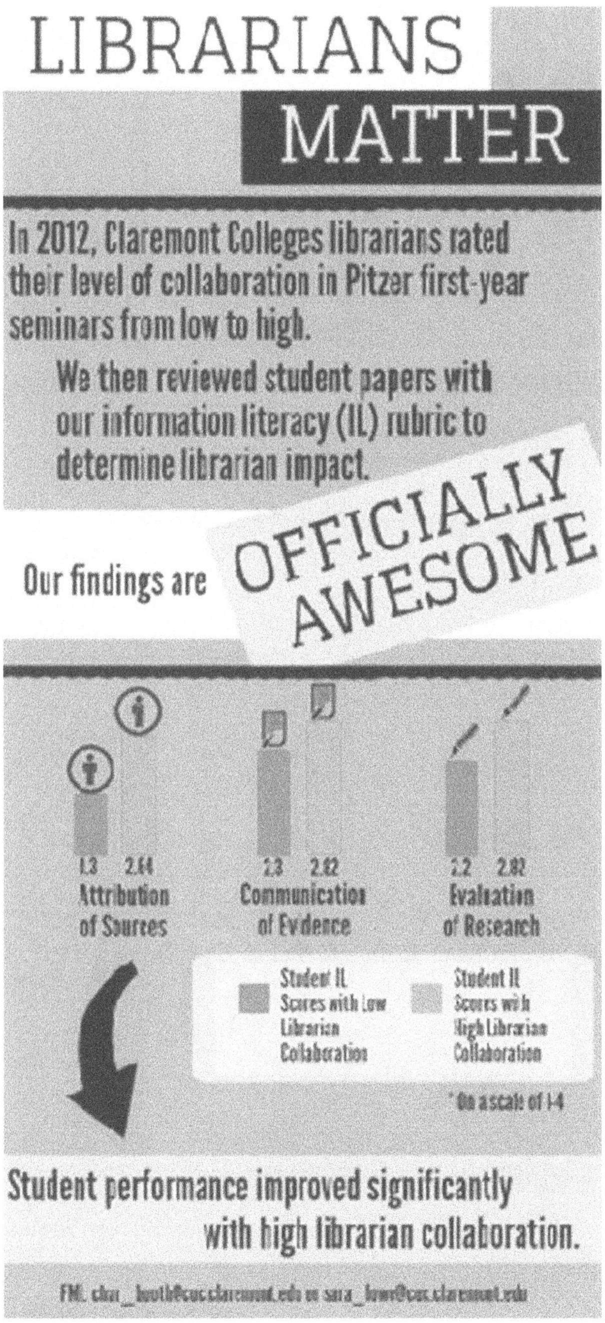

Figure 9.5. Librarians Matter. Created by Dani Brecher Cook, M. Sara Lowe, and Char Booth, Claremont Colleges Library, http://libraries.claremont.edu/informationliteracy/images/FYS_Infographic.jpg.

The analysis of the infographic that follows points out design and content aspects. The infographic is divided into the title and two sections: (1) the description of the study and (2) the results and conclusion. For clarity, each section is divided with a black line. The top of the infographic in figure 9.6 uses short text to explain the purpose, audience, and method used in the study.

- The color palette consists of blue-green and yellow with the yellow text emphasizing the main points.
- Boxed text draws the eye to important words.
- At the end of part 1, the reader is encouraged to read on about the findings of the study because of the word choice "officially awesome" enclosed in an angled yellow box that points downward to part 2.

Figure 9.6. Top of Infographic. Created by Dani Brecher Cook, M. Sara Lowe, and Char Booth, Claremont Colleges Library, http://libraries.claremont.edu/informationliteracy/images/FYS_Infographic.jpg.

Using separate bar charts for each question librarians explored in the study, part 2 in figure 9.7 explains the results.

- Two accent colors point out the results of low and high librarian collaboration.
- Small icons—a figure, paper pad, and pencil above the bars also help to identify the type of question. A legend is given to explain what each bar represents.
- A large black arrow points to the conclusion, also enclosed in a yellow box for emphasis.
- Contact information is available at the bottom if the reader wants more information about the program.

This infographic is an excellent way to highlight the results of a study, provide information about a faculty-librarian partnership, and above all show the importance of librarians as they use their expertise to provide students with necessary twenty-first-century research skills.

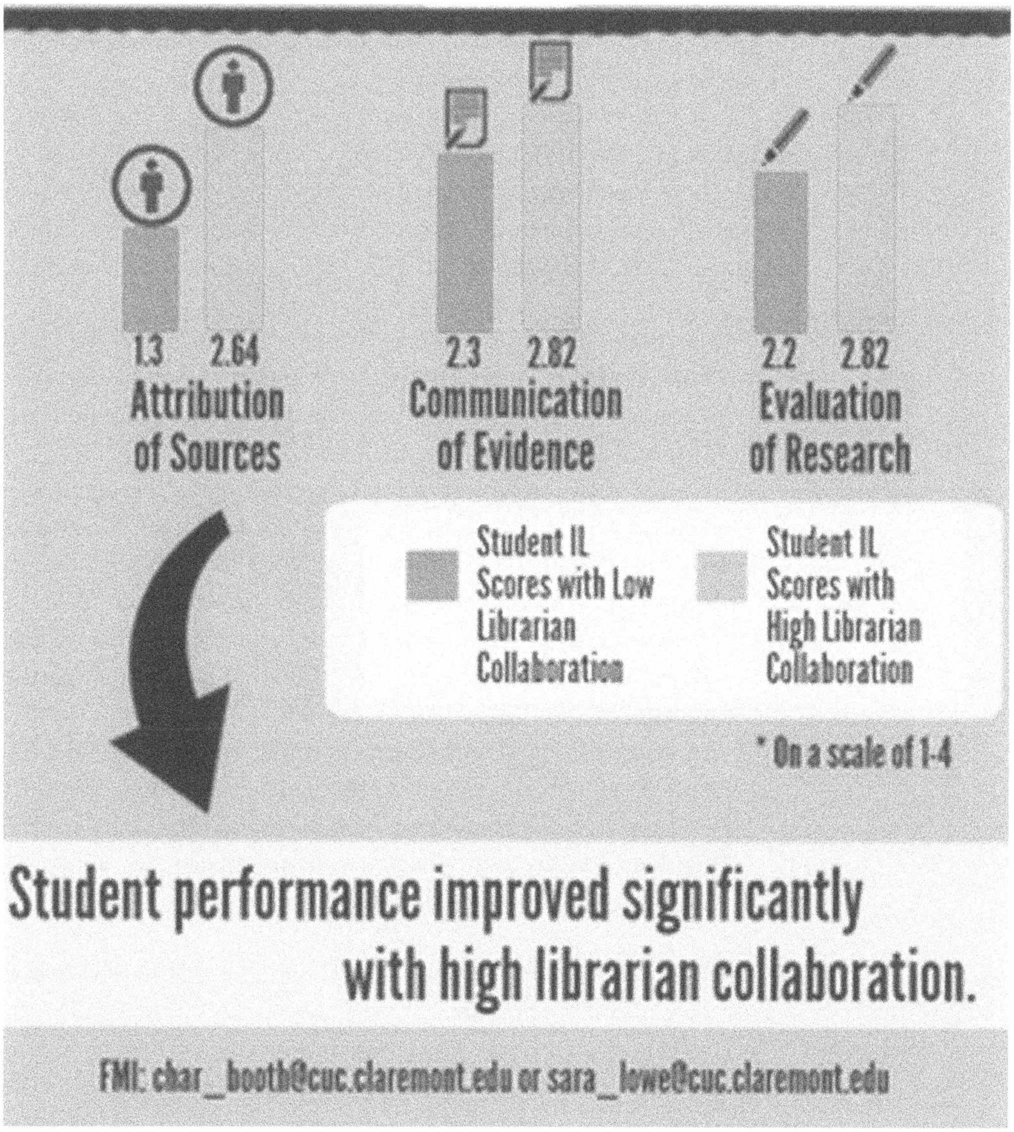

Figure 9.7. Bottom of Infographic. Created by Dani Brecher Cook, M. Sara Lowe, and Char Booth, Claremont Colleges Library, http://libraries.claremont.edu/informationliteracy/images/FYS_Infographic.jpg.

Example 7: Advocating for School Libraries

All libraries have and continue to experience the effects of budget shortfalls, but none more than school libraries. School districts face difficult decisions that they do not want to make, and, unfortunately, school library programs are often at the top of budget cut lists. The library's response needs to be immediate, accurate, positive, coordinated, consistent, and clear. The American Association of School Librarians (AASL) infographic, titled "School Librarians Transform Learning," provides a detailed view of a school library's advocacy approach using infographics (Stripling, 2014).

Research states that school libraries staffed by credentialed librarians have the ability to improve student learning (Kachel and Lance, 2013). Stories the library advocate can tell that point out higher test scores, reading improvement, and a child-centered approach emphasize the library's value and its return on investment (ROI). The infographic communicates a story about school librarians and learning. It can be a valuable visual aid to advocate for the importance of employing certified school librarians and the advantages of partnerships between teachers and librarians. Go to http://www.ala.org/aasl/sites/ala.org.aasl/files/content/aaslissues/advocacy/AASL_Infographic_FINAL.pdf to review the complete infographic in color.

Look first at the content to see the ways in which the infographic emphasizes the advantages of teacher-librarian collaboration at the school level. To impress upon its readers how librarians can transform learning, the infographic tells the library's story using statistics; short, hierarchical text; catchy phrases; images; and color. At the top of the infographic, the beginning of the story sets up the purpose, audience, and main message.

- The title, "School Librarians Transform Learning," makes the reader question "how" the librarian is transforming learning and encourages the reader to continue. A subtitle in dark blue reinforces the title, making the point that school librarians "ensure their students have the best chance to succeed."
- A text bubble at the top right communicates a message to teachers from one of their own—the 2012 Kentucky Teacher of the Year. She indicates that coplanning and coteaching with the librarian provides students with the necessary information literacy skills to succeed in college and the workplace. Whether you are a teacher, administrator, parent, or school board member, this short text is meaningful and emphasizes the importance of the librarian as an equal partner in learning by all students.
- An image of a hand with fingers pointing to text directs the reader's eye to provocative statements the author wants the reader to think about: the Internet can help with research, *but* if students don't have the important information literacy skills, they may not do their research well. This leaves viewers wondering why students may do poorly and how they can do better. Again, it entices them to read on.

The next part of the infographic expands on the theme with several subpoints in the second part of the infographic.

- Another hand directs the reader to the second part of the infographic. Notice the mobile phone image, which represents what students often use for googling their research question. Three short text messages make the point that students use Google as their research tool, do not use authoritative sources available to them, and lack the skill to evaluate the information they retrieve. This image appeals to students who so often communicate by texting.

- The iPad image to the right of the phone contains statistics from teachers to reinforce the message that students use few sources outside of Google, and the amount of information retrieved in their Google searches is so overwhelming that they do not develop the evaluation skills necessary to select the appropriate information.
- On the far left, subpoints show statistics in hierarchical bubbles to represent the amount of each type of source that students use for their research. Google, the online encyclopedia *Wikipedia*, and social media lead the way, followed closely by asking their peers. Authoritative sources, including online databases, the librarian, news, and textbooks are outdistanced. These statistics reinforce the previous statements by teachers. A statistic of billions of Google searches is shown separately in its own box so the huge number stands out.
- Another point made about student research is student access to technology. The three images—student, house, and dollar sign—indicate that technology can help students no matter what their learning style, although those who have technology at home may not be digitally literate enough, and many low-income students do not even have access to the technology.
- On the right side of the infographic, teachers note that their comfort level with technology determines how much they will use it in the classroom. An arrow pointing to "School Librarians" describes librarians' knowledge about technology and the help they can provide for teachers in answering questions, participating in learning communities, and training teachers to locate and evaluate digital content. This emphasizes the partnership.
- After telling the story of how librarians can help both teachers and students in their research to improve learning, the infographic brings the story to an end using bold text to state the main message—school libraries provide equitable access to resources and tools in a warm, stimulating, safe environment. Note, too, the image of the hands is carried through to the conclusion, showing one hand, the patron, and the other hand, the librarian, reaching to meet, again emphasizing the importance of partnerships.
- At the bottom right side of the infographic, a diverse list of sources emphasizes the need for comprehensive research, an important point in the infographic.

This infographic brings together the content and design to communicate the story. Moreover, the bold shades of orange and blue colors on a light yellow background lend emphasis to the message, and the warm orange color reflects the "warm environment." The hands, the vertical blue bar, and the handle of the Google magnifying glass guide the reader from point to point through the infographic. Lastly, the reaching hands at the bottom right bring both sides of the infographic together and conclude the story that the library and librarian have the resources to help students in the twenty-first century.

This library's story is now packaged on a single sheet of paper that can be posted in the library, on bulletin boards in the school, and on its website. It can be distributed in library newsletters, sent to parents, and posted on social media. It can even be put in an annual report to the school board or sent to the legislative representative. This infographic tells a compelling story about the school library but could also be modeled for an academic library. Review the following checklist for further tips on promoting your infographic.

Tips to Promote Your Infographic

Making your infographic unique and visually appealing while keeping it simple with a design that will captivate your audience and urge them to read on is the combination that will result in success or failure of your infographic going viral. Here are some additional tips:

- Combining text with graphics is more effective and understandable than either one presented alone.
- Visual elements can generate more views than blocks of text. Even adding photos to an article or press release can increase the number of viewers. Your target audiences who see your infographic will more often "like," comment, and share it to help make your content go viral.
- Infographics with visual elements that are relevant to your target audience's needs are usually more engaging. Non- and limited-English speakers find them more understandable.
- The key to success when using infographics for marketing is to provide clear and concise pieces of information in understandable and graphically appealing ways.
- Using graphical elements like tables, charts, graphics, and pictures, well researched from reliable sources and studies, can establish you as an expert in this field.
- Linkable content that is visually satisfying to attract attention and provide good, useful information makes others want to share your work on their social media and websites.
- Infographics are portable and easily embedded. By including an embed code with your post or uploaded infographic, people can easily integrate the embed code into their blogs or websites. The embedded infographic is then automatically linked to your site.
- Your infographics with your content information shared or embedded in social media or other online channels can generate links back to your content (backlinks). An abundance of inbound links can boost your search rankings, generating more followers to your site and reaching a broader audience every time your infographic is shared.
- Infographics are designed to attract inbound links and increase the amount of time users stay on your site. The longer they remain, the higher your chances of getting search engines to understand the importance of your content as a reliable source.
- The visual format can make infographics popular beyond online marketing as they can be applied to print materials, brochures, newsletters, slide presentations, and more.
- Infographics are easy to track with analytics. This will give you a greater understanding of how your targeted audience behaves and thinks so you can modify and make even more interesting and relevant infographics.

These tips on creating effective infographics can be good for search engine optimization (SEO), using your content to drive better rankings and better results. Chapter 3 contains more details on promoting your infographic with SEO.

Dos and Don'ts When Creating Your Infographic Script

It is important to think through what you will say as an advocate for your library. What should you include in your story? What points about your library will most interest your audience? What audience of stakeholders do you plan to address? These questions and many others must be carefully pondered. Any infographic message must consider its purpose, audience, and structure.

Your target audience can greatly affect the visual presentation of data you convey. For example, you may choose to share similar data in a board report and a patron handout but with a different message. In a report to the board, you want them to understand how interlibrary loan transactions are increasing so they can help evaluate the staffing and collection development implications. For patrons, you may want to highlight the increase in interlibrary loan as an expansion of material they can check out. You are using the same data but potentially different stories, targeted at specific audiences. The following tips should help you get started writing your script.

Dos

- Choose your message and the focus of your story based on the purpose and audience. This will direct your choice of points and data to support your story.
- Keep your message short. A laundry list of the wonders of your library is too much to digest, and the message gets lost in amounts of verbiage.
- Pick a story that matters to you and makes data memorable. If it is important to you, your audience will feel that when you tell the story.
- Select catchy words to capture the interest of your audience. Subpoints reinforce main ideas and repeat your message without its seeming redundant.
- Tell your story truthfully, remembering that it should have a beginning, middle, and end that shows the character, obstacles, and outcome.
- Conclude with a call to action, something you want your audience to do.

Your story should allow your audience to experience the data and provoke empathy between your story and the reader.

Don'ts

Although your infographic may be visually appealing, try to avoid the following when you create your story:

- An unclear thesis/purpose
- A mixed message that confuses your audience
- Questions by the reader about what to do with the information
- A cluttered layout with little white space between images
- Too many colors so the reader's attention is not focused
- Unclear relationships between the data
- Data that has no empathy

Finding Data to Tell Your Library Story

The impact of your message depends on how the data is tied to your intended audience. The more you can localize the data used for reporting and compare it against your own demographic, the more powerful and memorable the message. Relating data to national trends can also be effective in layering the story and highlighting similarities and differences of your target audience with a larger population. Two sources provide reliable data about libraries. The Institute of Museum and Library Services (IMLS) at http://www.imls.gov/research/public_libraries_in_the_united_states_survey.aspx collects data on public libraries and is an excellent source for comparison analysis, especially geared toward services, collections, staffing, and budget. Pew Internet data sets at http://pewinternet.org/Data-Tools/Get-The-Latest-Statistics.aspx provides research-based studies with data for illustrating the impact of libraries on society.

Libraries generally submit annual reports that contain demographic data related to their service area. Investigating census data can provide key statistics on interesting trends and specific data elements to include in reporting and visualizing data. Of course, your own library statistics—circulation, budget, and funding data—offer a rich source of information for building a compelling story about your library. Correlations and reasons for changes to the data can also be visualized.

Although it is nice to have data that is both informational and pleasing to the eye, most important is that it must be credible and accurate. Make sure to check the following:

- Your data is properly cited.
- Methodology for data collection and reporting is included.
- Supplemental data that relate to your own library service area is given.
- Your math is correct.
- Data is presented in an easy-to-understand format.

In summary, the most critical part of creating an infographic is the work required in gathering information and graphic assets.

- Plan the project: Why do you think an infographic is needed? Who is the target audience? Will you convey the information in different ways for different audiences? Is your data appropriate to be visualized in an infographic?
- Research: Gather your data and possible graphic elements (e.g., icons, imagery). The more local and personalized your data is, the more effective it will be in telling your library's story.
- Tell a story: Develop a plot that serves as a platform for the presentation. Is there a metaphor that can reinforce the message?
- Design: Consider color, images, typography, and layout as you design the infographic.
- Color guides you may wish to check include:
    - "The Psychology of Color" Infographic—http://nowsourcing.com/blog/wp-content/uploads/2012/01/louisville-painter.html
    - "Color Psychology in Logo Design"—http://hellotarte.com/blog/2012/04/26/color-psychology-in-logo-design-infographic/
    - "Color Science"—http://visual.ly/node/15845

Table 9.2 provides additional infographics and articles about library advocacy.

Table 9.2. Library Advocacy Resources

DESCRIPTION	URL
ALA advocacy guide	http://www.ala.org/united/sites/ala.org.united/files/content/powerguide/positioning-powerpoint.pdf
Advocacy resources specific to academic libraries	http://www.ala.org/advocacy/advocacy-university/academic-library-resources
ALA public library resources	http://www.ala.org/advocacy/advocacy-university/public-library-resources
Advocacy resources from the Public Library Association	http://www.ala.org/pla/advocacy
School library advocacy resources	http://www.ala.org/advocacy/advocacy-university/school-library-resources
"Teens Need Libraries," handout with main points and statistics	http://www.ala.org/yalsa/sites/ala.org.yalsa/files/content/professionaltools/Handouts/districtdays_web.pdf
Executive Summary: The Future of Library Services For and With Teens: A Call to Action	http://www.ala.org/yaforum/sites/ala.org.yaforum/files/content/YALSA_nationalforum_ExecutiveSummary_Final_web.pdf
"What Public Libraries Do for Teens"	http://www.ala.org/yalsa/sites/ala.org.yalsa/files/content/Infographic2_FINAL.pdf
"Libraries as Champions of Academic Freedom and Balanced Copyright"	http://www.iaml.info/en/node/1201
"Good News Story about Fair Use and Libraries"	http://www.pijip.org/2013/08/21/new-infographic-tells-the-good-news-story-about-fair-use-and-libraries/
State of America's Libraries Report 2014	http://www.ala.org/news/state-americas-libraries-report-2014

Key Points

Using infographics to tell their own library stories, librarians can advocate for their libraries.

- Telling an effective story through infographics requires accurate data, compelling design, and visualization tools. Using icons, design, and visual metaphors are critical in communicating the message.
- Infographics can visually represent library collections, circulation statistics, outreach successes, instruction outcomes, return on investment, and more.
- Infographics can be placed in annual reports or orientation materials, on social media and websites, and displayed at faculty/staff meetings.
- When creating an infographic, remember: start with data, then design; tell a story; contextualize your information; and keep it visual and simple.

When you know what your message is, how you want to position the library, and how you want the library to be seen, you can more effectively advocate for the library. You can build community support and get others to carry your message for you. That's what advocacy is all about—to inspire and energize others to take action for your library.

Exercises for Chapter 9

To reinforce what you learned in this chapter, try the following:

1. Analyze two infographics on reading from the following list. Consider these questions as you analyze them: What works well? What would you change? What story is being told? How does the layout and design of the infographic help to tell the story? What emotion, if any, does the infographic make you feel? Does the data support the claims? What is the call to action? Do the sources support the data? What other questions would you consider?
    - "The Benefits of Reading Together with Kids"—http://ebookfriendly.com/benefits-reading-with-kids-infographic/
    - "The Growing Popularity of E-reading"—http://ebookfriendly.com/e-reading-popularity-infographic/
    - "A Record Year for Ebooks and Libraries"—http://ebookfriendly.com/digital-reading-2014-infographic/
    - "Is Your Child Ready to Read?"—http://ebookfriendly.com/kids-ready-to-read-infographic/is-your-child-ready-to-read-infographic/
2. Select one of the above infographics and see if you can fact-check the data. Is it from authoritative sources? Can you tell if it's accurate, reliable—why or why not? Is the data correctly represented visually? How would you characterize the data in relation to the story?
3. Plan an infographic to advocate for your library. Write a script for your story.
    a. Choose the audience and the action you want to accomplish.
    b. Select something about the library that is unique, interesting, and will generate feelings and action from the target audience (e.g., a special reading program, a collection of unique databases, job training).
    c. Write a title to catch the reader's attention. Select two to four subpoints.
    d. Select data from research, annual reports, or library statistics to support the thesis.
    e. Create a draft of the infographic—what comes first, second, third; how you'll divide subpoints; colors and font to use; images that best portray the data.
    f. Review the infographic outline with several colleagues in your library.
4. Extra: If you are a teacher-librarian, how would you use infographics to teach a specific lesson, workshop, online class? How would you integrate it into your lesson? Create a plan to incorporate infographics into instruction you are planning.

References

ALA (American Library Association). 2015. "Getting Started as a Library Advocate." ALA.org. http://www.ala.org/offices/ola/gettingstarted.

Braun, Linda W. 2011. "How to Use Infographics for Library Advocacy." *YALSA* (blog). September 17. http://yalsa.ala.org/blog/2011/09/17/30-days-of-how-to-17-how-to-use-%09infographics-for-library-advocacy/.

Braun, Linda W., Maureen L. Hartman, Sandra Hughes-Hassell, and Kafi Kumasi. 2014. *The Future of Library Services For and With Teens: A Call to Action.* YALSA report. January 8. http://www.ala.org/yaforum/sites/ala.org.yaforum/files/content/YALSA_nationalforum_Final_web_0.pdf.

Cruz, Rebecca. 2013. "Infographics: Share Your Story in Pictures." *Public Libraries Online*, December 13. http://publiclibrariesonline.org/2013/12/infographics-share-your-story-in-pictures/.

Kachel, Debra E., and Keith Curry Lance. 2013. "Latest Study: A Full-Time School Librarian Makes a Critical Difference in Boosting Student Achievement." *School Library Journal*, March 7. http://www.slj.com/2013/03/research/librarian-required-a-new-study-shows-that-a-full-time-school-librarian-makes-a-critical-difference-in-boosting-student-achievement/#.

Sheketoff, Emily. 2015. "Education Businesses, Associations Demand Increase in School Library Funding." *District Dispatch* (blog). March 19. http://www.districtdispatch.org/2015/03/education-businesses-associations-demand-increase-in-school-library-funding/.

Stripling, Barbara. 2014. "School Librarians Transform Learning." *American Libraries*, Digital Supplement (September/October): 6–7. http://edition.pagesuite-professional.co.uk/Launch.aspx?EID=6c7cb940-d8fb-43d8-8ad8-864bf0e83f38.

TLA (Texas Library Association). 2014. "Texas Library Snapshot Day." http://www.texaslibrarysnapshotday.org/.

Further Reading

Balliett, Amy. 2011. "The Do's and Don'ts of Infographic Design." *Smashing Magazine*, October 14. http://www.smashingmagazine.com/2011/10/14/the-dos-and-donts-of-infographic-design/.

Library Research Service. 2013. "School Libraries & Student Achievement." http://www.lrs.org/data-tools/school-libraries/impact-studies/.

YALSA (Young Adult Library Services Association) Blog. 2015. "Speaking Up for Library Services for Teens, A Guide for Advocacy." Accessed June 5. http://www.ala.org/yalsa/sites/ala.org.yalsa/files/content/advocacy_final.pdf.

Zickuhr, Kathryn, Lee Rainie, and Kristen Purcell. 2013. "Younger Americans' Library Habits and Expectations." Pew Internet Organization. June 25. http://libraries.pewinternet.org/2013/06/25/younger-americans-libraryservices/.

CHAPTER 10

Bringing It All Together

Creating Your Own Infographic

IN THIS CHAPTER

- A step-by-step process to create your own infographic, using a model infographic created in PowerPoint
- An infographic step by step using Piktochart, an infographics program

THROUGHOUT THE BOOK you have learned about infographics. You've seen examples, identified their characteristics, and reviewed numerous applications where you might use infographics in your libraries. Now it's time to try your hand at creating your own infographics using two different programs: PowerPoint, a program used to create presentations that is familiar to almost all librarians, and Piktochart, a program specifically designed to create infographics. The story that will be conveyed in the example infographics is about a reading program in a public library in New Mexico.

Story of the Infographic: Wags and Words Reading Program

The Vista Grande Public Library (VGPL, 2015) in Santa Fe, New Mexico, started a new free program in May 2014 titled Wags and Words. This popular program, designed for beginning and reluctant readers, brings youngsters to the library to read to dogs. Working in conjunction with Pet Outreach Services at the Santa Fe Animal Shelter, the library hosts a Reading Education Assistance Dogs (R.E.A.D.) program. The dogs are licensed as therapy dogs, and their handlers have training to participate in the program. The program is ideal for young readers who struggle with reading aloud or are beginning to read; they now have a nonjudgmental audience to practice with to improve their confidence. Those interested can sign up for fifteen-minute sessions with dogs that come to the library several days a week. The Albuquerque, New Mexico, television station KRQE also interviewed the library staff about the program (Younger, 2015). Wags and Words is the focus of the example infographics you will review next created in both PowerPoint and Piktochart.

Creating Your Own Infographic Using PowerPoint

As more people begin to know about infographics and their benefits for a wide range of uses, they are looking for a way to create their own. Many librarians have used Microsoft PowerPoint to create presentations using graphics as part of them, so it is a natural extension that they would turn to PowerPoint to try to create infographics. Teachers and librarians, graphic designers, nonprofit organizations, and more have put together infographics with PowerPoint.

The following infographic will serve as a model to show you how to create your own infographic using PowerPoint. You will select a template and following specific steps, learn how to create the title, enter and change the font type and size, insert images, change colors, and more. Once you've completed and reviewed each section of the infographic, you will learn how to put sections together to create the infographic.

A slideshow created by fppt.com at http://www.free-power-point-templates.com/articles/how-to-create-infographics-using-powerpoint/ shows three different infographics created with PowerPoint. Three templates were used, each for a different purpose—to show a process, to inform, and to use data to communicate a message. The model you review next shows an informational infographic. You can also review the other templates and instructions in the slideshow.

As you review this example and plan your infographic, remember the principles of storytelling and design covered earlier in the book. Make sure you have a rough draft of your graphics and text you can follow before you start the actual infographic.

You also must think about the design tools available in PowerPoint as you begin. There are three essential elements (text, picture, and shape) and four essential tools that you will use to design your infographic in PowerPoint. They will help build your color scheme, shape style, and font styles.

- Fill—determines the primary color of an object or text.
- Line—creates the outline surrounding an object. You can use the line of an object to make it stand out among colored backgrounds or just to give it a border.
- Effects—adds design elements to your infographic. These include shadows, outer glows, 3D effects, and frames.
- Shape styles—give you the option to choose from a number of predesigned colors, lines, and effects that can be applied to your infographic. You can use the effects for objects, lines, and text.

Follow these steps that are used to create the Wags and Words infographic. For steps 1–4 you are using PowerPoint. Step 5 employs Pixlr, a free editing program, to piece together the slides into an infographic. Note that you can select your own image, font style, and color; you do not have to select the ones in the example.

Step 1: Decide the Theme and Gather Content

The Vista Grande Public Library (VGPL) creates a monthly newsletter with information about the library and its programs. An announcement about Wags and Words appeared here first. As the program became more popular, updates were mentioned in subsequent newsletters. The KRQE news station in Albuquerque picked up the story, interviewed the librarian, and created a video to publicize the program. The video provided pictures as well as quotes from the children and the dog handler that could be used to tell the program's story. Not your usual library program, Wags and Words provided a unique twist to promote and improve reading for children at the library.

Step 2: Create the Header

Begin with the title and any other information you want to put in the header, such as the name of the featured program, the organization, and an image that represents the program.

- Start with a new slide. Change the orientation from Landscape to Portrait. Change the size of the slide to fit in a blog post (about six inches wide and eleven or twelve inches high) (Gauthier, 2013).
- Click the top of the slide, and the handles of the textbox will appear to size the textbox. Highlight the sample title text in line one and type in your own title text. From the drop-down boxes under Font, change the font type to Tahoma and size 40 points. Peruse other effects such as WordArt from the Insert menu to create the 3D-style letters for the title and subtitle. Make the subtitle the same but smaller font in the same 3D-style letters and color. See figure 10.1.
- Add an image—one of the dogs in the reading program—to increase interest and represent the main theme of the infographic. Customize your font, color, and image.
    - For the title name—Under Drawing Tools > Format > WordArt Styles, select a 3D text in an uneven blue color.
    - For the organization name—Under Change Styles, change the font to Office 2, Calibri Cambria.
    - For the image—Under the Shape Effects drop-down menu, select Soft Edges to blur the edges of the image. Mouse over different levels of blurring to select the best effect.

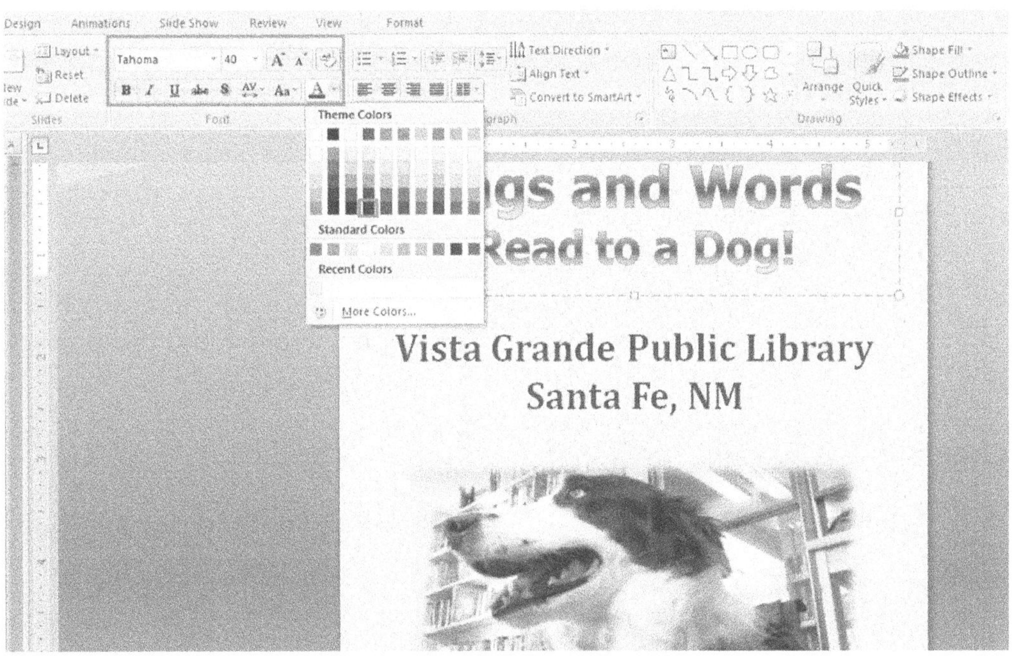

Figure 10.1. Beginning of the Infographic.

Step 3: Determine Number of Sections

Using your script and design draft, determine the number of sections and where they will begin and end.

- Select a divider to separate sections. Under Insert > Shapes > Line, click the line shape and draw a blue bar consistent with the blue color palette in your title. Click the line and from Format select the line width and color.
- Choose a shape to input the main message text for each section. Under Format > Shape Styles, select a box style and color; then input the message for your second section, including the font type and size from Text Outline.
- Add dark blue text to emphasize the benefits of reading to dogs to go with each image. Select the type and size of the font from the drop-down box.
- Soften the outline edges of the dog images for interest.
- Add the same line to divide section 2 from section 3. See figure 10.2.

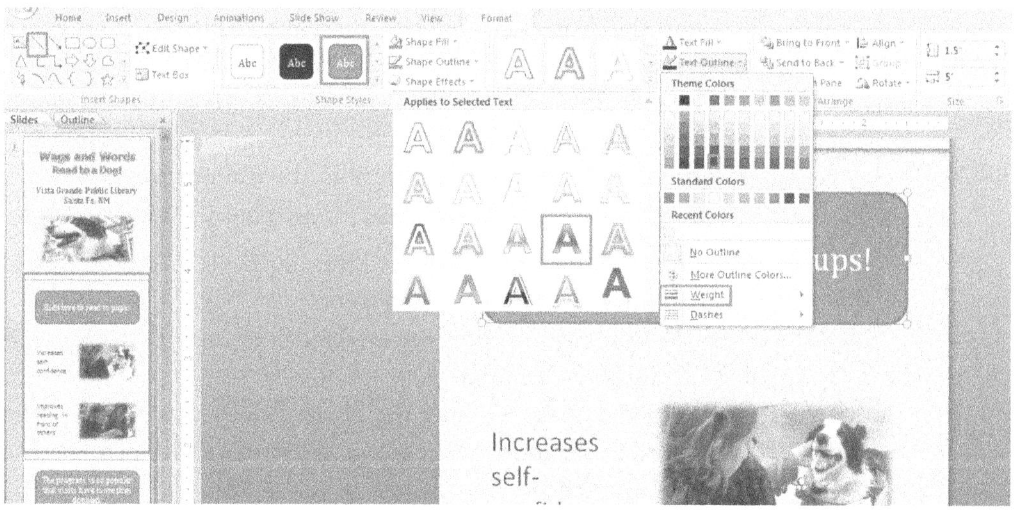

Figure 10.2. Editing Slide 2.

Step 4: Add Data

Add data to your infographic to illustrate the increase in popularity of the Wags and Words program.

- Continue with the same section divider line, shape box and font type, color, and size.
- To add the data, click Insert > Chart > Column. Select a basic bar chart, and click OK.
- Type data into the Microsoft Excel spreadsheet that displays. Copy and paste it into the PowerPoint slide. See figure 10.3.

Step 5: Connect the Slides

After you have reviewed the slides for the final time, you are ready to put all the slides together as an infographic.

- Save the slides as PNG images using File > Save As > PNG format. This is the only file type that gives your infographics the high quality needed for publishing.

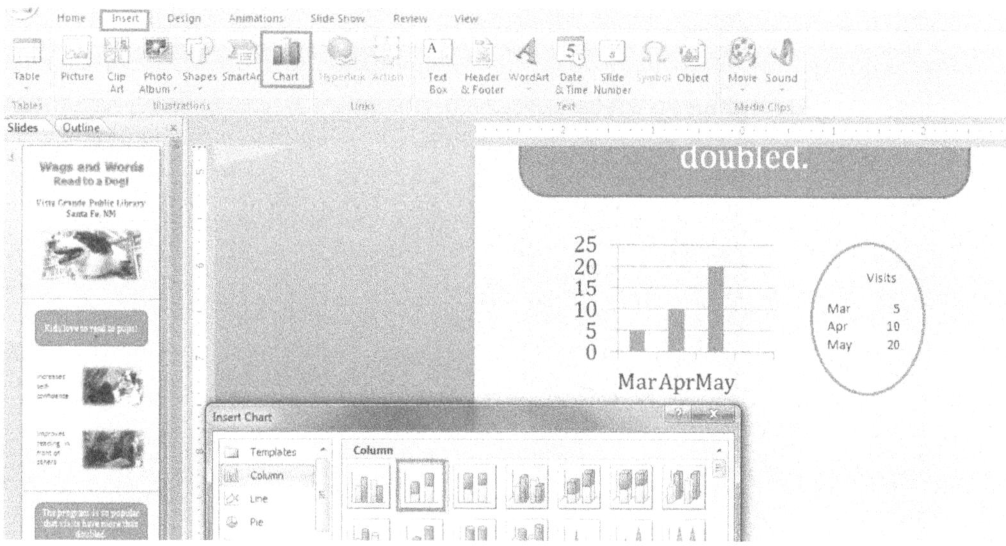

Figure 10.3. Inserting Data.

- From your browser go to Pixlr, a free online editor at http://pixlr.com/editor/.
- From the Pixlr Editor screen, select Open Image from Computer, find the folder in which you saved your PowerPoint slides, and select the first slide for the top of the infographic. See figure 10.4.
- From View > Zoom, adjust your zoom number in the bottom left-hand corner to 20 percent. See figure 10.5.

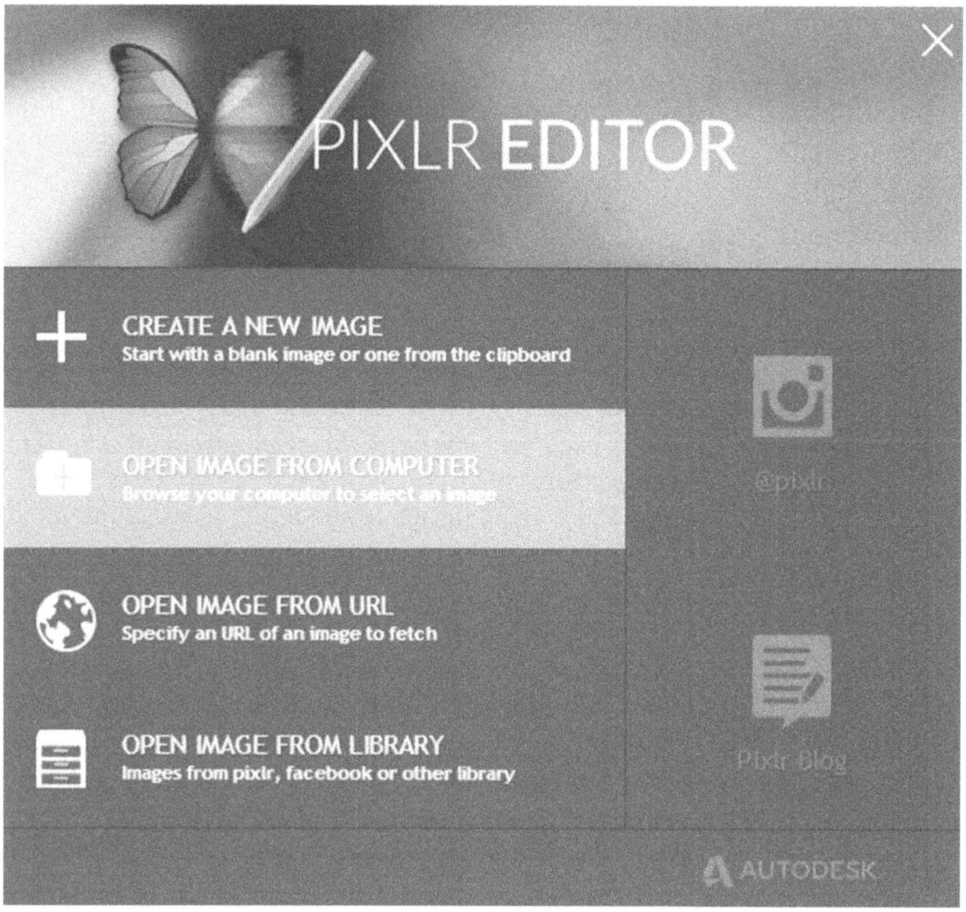

Figure 10.4. Pixlr Editor.

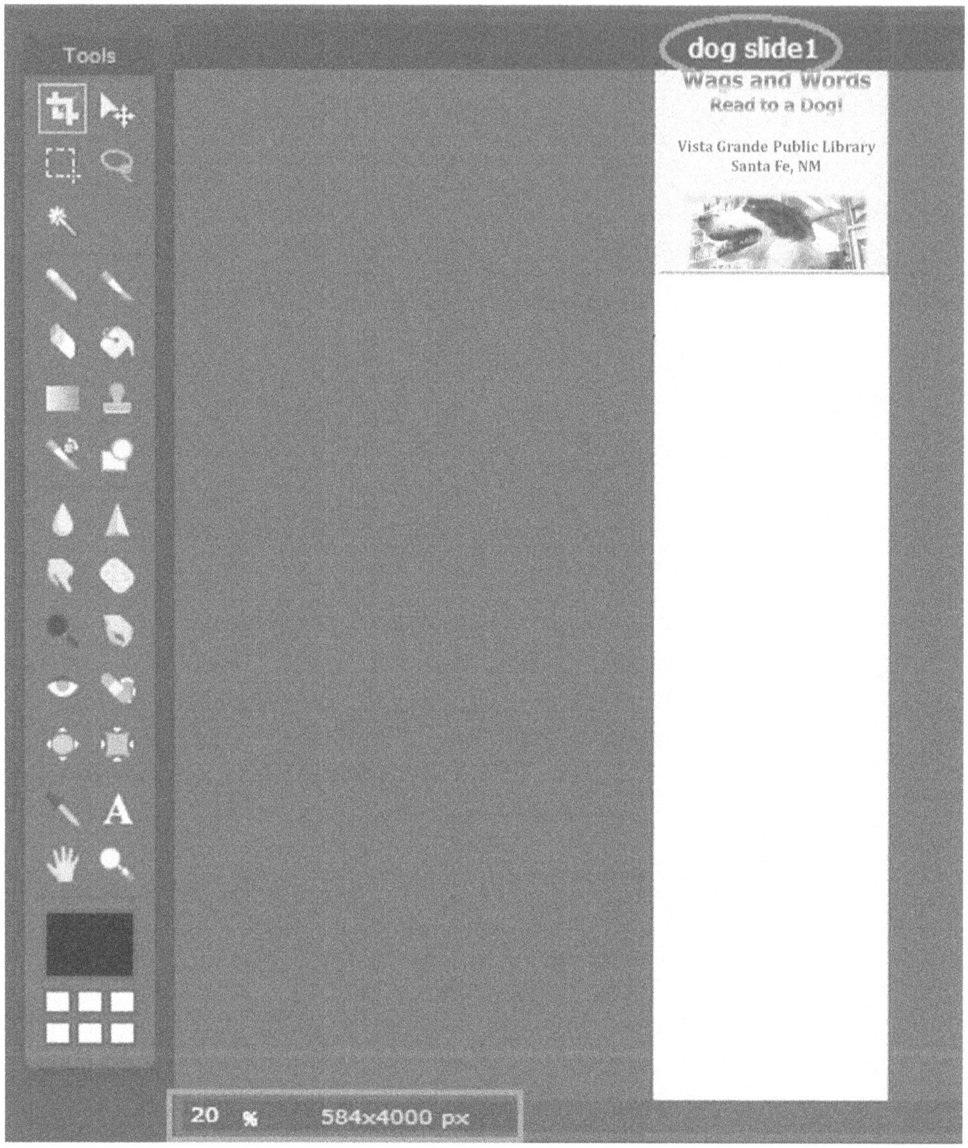

Figure 10.5. Edit Slide 1.

- From the top navigation bar, select Image > Canvas Size and change the height to 4000. This allows your canvas to be long enough to paste in each PowerPoint slide to build the infographic. You can increase this height number when needed or crop it later.
- Using File > Open Image, select Slide 2, saved as a PNG. Adjust the zoom to 20 percent. Click the slide and use Ctrl+A to select the entire Slide 2. Then click Edit > Copy.
- Click the Slide 1 image with the increased height and Edit > Paste Slide 2 below Slide 1. From the toolbar, use the Move tool to move the new image around on Slide 1, to ensure all the slides are lining up correctly. See figure 10.6.
- Continue to copy and paste your slides until your entire infographic is pieced together. You can use the Crop tool in the toolbar to eliminate any extra white space added by adjusting the canvas height. See figure 10.7.
- When the infographic is pieced together, save it in PNG format. Note when you exit Pixlr, all your content will be lost if you have not saved it as you go. See table 10.1 for more resources on creating infographics with PowerPoint.

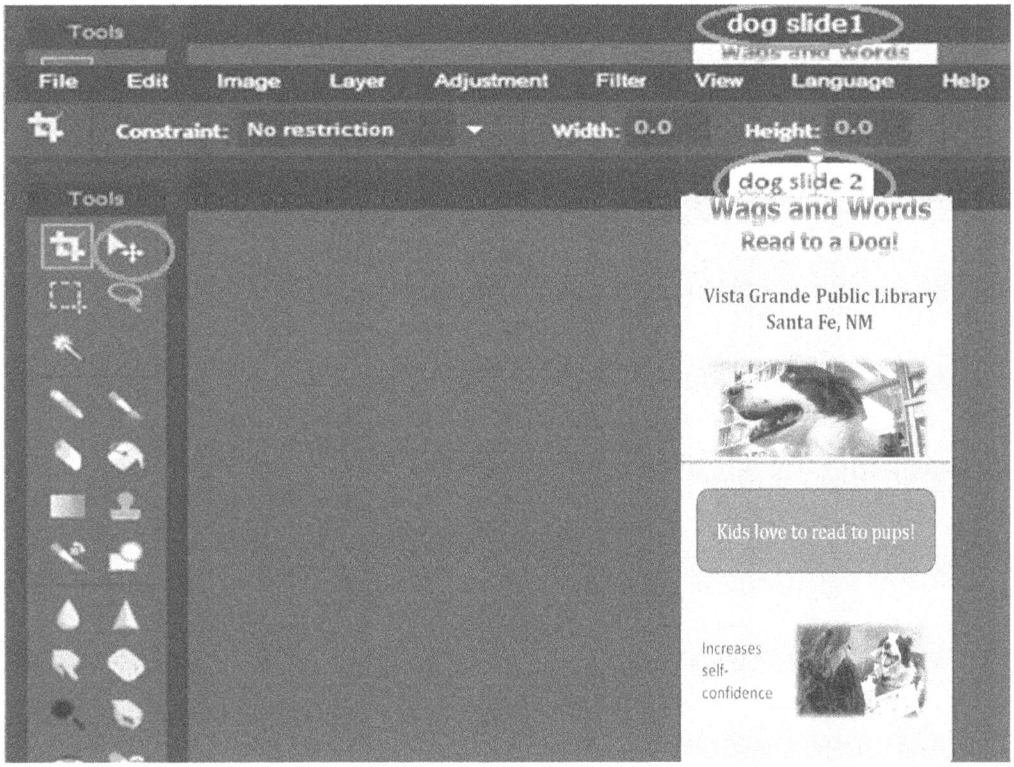

Figure 10.6. Adding Slide 2.

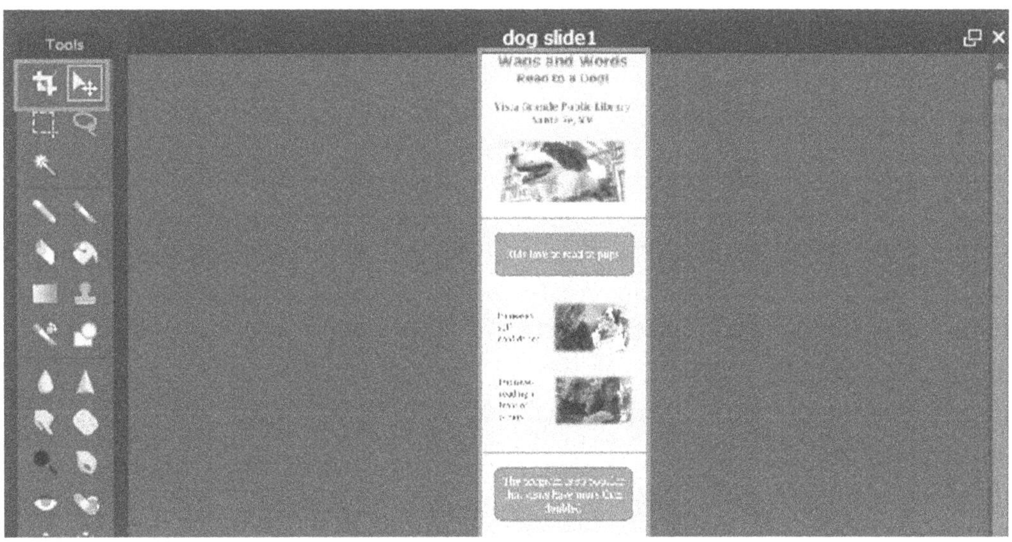

Figure 10.7. Completed Infographic.

Table 10.1. Support Resources for PowerPoint

DESCRIPTION	URL
"How to Create Infographics Using PowerPoint"	http://www.free-power-point-templates.com/articles/how-to-create-infographics-using-powerpoint/
"Infographic Templates for Free"	http://www.free-power-point-templates.com/articles/free-infographic-templates/
"Free Simple PowerPoint Templates"	http://www.free-power-point-templates.com/category/ppt-by-topics/simple/

Creating Your Own Infographic Using Piktochart

The easy-to-use Piktochart program enables you to make infographics using precreated templates. It is available in both free and paid-for versions. You can insert hyperlinks into content, add multiple clickable tabs to separate sections of an infographic to view it easily, share them on social media networks, and embed them on websites. Other programs to create infographics are discussed in chapter 4.

Create an account, and you are ready to start creating your own infographics. Go to http://www.piktochart.com, and sign up for an account. There are different types of accounts from which to choose:

- Free standard with limited number of templates
- Education for a single individual or a classroom, both at minimal cost
- Free nonprofit or with a small yearly fee that has the features of the pro account
- Pro with a monthly fee

Information about each type of account is available from the Piktochart home page under Pricing.

It takes one step only to sign up. You can register through your Facebook or Google account or create a new account by entering a user name, e-mail address, and password. By clicking the newsletter box, you will also receive a newsletter with tips about using Piktochart. Click Create My Account, and your account is automatically set up, and you are ready to start creating. Once you have an account, log in with your account ID (e.g., e-mail address, or via Google or Facebook).

When you have signed in, your infographic-making journey begins. Just follow the steps in the process. Go to http://www.piktochart.com to get started.

Step 1: Pick a Template

Scroll through the templates according to their different formats—Standard, Report, Banner, and Presentation. Just click the one you want. Below the formats you can choose from eleven free themes or more than six hundred pro themes, depending on your account. The demonstration will be for a free account. You can also create your own infographic with a "blank canvas" without using a premade template. If you know the theme you want, you can type it into the Search box. Mouse over each template, and click the Preview button to see a larger version of a template. See figure 10.8, with the template used in this example highlighted.

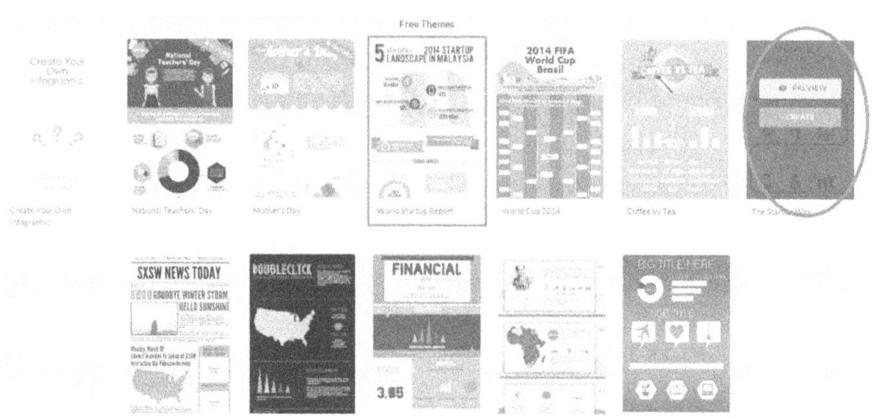

Figure 10.8. Free Themes.

The templates encompass different types from Coffee vs. Tea, showing a comparison, to How to Make Money, a process, to ones that contain different kinds of data—charts, maps, and graphs. As you are selecting the template, consider the way your eye will move from one point to the next and the way sections are divided. Next, you will see how to customize many items on the template, such as font size, color, images, interactive maps, and more.

Step 2. Explore the Toolbars

Click the template you want, in this example World Startup Report at https://magic.piktochart.com/. Click the Create button to start. Your template will load. You can now make changes to your template. First, become familiar with the Piktochart toolbar on the left and Edit tools at the top left and right of the template. Review the toolbars in figure 10.9.

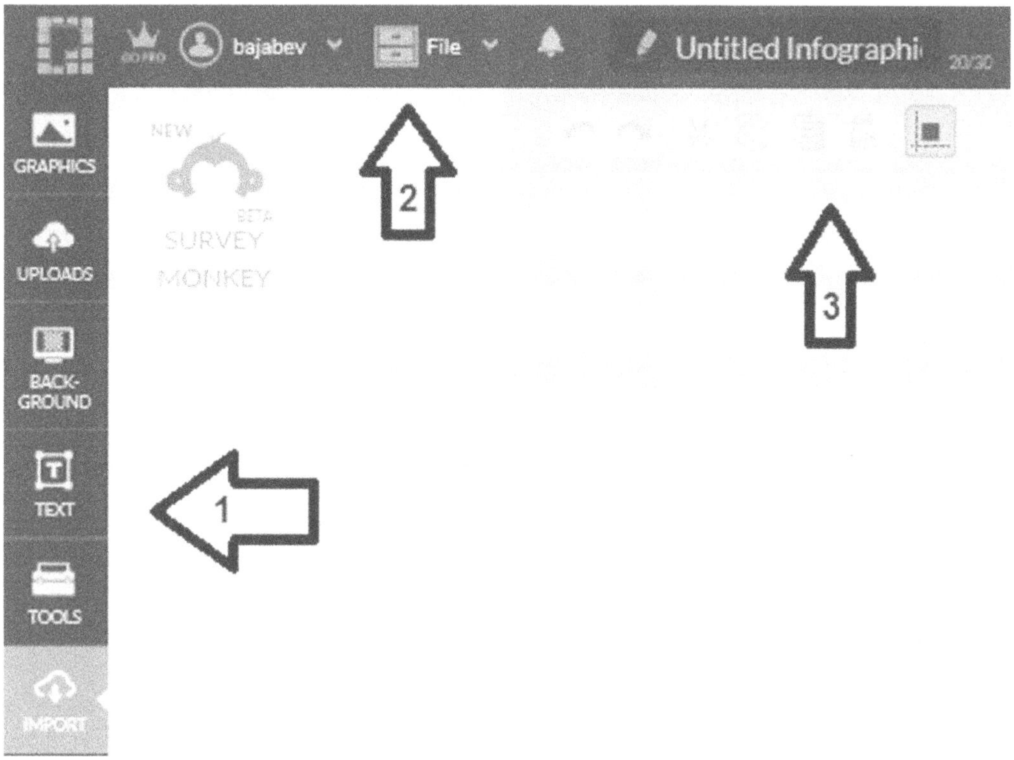

Figure 10.9. Toolbars.

Left Toolbar

The left toolbar contains Graphics, Uploads, Background, Text, Tools, and Import Poll Tool. Each heading contains more choices as shown next.

Graphics. Click the Graphics buttons to see Shapes & Line, Icons, Photos, and Photo Frames. For example, Shapes & Line contains basic shapes and dotted and solid lines. Click Shapes & Line and the chosen object. Drag it to the location where you want to locate it. To collapse Shapes & Line, click the down caret next to the title of the category.

Icons include a drop-down menu with categories from Arrows to Weather. You can also enter the name of an icon in the Search box to locate it. *Note:* To edit a line style and thickness, use the Properties toolbar and drag and drop. Photos are divided into categories and are available from a drop-down menu.

Photo frames are the last category of graphics and can be dragged to the appropriate spot on the template. All graphics work in the same drop-and-drag manner. See figure 10.10.

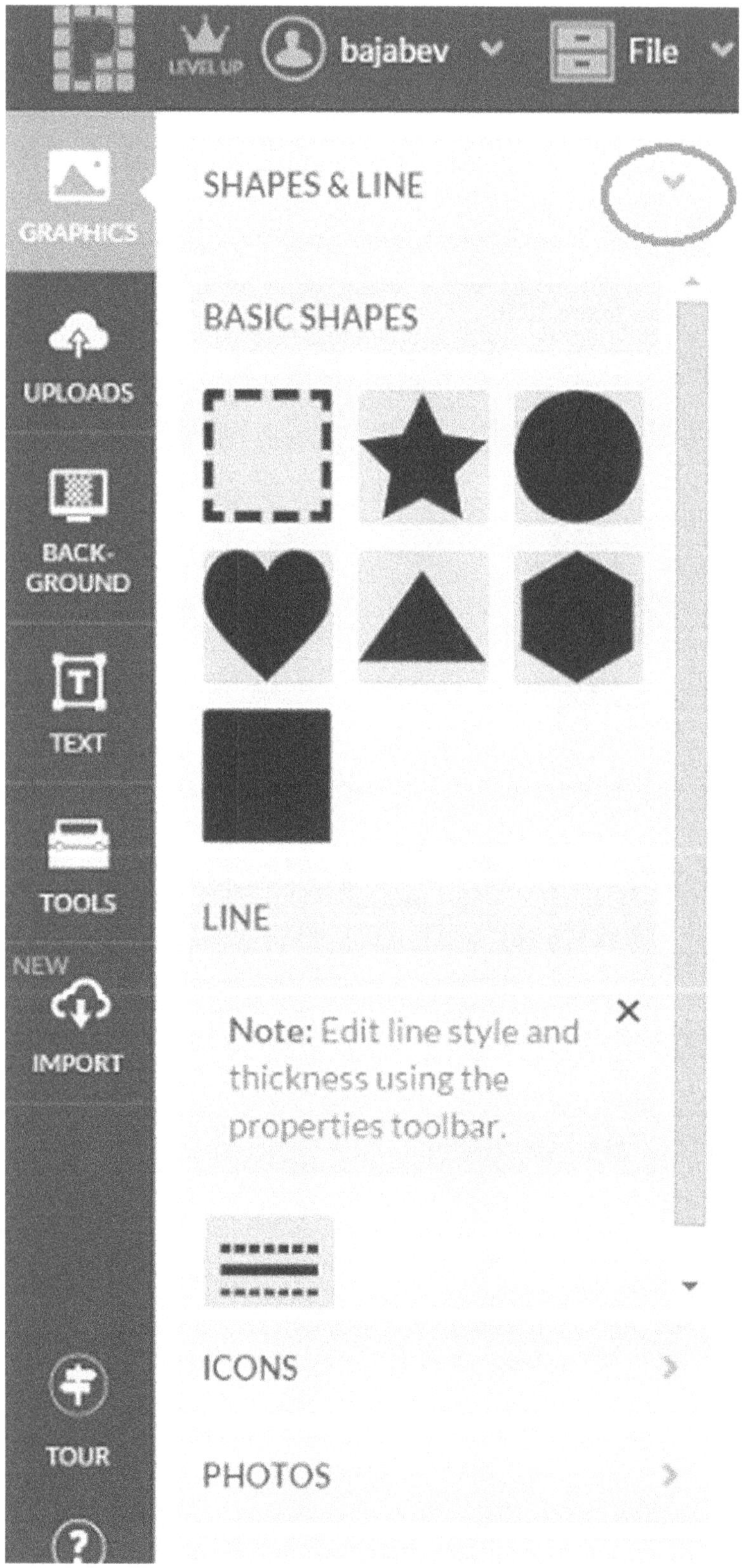

Figure 10.10. Graphics > Shapes & Line.

Uploads. From Uploads, you can select an image from your computer and drag it to the dotted image box or directly onto the canvas.

Backgrounds. You can change the backgrounds and adjust them to varying levels of opacity by dragging the bar to the right. They are available in a variety of colors and textures. You can also change the background color by clicking the appropriate color square.

Text. Under the Text button is a range of text sizes, including lettering for titles, subtitles, and body text. Text frames make the lettering stand out. To edit text, double-click the text and click the style of interest. You can also move the text. Double-click the text you want to change. When the highlight around the text appears, you can type new letters and words.

Tools. Different tools enable you to create charts, maps, and videos. Subsequent menus provide instructions to illustrate how to edit charts and create maps and videos.

Click each category to view the subcategories available. You will see demonstrations of these tools as you create the sample infographic.

Upper Right Toolbar

The toolbar on the upper right of the screen contains four buttons.

- The Preview button allows you to view changes you make to your template as you create the infographic.
- With the Download button, you can change the size for viewing on specific devices and save as a PNG or JPEG format. You can also download the infographic at a higher resolution, download it in PDF format, and remove the Pictochart watermark.
- When you have completed the infographic, click the Publish button to make the infographic go live so those whom you want to see the finished version have access.
- The Share button enables you to share the infographic via e-mail; export it to Slideshare and Evernote; or share it on social media, including Facebook, Twitter, Google+, and Pinterest. You can add the icons for social media to your infographic. More on this later. See figure 10.11.

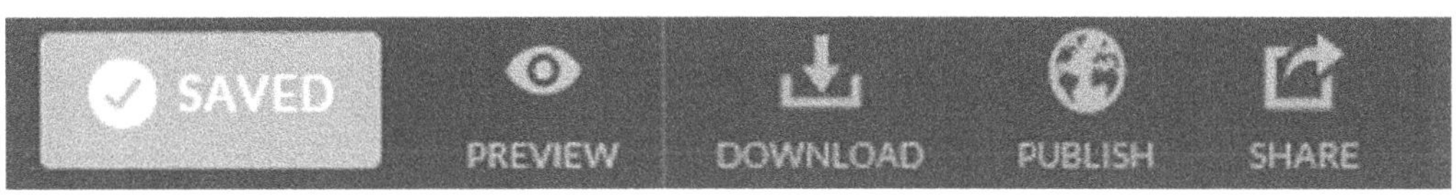

Figure 10.11. Upper Right Toolbar.

Now that you've explored the toolbars, it's time to use them to create your infographic. Open the Piktochart program, and follow along with these instructions.

Step 3: Decide the Theme and Gather Content

As in the PowerPoint infographic, interviews with library staff, the monthly newsletter at the Vista Grande Library, information from the KRQE interviews, and video provided content for the Piktochart infographic. The Piktochart infographic and the PowerPoint infographic are not exactly the same. More ways to expand the story are illustrated in the Piktochart example.

Step 4: Determine the Layout

You will need to decide on content for the infographic and determine the layout. Based on the content (e.g., pictures and text) extracted from the KRQE video and interviews with the Vista Grande staff, the infographic is divided into six sections, to illustrate different ways to modify the infographic. Like any good story, the infographic has a beginning, middle, and end.

- The beginning in section 1 contains the name of the library, the name of the program, and a short text description of it.
- Sections 2 through 5 provide the middle—details about the program.
  - In section 2 pictures of the dogs and children and quotes from the children and dog handler illustrate the story. A tagline at the end of section 2 emphasizes the purpose and results for the children.
  - Section 3 uses the KRQE news coverage to promote the program further. Note that the video created by KRQE could be inserted into the infographic and clicked to hear the actual interview.
  - Section 4 lists the benefits and a bit more about the program.
  - Section 5 uses data in the form of a bar graph of reading visits for three months to show the program's increase in popularity.
- Finally, the end in section 6 provides a call to action: how you can contact the library to participate. The library logo restates the organization involved. Also, social media icons can be clicked to share the infographic, an important advantage to promote the program.

Step 5: Design and Create Each Section of the Infographic

With an outline created, you are ready to decide on and create your design.

- Preview each of the free templates and decide which one fits best with your outline. Remember that you can also use a blank template to create your design from scratch. The choice here is the World Startup Report, highlighted earlier in figure 10.8.
- Think about your graphics, color palette, and text fonts. Click inside the top of the template to highlight each block as you proceed down the page. Note the following issues.

Section 1 will contain your title and subtitle. You can use Photo Frame, a feature of Piktochart, to select ready-made designs. Scroll down and click the design you want, in this case the banner. Select the font type from the drop-down box and type the text in the textbox within the banner. The text will automatically resize to fit the design. Notice the Save button automatically saves your work as you create and edit.

Designs display in different colors so this may help you select your color palette and font size that fits within the graphic. The banner in navy blue with the name and location of the library clearly identifies the organization. Blue will be one of the main colors for the infographic. The text chosen stands out in the graphic, and the banner welcomes the viewer into the graphic. See figure 10.12.

Between sections 1 and 2, there is a subtitle centered between two dotted bars. This same designed subtitle, font type (League Gothic), and font size (28 points) appear between each section. Depending on the amount of information in each section, you can

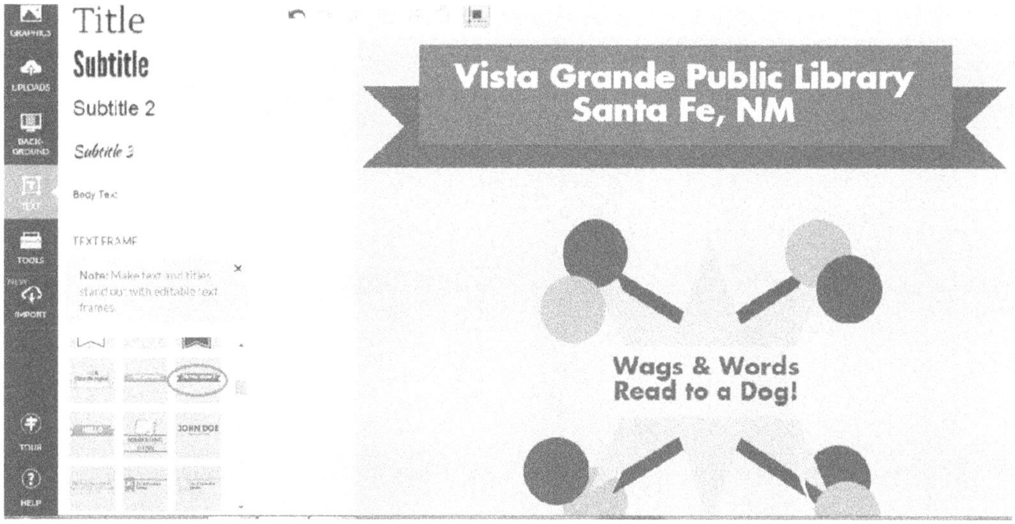

Figure 10.12. Title.

resize each section by selecting the appropriate arrow and dragging the dividers up or down. You can also delete and add sections by clicking a block.

Section 2 starts with descriptive text in a fun font (Comic Sans) to describe the message for this section. For consistency sections 2 through 6 use the same text font and size.

The image that appeared in the template is the focal point of this section. Click and mouse over the image to see the different parts you can change. This section communicates the main message of the story.

From the toolbar on the left, click Upload and drag pictures of the dogs that you have already uploaded from your own computer onto the large graphic in the center of this section. Size all the images to be the same width and height; select color, in this case a turquoise blue and complementary color orange. The navy, turquoise, and orange form the color palette for the entire infographic.

Under Graphics > Shapes & Line, add other accent design elements like the circles in blue and orange and the same color lines. Note that the orange and turquoise circles and lines lead the viewer's eye through Section 2.

At the bottom of section 2, short text in an orange banner, similar to the title banner, emphasizes the benefits of Wags and Words. Small icons of a book and a "thumbs up" hand, dragged from Graphics > Icons onto the banner, reinforce the text. See figure 10.13.

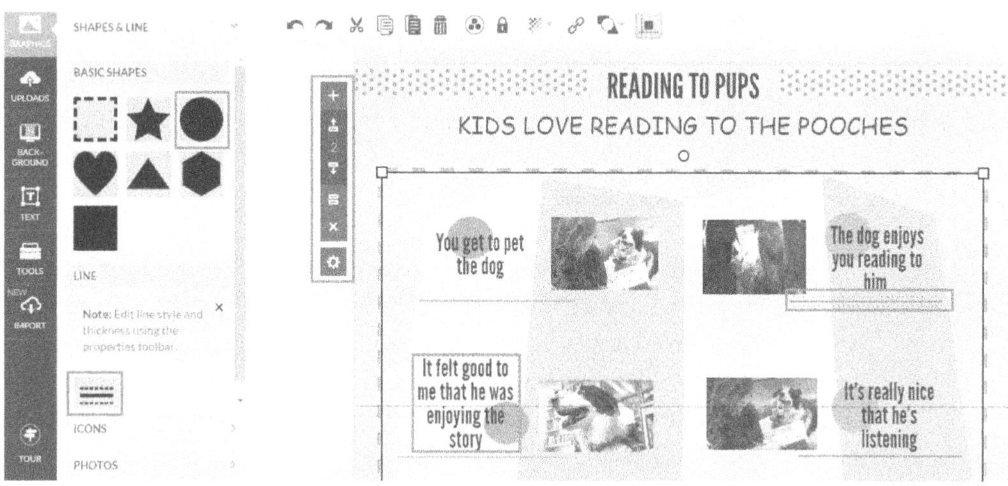

Figure 10.13. Wags and Words.

Section 3 displays an image about the News Coverage from the KRQE TV video. By clicking Uploads and Select Image from Computer, the image displays in the box that appears. Then drag and drop it into section 3 and resize it using the "handles." This could be created as an interactive image so that clicking the image would play a section of the video about the Wags and Words program. See figure 10.14.

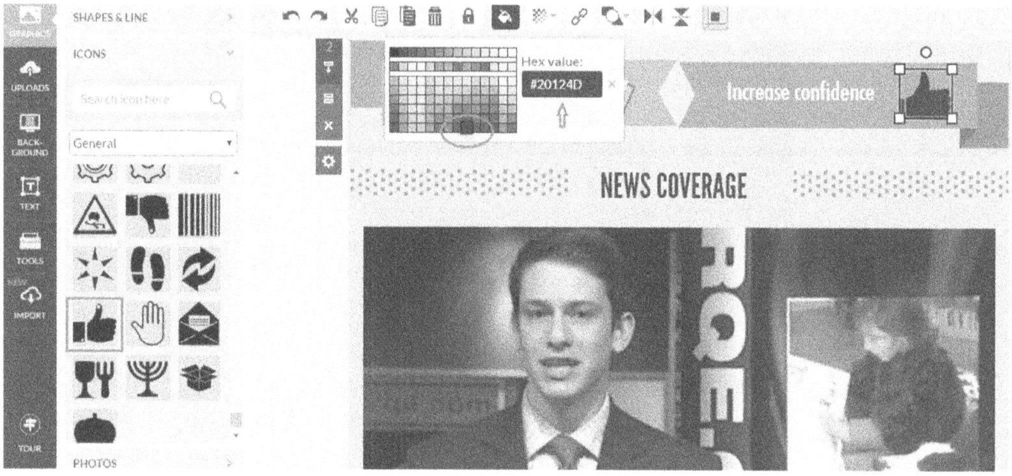

Figure 10.14. News Coverage.

Section 4 highlights the information about the Wags and Words program and its benefits. The text in a readable font fits inside turquoise-colored bars. Colors and text size and color continue the theme. See figure 10.15.

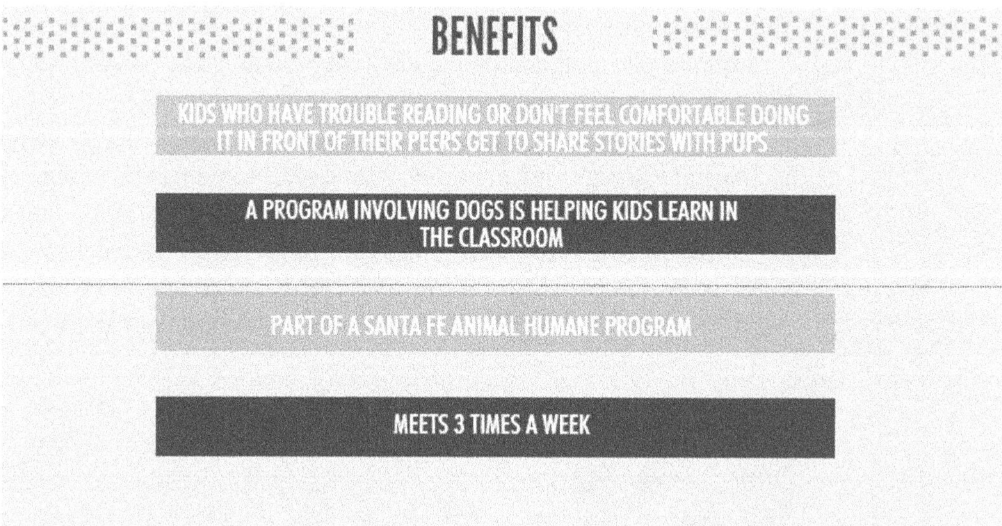

Figure 10.15. Benefits.

Section 5 presents data illustrating the success of Wags and Words. The bar chart depicts the increase in number of visits over a three-month period by children reading to dogs. From Tools, click Charts, and enter the data in the spreadsheet that displays, or import your data from a CSV, XLS, or XLSX spreadsheet. Again, you can carry the color scheme through by clicking the Settings button and selecting the colors you have used previously. See figure 10.16.

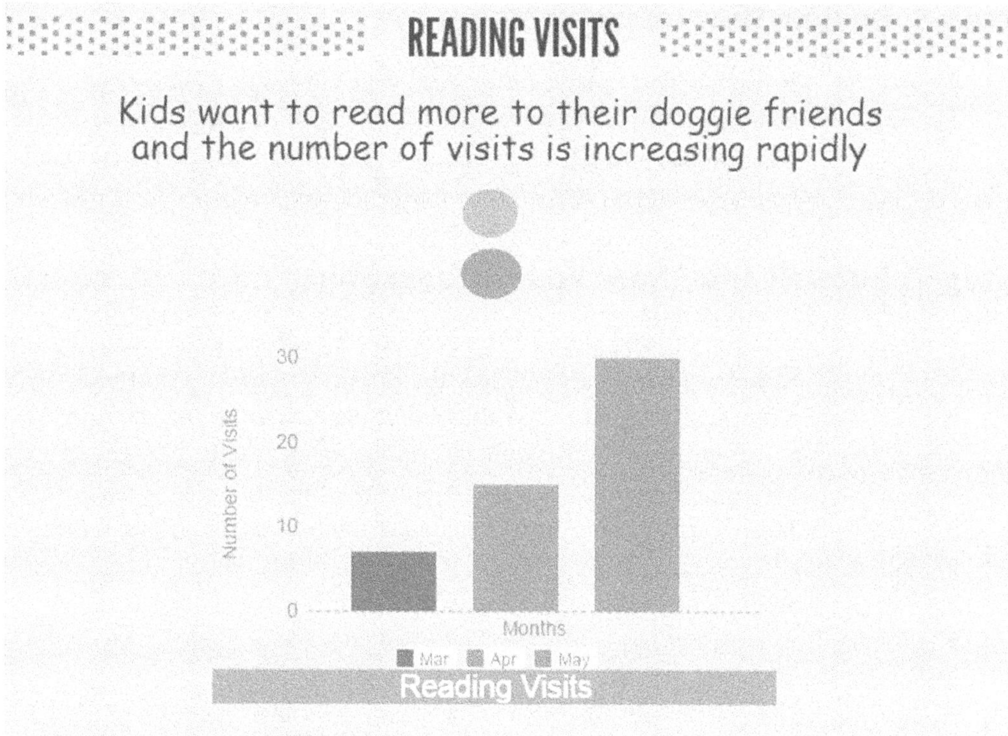

Figure 10.16. Reading Visits.

Section 6 concludes the infographic with a call to action to obtain more information about the program from a URL linked to the library website. Adding social media icons on the left linked to the library offer opportunities to share the infographic. The Vista Grande Library logo reinforces the organization name. See figure 10.17.

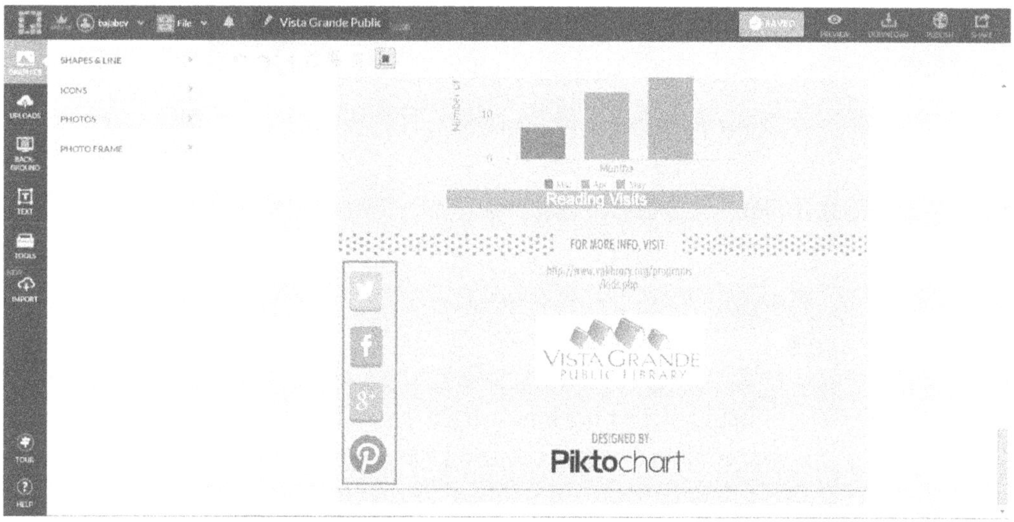

Figure 10.17. Call to Action.

You can also change the background to make it more color compatible with the palette. Click Background and select the appropriate color/texture. The entire background of the infographic changes to the new color. Notice the infographic continues to be automatically saved.

The next steps are a vital part for producing both the PowerPoint and Piktochart infographics.

Step 6: Review Your Infographic

It is important to have others read your infographic before publishing it. Many eyes may spot something you overlooked. Make sure the sections you've included tell your story in a logical manner. Check grammar and spelling. Review for consistency of color, text font and size, spacing, and alignment. Edit as needed.

Step 7: Publish and Share Your Infographic

You can download as an image, publish to the web, e-mail, and post your infographic directly to social media. Click the Publish to the Web button so it can be seen publicly. View your infographic on the output page by following the provided URL.

Your infographic is done. Continue to use your infographics to promote your library's services, programs, and expertise using other methods mentioned in this book. Review table 10.2 for more support material on creating infographics using Piktochart.

Table 10.2. Support Resources for Piktochart

DESCRIPTION	URL
How to make an infographic in five steps	http://support.piktochart.com/hc/en-us/articles/202363710-How-can-I-make-an-Infographic-in-Five-Steps
YouTube videos on making your own infographics with different programs	http://www.youtube.com/watch?v=OzYAFaHu2Ys&feature=youtu.be
"All about Piktochart's Infographic Editor"	http://support.piktochart.com/hc/en-us
"What Are Presentation Infographics?"	http://support.piktochart.com/hc/en-us/articles/202202020-What-are-Presentation-Infographics
How to publish a Piktochart using HTML	http://support.piktochart.com/hc/en-us/articles/200631345-How-do-I-publish-my-Piktochart-using-HTML
"What Are Standard Infographics?"	http://support.piktochart.com/hc/en-us/articles/202201870-What-are-Standard-Infographics-
"What Are Report Infographics?"	http://support.piktochart.com/hc/en-us/articles/201951964-What-are-Report-Infographics-

Key Points

Throughout this book, you have learned about infographics and using them to enhance and promote a library's programs and services. Microsoft PowerPoint and Piktochart provide different ways in which you can create your own infographics to facilitate different uses in your libraries.

- Create an infographic to tell your library's unique story, supported by authoritative content and data in a well-designed format.
- PowerPoint is a program known to librarians that they have used to create presentations; thus using its tools offers a familiar way to create your own infographics.

- Numerous infographics tools, such as Piktochart and others described earlier in this book, are easy to use to design your infographics with ready-made templates or starting from a blank canvas.
- Step-by-step instructions provide a model to follow, including how to use images, fonts, color, and data.

Infographics have become a popular resource for accessing complex information quickly and effectively. Librarians can enhance their physical and virtual collections by creating quality materials that incorporate infographics. In addition, twenty-first-century learners need to be able to use these infographics effectively. Engaging activities that involve students in evaluating, using, and creating their own infographics can enhance their information literacy and technology skills. Finally, the popularity of infographics provides a wonderful opportunity to enhance library marketing activities through displays, posters, handouts, and other items that incorporate infographics.

It's now more important than ever for libraries to heed users' advice and "sell" their value. For many Americans, the library experience is new or renewed. This creates a great opportunity for libraries to discover more about what is needed, what is valued, and what more can be provided to a new set of users who are looking to the library as a valued asset.

Studies mentioned earlier have shown that the value of libraries is high. A strategic priority must be to encourage users, students, and colleagues to tell their stories—repeatedly, online and in person. Infographics have a place in almost any message. They are especially great at making data more appealing and instantly understandable. To be successful, your library's awareness campaign must do two things:

- Wake up potential supporters to the fact that the library is relevant in the twenty-first century.
- Activate conversations about the vital and transformative role that the library plays and its value to schools, businesses, academic institutions, and the community.

Libraries are finding innovative ways to engage users and meet their twenty-first-century needs. In their popularity with today's users, infographics are and will continue to be a vital part of the library's playbook. Get started now to integrate infographics into your library resources.

Exercises for Chapter 10

In chapter 9 you compiled and reviewed content for a project that might be used in your own library. Reinforce what you learned in this chapter by using the information from the exercises in chapter 9 to create your own infographic.

1. Based on the draft of the infographic you wrote in chapter 9 exercises (number 3), select either PowerPoint or Piktochart to create an infographic.
2. Select a template or start from a blank canvas and divide your content into sections based on your choice of programs.
3. Follow the steps outlined in this chapter. Pay attention to color, font type and size, graphics, data, and placement.

4. After completing a draft, have your colleagues review and edit your infographic.
5. Identify social media and other methods you will use to promote your infographic.
6. Write a blog post about your infographic and publish the post with your infographic to your library website. Send it out via social media.
7. Analyze the process of creating the infographic (e.g., what went well, what was difficult, what you would do differently on your next attempt) and share the information with colleagues and your personal learning network (PLN).

References

Gauthier, Kimberly. 2013. "How I Created Easy Infographics Using MS PowerPoint." SlideShare. August 25. http://www.slideshare.net/kimberlygauthier/creating-infographics-with-ms-power-point.

VGPL (Vista Grande Public Library). 2015. "Wags and Words." http://www.vglibrary.org/programs/kids.php.

Younger, Emily. 2015. "Kids Read to Dogs." KRQE News 13. January 17. http://krqe.com/2015/01/17/kids-read-to-dogs-improve-their-confidence/.

Index

About the Author

Beverley E. Crane received a bachelor of arts in curriculum and instruction, with a dual major in Spanish and English, and a master of education in bilingual education and English as a second language, from Penn State University. She obtained a doctorate of education in curriculum and instruction, with emphases in instructional technology and language arts from Oklahoma State University. She has taught English/language arts and English as a second language at the middle, high school, and college levels. She also taught education courses in the Teacher Education Program at San Jose State University.

While working on a grant for a five-state multicultural resources center, she conducted workshops for teachers and librarians on such topics as literacy, writing, English as a second language, and integrating technology into the curriculum. For twenty-four years, she also worked for Dialog, now a business of ProQuest, where she created educational materials and conducted workshops and online training, teaching academic, public, school, and special librarians about online searching. She has presented at conferences throughout the United States—including those of the American Association of School Librarians, the International Society of Technology Educators, the American Educational Research Association, and the California Media and Library Educators Association, among others—on such topics as using online searching in the curriculum, computers and writing, and online research across the curriculum. Her most recent presentation in 2014, titled "Perceptions of the Roles of Librarians/Information Specialists in Media and Information Services," was at the conference of the Association of Caribbean University, Research, and Institutional Libraries (ACURIL) in the Bahamas.

As director of the English Education Program at San Jose State University for five years, she worked closely with classroom teachers, administrators, and librarians to provide guidelines for mentor teachers who supervise English student teachers. She currently continues to provide educational consulting via Crane's Educational Consulting to create training materials, videos, and self-paced modules for online learning. Her books include *How to Teach: A Practical Guide for Librarians* (2014), *Using Web 2.0 Tools and Social Networking in the K–12 Classroom* (2012), *Using Web 2.0 Tools in the K–12 Classroom* (2009), *Internet Workshops: 10 Ready-to-Go Workshops for K–12 Educators* (2004), and *Teaching with the Internet: Strategies and Models for K–12 Curricula* (2000). She lives in Santa Fe, New Mexico, where she paints Southwest landscapes and is involved with local art associations. She continues to maintain a presence in the educational community.

www.ingramcontent.com/pod-product-compliance
Ingram Content Group UK Ltd.
Pitfield, Milton Keynes, MK11 3LW, UK
UKHW051933150926
475560UK00005B/367

9 781442 260351